The FUTURE
of NATURALISM

The FUTURE of NATURALISM

EDITED BY
John R. Shook
AND
Paul Kurtz

Humanity
Books

an imprint of Prometheus Books
59 John Glenn Drive, Amherst, New York 14228-2197

Published 2009 by Humanity Books, an imprint of Prometheus Books

Inquiries should be addressed to
Humanity Books
59 John Glenn Drive
Amherst, New York 14228–2119
VOICE: 716–691–0133, ext. 210
FAX: 716–691–0137
WWW.PROMETHEUSBOOKS.COM

13 12 11 10 09   5 4 3 2 1

Library of Congress Cataloging-in-Publication Data.

The future of naturalism / [edited] by John R. Shook and Paul Kurtz.
    p. cm.
    Essays originated in presentations at a conference at the Center for Inquiry Transnational in Amherst, N.Y. in 2007.
    Includes bibliographical references.
    ISBN 978–1–59102–731–7 (hardcover : alk. paper)
    1. Naturalism. I. Shook, John R. II. Kurtz, Paul, 1925–

B828.2.F88 2009
146—dc22

2009013294

Printed in the United States on acid-free paper

Contents

Preface
John R. Shook and Paul Kurtz   7

PART ONE:
WHAT KIND OF NATURALISM
DESERVES A FUTURE?

1. *The Future of Naturalism:*
   Nature and Culture in Perspectival Duality
   Nicholas Rescher   15

2. *Reclaiming Naturalism*
   Joseph Margolis   25

3. *Advantages and Limits of Naturalism*
   Mario Bunge   43

4. *Primitive Naturalism*
   John Lachs   65

PART TWO:
CAN PRAGMATISM ASSIST NATURALISM?

5. *Pragmatic Natures*
   Sandra B. Rosenthal   77

6. *The Value of Pragmatic Naturalism*
   John Ryder   97

7. *Wayward Naturalism:*
   Saving Dewey from Himself
   Isaac Levi   115

5

8. The Fecundity of Naturalism:
   Reflections on Dewey's Methodology
   James Gouinlock   137

9. Pragmatism and the Naturalization of Religion
   John Peter Anton   155

PART THREE:
NATURALISM APPLIED?

10. Eupraxsophy and Naturalism
    Paul Kurtz   179

11. Naturalizing Jurisprudence: Three Approaches
    Brian Leiter   197

12. How Knowers Emerge, and Why This Is Important
    to Future Work in Naturalized Epistemology
    Lynn Hankinson Nelson and Jack Nelson   209

13. Naturalism's Unfinished Project:
    Making Philosophy More Scientific
    Randall Dipert   231

14. Why Is There a Universe at All,
    Rather Than Just Nothing?
    Adolf Grünbaum   249

About the Editors and Contributors   269

Preface

John R. Shook and Paul Kurtz

I.

Before we can discuss the future of naturalism, we need to define it. Succinctly, *naturalism* seeks to apply the methods of the empirical sciences to explain natural events without reference to supernatural causes; and it derives ethical values from human experience, not theological grounds.

Naturalism has deep roots in the history of philosophical and scientific thought. It can be traced back to the first pre-Socratic philosophers who eschewed occult explanations and sought material causes. These thinkers included Thales, Democritus, and Leucippus, among others. It even included Aristotle, who attempted to use the science of his day to explain nature by reference to observable causes. Naturalism encompassed a wide range of thinkers historically, including Epicurus and Lucretius, Spinoza and Voltaire, Galileo and Darwin. Indeed, modern philosophy focused on the epistemology of science, in recognition of the importance of science in unlocking the secrets of nature—from Bacon and Hobbes, to Locke and Hume, Kant and Russell. There were of course differences between rationalists and empiricists as to whether mathematical coherence or empirical observation was more important in testing truth claims. This controversy was eventually resolved with the recognition that both are incorporated in scientific methodology.

The first sense of naturalism is *methodological*. As such, it has been the most influential philosophical movement in the modern world, encompassing a broad range of philosophical schools including empiricism, rationalism, logical positivism, analytical philosophy, and pragmatism. Charles Peirce, who is often not consid-

7

ered a naturalist, because of his free-wheeling speculations, nonetheless maintains in his famous essay "The Fixation of Belief" that the method of science is the most effective way to overcome doubt and establish beliefs, for in the last analysis it is based on real things, and it is tested pragmatically in comparison with other methods.

Given the progressive advance of scientific knowledge and the impact of technology on the modern world, naturalism represents the philosophical recognition of the power of the methods of science. Indeed, this has been the dominant theme of contemporary American philosophy. Among the most influential naturalists have been John Dewey and George Santayana in the first half of the twentieth century, and it continues with naturalists later in the century with thinkers such as Ernest Nagel, Sidney Hook, Hilary Putnam, Donald Davidson, Daniel Dennett, and others, including many of the distinguished contributors to this volume.

The logician W. V. Quine defended a "naturalized epistemology," maintaining that the natural sciences provide the most reliable method for confirming hypotheses, for they refer to physical, material, and natural causes. Quine said that the scientific method should be used in philosophy as well.

There is a second version of naturalism that is *ontological*. This position goes further than methodological naturalism by asserting that only the world of nature is real and that supernatural entities do not exist, at least there is insufficient evidence for a transcendental or spiritual realm. This no doubt was influenced by earlier forms of materialism. A key point of metaphysical naturalism is that its proponents are either atheists or agnostics. They find the God concept unintelligible at best and in any case without sufficient evidential or rational grounds for accepting His (or Her) existence.

The naturalism-theism controversy has taken many forms historically. In America it has focused on creationism versus evolution. This controversy has led fundamentalist and evangelical theists to reject the Darwinian theory of evolution. The influence of Darwin on naturalism is unmistakable, for Darwin was able to provide accounts of the origin of species and their extinctions in terms of natural selection. There is no need to postulate "intelligent design" to explain biological phenomena, say naturalists, for there is abundant evidence for evolution. Naturalists point to genetic mutations, differential reproduction, and adaptation as causal factors that more adequately account for the change of species through time.

Theists attempt to separate the human species from the rest of nature, and they postulate an immortal soul. A central issue for naturalists is whether "consciousness" exists independently of the body. This is the well-known mind/body dualism that Dewey had criticized earlier. Although naturalists consider human beings and their psychological behavioral functions to be natural in every sense, there are disagreements as to whether mental characteristics can be reduced to micro events, or whether they can be considered as natural emergent qualities to be understood in terms of conceptual hypothesis developed on the macro level. Supervenience is often cited. This means that mental characteristics are supervenient or dependent on physical characteristics, complimentary to neurological explanations. Reductionists insist that the basic physical-chemical laws on the micro level can best explain cognitive and other psychological experiences. Many naturalists differ on this point, claiming that linguistic and other transactions of the human organism in the social environment are important in understanding cognitive behavior.

Similar considerations apply to complex social and cultural phenomena, and whether the explanation of social institutions, such as the economy and the state, are reducible to basic physical-chemical laws. Incidentally, many naturalists eschew the language of "spirituality," for it seems to smack of religion; others are willing to naturalize it by relating it to the aesthetic and moral dimensions of human experience and the pagan sense of oneness with nature. The future resolution of these ontological questions no doubt depends on the progress of science and which kinds of explanations are more effective. This may be more a matter of competing programs of research than ontological differences.

A third area for intense discussion is whether ethical values have any status, independent of human experience. *Ethical naturalism* asserts that in spite of the fact that ethical principles are relative to human experience, they are amenable to objective rational evaluation and modification in the light of their consequences. Naturalists reject the need of a theological basis for morality. They maintain that it is possible to avoid complete subjectivity and to develop shared principles and values that cut across cultural differences.

Although there are many varieties of naturalism, and some philosophers may adopt only one version of naturalism—in methodology, ontology, or ethics—naturalism in its full sense is committed to a naturalized epistemology, scientific ontology, and naturalistic ethics.

II.

The above issues are among those discussed in this volume, which consists of fourteen entirely new essays by prominent philosophers about the naturalistic worldview and the serious challenges to its principles. Naturalism has long claimed to be the most reasonable philosophy, and here our authors consider how naturalism might best evolve in order to uphold this ambitious claim. We address the timely question of the future of naturalism by pondering its philosophical credibility and value. Fresh challenges from nonnaturalisms, along with new developments among naturalist philosophers, are severely testing philosophical naturalism's ability to offer a comprehensive worldview. Dualisms, transcendentalisms, supernaturalisms, idealisms, and positivisms, while impressed by empirical science and the power of naturalistic explanations, hardly feel compelled to finally rest in peace in the cold chapters of intellectual history.

Philosophers should pay close attention to naturalism and its destiny, even if their own research interests neither depend on nor engage the changing fortunes of naturalism. Those who are concerned about the future course of the naturalistic outlook need to ask, what are the prospects for naturalism surviving in a culture in which religious sensibilities play such an inordinate role?

Naturalism is still widely regarded today as the dominant philosophical outlook in the West. The prestige of science and the power of technology have driven naturalism to prominence, even as deep questions mount on all sides. Religion continues to demand that the existence and orderliness of nature itself require explanation from the mysterious beyond. Advocates for the preciousness of "consciousness" and "rationality" worry that science cannot find a place for free will, reason, morality, or the creative spirit somewhere among the whirling particles. The controversies surrounding scientific knowledge, naturalistic explanation, and the nature of the human mind itself all eventually impact every field of philosophical endeavor.

Perhaps we also need to be reminded that nonnaturalisms are hardly the only, or most serious, source of criticism and controversy. Science itself has proven to be just as challenging to naturalism. Stunning scientific advances force naturalists to continually revise their general understanding of the universe and humanity's place within it. Naturalism itself must adapt, evolve, or perish. All participants in the debates over naturalism and its future are watching these developments closely. Failure to keep up with science itself may prove fatal to philosophical naturalism. A common criticism of naturalism is that it is either ill prepared for, or quite incompatible with, some fresh mystery discovered by science or some radical new theory proposed by science. Philosophers favorable toward naturalism had better prove to be as adventurous as scientists themselves.

The authors of this volume's essays consider a wide variety of challenges for naturalism, proposing improved defenses and novel developments for naturalism. Some essays question whether naturalism is a coherent and unified philosophy and try to determine how one or another variety of naturalism has an advantage. Other essays defend naturalism's approaches to morality, law, religion, and society. Confident that naturalism has a strong future, most of this volume's authors are willing to help reformulate its principles for the twenty-first century and beyond.

Most of this volume's essays originated in presentations made at a conference titled "The Future of Naturalism" at the Center for Inquiry/Transnational in Amherst, New York, in 2007. We gratefully acknowledge the co-sponsorship and financial assistance of the State University of New York at Buffalo's Philosophy Department and its chair that year, Carolyn Korsmeyer, along with support from the C. S. Peirce Professorship in American Philosophy, the Marvin Farber Fund, and the George Hourani Fund. The Center for Inquiry/Transnational, which is committed to science, reason, and free inquiry in every area of human endeavor, provided funding as well. Last but not least we are grateful that Prometheus Books has agreed to underwrite the publication of this volume.

PART ONE:
WHAT KIND OF NATURALISM DESERVES A FUTURE?

1.

The Future of Naturalism: Nature and Culture in Perspectival Duality

Nicholas Rescher

1. TWO MODES OF "NATURALISM"

Naturalism has two principal senses. In one sense it is simply a euphemism for scientism, the idea being that science—and natural science above all—has all the answers, so that if there is going to be any answer to a question about reality, it will be forthcoming from science. The stance of this mode of naturalism is effectively that of a science-geared reductionism that sees the key to understanding reality as being provided by the instrumentalities that account for the fundamental processes of observable phenomena. The other version of naturalism—nowadays far less notable—envisions nature as a developed—virtually even intelligent—organism. The crux of this *idealistic* (rather than *scientistic*) version of naturalism lies not in the idea of a *reduction* of intelligence and its works to the material realities of nature, but rather in seeing the latter as so constituted as to facilitate and favor the emergence of intelligent beings. Accordingly, there is both a positivistic or scientistic and an idealistic construal of naturalism—typified on the one hand by a neo-Darwinist approach and on the other by the emergent evolutionism of Bergson and Teilhard. Both versions envision the fundamentality of natural process—

one focusing on the *evolution* of *life* in nature and the other on the role and impact of *intelligence* in nature.

2. A DUAL REALITY

In line with this duality of approach, the ontological perspective of Western philosophical thought has from its very outset been dualistic. From the days of the pre-Socratics it has distinguished the realms of *phusis* (nature) and of *nomos* (artifice)—of physical reality on the one hand and human contrivance such as language or custom on the other. And various Greek thinkers transmuted this distinction into one between two existential levels—the one deep, fundamental, and natural, the other shallow, derivative, and artificial; the former geared to realty, the latter to mere appearance. (Think here not only of the Atomists but also of Heracleitus and Pythagoras.) Plato picked up these threads of thought and in the Myth of the Cave wove them into a distinction between the sensory world—the world of the observation of everyday life—and an ideal world accessible to reason alone. As he saw it, it is the mind rather than the senses that provides the proper pathway to reality. And Judeo-Christian thought reinforced this dualization, taking the line that after the expulsion from Eden, humankind was constrained to have its life in this imperfect world, albeit ever conscious of (and yearning for) an ideal world inaccessible to mundane experience. Neo-Platonism and the church fathers followed along the tracks of this tradition.

And so, the perspectival duality of nature and nurture, the physical and the conceptual realm, has been among the most fundamental and pervasive features of Western philosophy. Its dialectic of philosophical deliberations has moved within the range defined by the two poles of mind and matter, with humankind generally seen as an amphibian able to live in two different realms.

With Leibniz this dualization took the form of two distinct orders—the kingdoms of nature and of grace—the former entirely mechanical, the later entirely teleological, and the two coordinated by a preestablished harmony between matter and spirit. Immanuel

Kant moved this dualization forward. For him, too, man is an amphibian living in two distinct realms, the experiential world of nature ruled by natural law and efficient causation and a nominal world of intelligence, rationality, and free will governed by the agent-causality of rational beings. On the one hand, scientifically inquiring reason can and should proceed to explain everything in scientific principles; but on the other side a different order with its own teleological principles is free to explain human activities in very different terms of reference. Two distinct explanatory worlds are thus at issue: the realm of natural causality (causality of nature) and that of nomic causality (causality of thought). These correspond with the duality of our living at the same time in the realm of nature and in that of the thought-artifice characteristic of *Homo sapiens*.

3. AN AMBIDEXTROUS TRADITION

While German idealism rebelled against Kant through its impersonalistic naturalization of "Spirit," its post-Hegelian successors—specifically Friedrich Rickert, Johann Eduard Erdmann, and Wilhelm Dilthey—returned once more to a Kant-reminiscent dualistic perspective, with the idea of humankind's occupancy of a dual world again coming to the fore. Thus Dilthey envisioned a two-sided domain of thought and inquiry, encompassing both naturalistic, world-oriented empirical science and a humanistic and normatively oriented study for the human condition. On the one side lay the natural world (*Naturwelt*) of the natural and exact sciences (*Naturwissenschaften*); on the other the world of everyday life (*Lebenswelt*: life-world). The latter is predicated on the artifacts of culture and society whose lineaments inhere in the thought-framework afforded us by processes that we study in the human rather than the natural sciences (the *Geisteswissenschaften* rather than the *Naturwissenschaften*). And as these thinkers saw it, the domains of nature and culture should ideally complement one another. They do not—cannot—really conflict, both because they deal with different matters (physical processes and conceptual processes) and because they must in the final analysis be comparable, given that human thought transpires within the format of nature.

And so two distinct modes of natural reality were deemed to be at issue throughout this tradition, returning time and again to a dualistic leitmotif. The twentieth century affords ample illustrations of this. C. P. Snow's two intellectual cultures have often figured in the thought and discourse of academic inquirers. Think here of Sir Arthur Eddington's two tables—that of physics and that of the plain man—or Wilfred Sellars's distinction between the "scientific image" of things and the "manifest image" by which we deal with them in everyday life. Or, again, think of John McDowell's distinction between the scientific-explanatory space of causes and the anthropocentric-conceptualistic space of reasons—as well as the present author's distinction between the natural order of causality and the thought-order of ideals. All of these are, at bottom, simply so many later-day variations on the theme of Dilthey's fundamental duality.

What became particularly prominent in the twentieth century is a dualism of fact and value, of observational information about the world and affective judgments from a humane perspective.

And this line of thinking confronts us with a duality of realms: natural science and humanistic culture. Science uses causal explanation to embed the life-world within the natural order; humanism uses hermeneutic explanation to fit science into the life-world as a human project. The scientific order is causally reductive; the humane order is hermeneutically constructive.

4. A PRAGMATIC LINKAGE

Which of these two competing perspectives upon reality at large, the humanistic and the scientistic, is the correct one—or at least, which is the more fundamental and deserving of prioritization? The answer in the final analysis is neither one. Like waking and sleeping in human life, both are coordinatively necessary to achieve a healthy balance in the human understanding of reality.

After all, how are the two worlds—the observational scientific natural-world and the experiential life-world—related to one another? The question is fundamental, and the answer is simple. The glue that links the two together is explanation. But different modes of *explanation* are at issue: the one, causal explanation, proceeds in the natural scientists' domain of matter and energy and the other, hermeneutical explanation, proceeds within the reference frame of a humanistic sphere of purpose and value. And the situation that results overall is one of coordinative unity engendered by the realities of humankind's place within nature.

One can, of course, choose to be one-sided about it. If you want to be a reductive scientific materialist, you opt for the perspective of natural science. If you want to be a cultural idealist, you opt for the perspective of an imaginative humanism. However, if you want to be a synoptic realist, you will do well to take both into account at once as per the two-sided synthesis in figure 1. You will then accept a complex reality that envisions a two-sided intertwining of the two, effectively adopting a complex-reality perspective that combines and coordinates causal naturalism with hermeneutic idealism.

A human being indeed is an amphibious creature, destined to live in the realm of physical materiality and mental conceptuality. And given that we actually can "have it both ways," there is no good reason why we should not.

And so what we do well to accept in the end is a systemically integrated perspective that comes to terms with two fundamental facts: (1) that *Homo sapiens* exists and has his being within the world of nature as science studies it; and (2) that science itself is a human construction whose ideas, concepts, and theories are cultural artifacts of the conceptual order.

A theory of nature that cannot be articulated via artifice-devised conceptualizations is simply inaccessible to us. A combination of concepts that cannot come to grips with natural reality through application and prediction is blind. To achieve cognitive health, the two sectors must collaborate and interact in fruitful symbiosis to facilitate a Janus-faced duality of perspective that looks alike to the workings of nature and of mind.

Figure 1

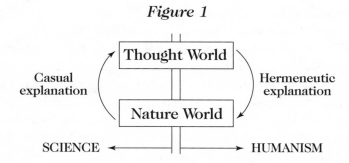

The difference between scientistic naturalism and idealistic naturalism is illustrated by two different approaches to the relationship of mind to body. When nature and thought interact, who is in charge? When we act within nature on the basis of our thoughts, are we not once more in the grips of the causality of nature? How are we to unravel the Kantian knot of two modes of causality?

5. THE FALLACY

In this connection, consider the following oft-maintained contention:

> An act can be free only if its productive source is located in the thoughts and deliberations of the agent. But this is never the case because the tight linkage of mind-activity to brain-activity means that the thoughts and deliberations of the agent's mind are always rooted in and explicable through the processes at work in the agent's brain.

To see what is amiss here, consider the classic freshman-physics setup of a gas-containing cylindrical chamber closed off by a piston at one end. The temperature inside the chamber is lockstep coordinated with the distance of the piston wall from the fixed wall: when the piston moves, the temperature changes correspondingly, and conversely, when temperature-changes are induced, the piston moves correspondingly. But this condition of functional lockstep coordination leaves the issue of initiative wholly open: one may either be changing the temperature by moving the piston or be moving the piston by changing the temperature. Thus, lockstep coordination as such does not settle the question of which of those coordinated variables is free and which is dependent. The fact that two parameters are lockstep coordinated does not settle—or even address—the issue of processual initiative.

In further illustration of this point, consider a teeter-totter or, alternatively, a pulley arrangement, such as the one illustrated in figure 2.

Figure 2

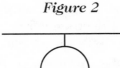

Here the up-or-down motion of the one weight is inseparably tied to the corresponding motion of the other. And this illustrates the larger point: however tight and rigid the functional coordination between two operative agencies may be, the issue of initiative and change-inauguration is something that yet remains entirely open and unaddressed. Mark Twain's tendentious question, "When the body is drunk, does the mind stay sober?" is perfectly appropriate. But then the inverse question, "When the mind panics does the body remain calm?" is no less telling.

All of the myriad illustrations of a coordination between thought and brain activity are simply immaterial to the issue of who is in charge. For what is involved cannot answer the question of whether mind responds passively to brain-state changes or whether it actively uses the brain to its own ends.

For the determinist, to be sure, agents are productively inert—what they do is always the product of what happens to them: they simply provide the stage on which the causality of nature performs its drama. The voluntarist, by contrast, sees intelligent agents as productively active participants in the drama of the world's physical processuality. And the reality of it is that mind-brain correlation cannot effectively be used against him. It is simply fallacious to think that the intimate linkage between brain activity and thought puts the brain in charge of the mind.

For those who accept the fallaciousness of this idea, the brain/mind is seen as an emergent product of evolutionary development resulting in an evolved dual-aspect organization whose two interlinked domains permit the impetus to change to lie sometimes on the one side and sometimes on the other. For the *direction* of determination so far remains open. Given the interlocked variables, the question of dependent-v.-independent status is wholly open and the question of *initiative* unresolved. And the fact that mind and brain sail in the same boat is no reason why mind cannot occasionally seize the tiller. What is at issue is a partnership of *coordination*, not a state of inflexible master-servant *subordination*. In particular situations the initiative can lie on one side or the other—it all depends.

But it all depends on what? How does it get decided where the initiative lies? Well—think again of the pulley situation. When the cube rises, is this because someone is pushing up on it or because a bird has alighted on the sphere? The system itself taken in isolation will not answer this for you, but the wider context—the overall causality, synoptic and dynamic context—will decide where the initiative lies. It is all a matter of where the activity starts and what stands at the end of the causal line. And the free will situation is much the same. When I read, my mind responds to my body; when I write, my body responds to my mind.

6. THE FUTURE OF NATURALISM

What then of the future of naturalism?

How naturalism fares will very much depend on how the position is to be construed. At the outset we contemplated a naturalism that was scientistic and reductivistic in its orientation. And this stood in contrast to another sort of naturalism that was idealistic in orientation, in prioritizing the constructive intelligence in the world's scheme of things. It would seem plausible to think that the outlook for both of these perspectives is bleak, simply because each is too one-sidedly narrow in outlook and perspective to come to satisfactory terms with a complex reality. I myself am persuaded that the only sort of naturalism that can lay claim to a promising future will have to be one that is sufficiently broad in its range and its sympathies to allow *both* the nature-geared scientistic version of the doctrine (geared to *Naturwissenschaften*, broadly construed) *and* the thought-geared insights of the humanistic sphere (the *Geisteswissenschaften*, broadly construed) to figure in cooperative coordination. In the end, then, it seems to me that the sort of naturalism that has a promising future will be one that is neither exclusively scientistic nor exclusively idealistic in its ethos but is humanistic in the sense of being sufficiently ample in scope to do full justice both to the works of nature itself and to those of humankind and mind operating within its realm. Such an ampler humanistic naturalism would view the way intelligence works as an integral part of a nature that has facilitated the evolutionary development of a being able to act freely—that is, to make use of intelligence for the guidance of action to meet its needs and desires within the operative setting that nature affords.

2.

Reclaiming Naturalism

Joseph Margolis

I.

W hat I find particularly striking about the problematic we call naturalism is that its most strategic questions are all but invisible—philosophically. At any rate, I'll risk the dare for the sake of a fresh discovery and an eventual source of fresh agreement. Here, then, I offer five distinctions that are not likely to be featured in any usual academically informed analysis of what we should mean by "naturalism." For one thing, naturalism is a thoroughly historicized distinction: it has evolved in dramatically diverse ways, following the contours of philosophical fashion. It cannot possibly mean the same thing or raise the same puzzles for (say) Aristotle and ourselves; we realize that *our* answer to the questions *we* deem decisive cannot fail to reflect our particular grasp of what the entire history of philosophy has pertinently accomplished and needs still to resolve. But as soon as we admit this much, then, second, we find ourselves drawn to admit as well that what is most essential to our present grasp of the entire matter centers, precisely, on distinctions that were never explicitly formulated in the ancient world, or, for that matter, much before the second half of the eighteenth century and the beginning of the nineteenth. Third, if we follow the implications of this last admission, we cannot fail to acknowledge that a good many of the salient puzzles of naturalism advanced in the past are now thought to be unhelpful (possibly even benighted) versions of questions that any properly responsive naturalism would now have to answer if it were to claim a valid advantage over its rivals: earlier versions of the naturalism question might well be discarded outright as misdirected or simply useless, or allowed only by the barest courtesy. Certainly, a good many of Aristotle's, Descartes', and Kant's explanatory maneuvers would now be thought to exceed the resources of any unproblematic naturalism, even where their authors assign them to a larger Nature.

Thinking along these lines, without prejudice to the argumentative force of competing naturalisms (or anti-naturalisms), we would have to admit, fourth, that naturalism in our time must come to terms with the profound, ubiquitous, perfectly obvious—but as yet unresolved, perhaps ultimately benign—conceptual incommensurabilities that color the discursive fluencies of our favored accounts of physical nature and a fully formed human world: for instance, the struggle between reductive and anti-reductive forces, which is certainly central to contemporary philosophical dispute, hardly acknowledges the direct bearing of descriptive and explanatory incommensurabilities on the very coherence and right characterization of naturalism itself, in spite of the fact that that dispute already implicates the question of how to define any thoroughly naturalistic idiom. Think, for instance, of the usual idioms of mind and matter and of familiar modes of explanation addressed to bodily movement and deliberate action. The unity of science program may well assume, but it nowhere demonstrates, that the ineliminability of incommensurable explanatory idioms is, finally, incompatible with a thoroughgoing naturalism; and, of course, if the necessity of a completely reductive or hierarchically closed system of explanations, whether transcendental in Kant's sense or causal in the sense long sought in theoretical physics, cannot be demonstrated (as I believe is true), then naturalism and the admission of explanatory incommensurabilities cannot be shown to be incompatible for that reason alone.[1]

Finally, the fate of these questions draws us on to the deeper issue of whether naturalism, taken in its explanatory mode, can or must be cast as an inclusive or closed system of nature, or whether any such conception can be coherently formulated in cognitive terms or would, if allowed at all, problematize the very distinction between naturalism and the usual bounds of our canonical specimens (for instance, in terms of first causes, natural necessities, uncreated nature, the first of Kant's antinomies, or Creation itself). Here we are made to realize that the familiar innovations of "modern" modern philosophy— featuring (say) the inquiries of Kant and the German idealists (including Hegel)—account for both the historical transformation of the problematic now before us and the special force of the relatively invisible topics I've just trotted out that the academy would need to reclaim if we supposed it capable of constructing a satisfactory answer now. The invisible topics, let it be said, have to do, most prominently, with the prospects of a possible rapprochement among the main currents of Eurocentric philosophy now actively opposed to one another within the terms of the naturalism question.

I believe there are worthwhile answers to these questions, but they converge on our sense of the principal contests of our time—or they go toward redirecting our sense of such contests. For me, they settle in the leanest way on understanding the conceptual relationship between physical nature and human history and culture—and whether we could provide a convincing reformulation of what naturalism might now rule in or out of bounds (and why) regarding the recovered saliencies of our time. For present purposes, I trust this way of casting the question: that is, treating it as tantamount to judging the adequacy of pragmatism vis-à-vis the best forces of analytic philosophy (which oscillate between pragmatist and what we may call scientistic tendencies) and the best forces of continental philosophy (which, similarly, oscillate between pragmatist and what we may call extra-naturalist, or, indeed, supernaturalist tendencies). I confine myself, therefore, to selected issues thus constrained.

What I mean is this. Naturalism, in our time, tends to favor the primacy of the invisible topics I've mentioned (and others of the same gauge), which it is prepared to treat generously and informally, guided by the weight of accumulating arguments against the need for what we may call extranatural if not supernatural readings of the same topics. For example, the relative adequacy of reductionism and anti-reductionism is *not* ordinarily construed as a dispute between naturalism and extranaturalism; but, if it is so construed, then, since as a matter of fact, explanatory incommensurabilities are common-place among those who regard the physicalist reduction of the human world as having effectively failed, the elimination of such incommensurabilities cannot be deemed essential to the fortunes of naturalism as such; and if that is so, then the concept of nature as a closed system—whether in the conceptual sense originally featured in Kant's first *Critique* or, say, in the causal sense favored by the theoretical physicist Steven Weinberg, cannot now count as a compelling restriction on a viable naturalism.[2]

Nevertheless, Aristotle's account of *nous* (in the *De Anima*) and of the Prime Mover (in the *Physics*), Descartes' treatment of a rational knowledge of "eternal truths" (in *The Principles of Philosophy*), and Kant's and Husserl's faculties of transcendental reason yielding substantive necessities of thought that empirical science must accommodate are challenges from the extranaturalist side of cognition that the leaner naturalisms of our own day must either defeat or supersede or, failing that, admit the resultant diminished standing of the doctrines they had hoped to champion.

Here, naturalism's philosophical wager is perfectly plain: whatever is thought to be essential to an adequate account of the human world—language, intersubjective communication, and the sui generis nature and emergence of human cultures, for instance—must be admitted to be open (as such) to naturalistic explanation; privileged cognitive faculties yielding indubitable or necessary synthetic truths, whether "natural" or transcendental, must be defeated or replaced or reinterpreted along a posteriori lines; and doctrines that clearly exceed the limits of finite inquiry and intelligence and the cognition of what is true (notably, those that belong to the Kantian and post-Kantian tradition: truths about *noumena*, the infinite outcome of finite inquiry, knowledge of the completely and concretely totalized Absolute in the sense invoked by Hegel, closed systematicity in Kant's sense, and the like) must either be rejected outright or construed as no more than heuristic, rhetorical, confined to rational hope, or otherwise diminished. There's an endless glut of such presumptions to be scanned. But acknowledging them and the need to get beyond them suggests the strategic role of pragmatism within the compass of current Eurocentric debates. For pragmatism is preeminently committed to a moderate naturalism of the sort now being sketched—against the extremes of analytic scientism and continental extranaturalism. There's the thread of the argument I have in mind but not the argument itself.

II.

Here, the cunning of history comes to the rescue. For analytic philosophy remains noticeably weaker than either pragmatism or continental inquiry in its grasp of the conceptual revolution wrought by Kant and Hegel. All this affords an ample confirmation of just how far—and yet how far short of what is needed—the most perceptive (and courageous) analytic forays have dared to penetrate into the uncertain common ground of naturalism. Here (frankly, for the sake of an argumentative economy and a fashionable example) I single out the helpful candor of John McDowell's plan to recover an adequate naturalism by way of an inventive reading of certain philosophical sources that he finds neglected. McDowell proceeds, in *Mind and World* (1996), his John Locke Lectures, by seemingly co-opting Hegel's concept of *Bildung* in the service of correcting Kant's transcendental extravagance among the largely ahistorical and "pre-Kantian" inquiries of the best of contemporary Anglo-American analytic philosophy. Quite a complicated undertaking; and yet it collects the pivotal issues most effectively—in fact, unintentionally, against its own argument.

I believe McDowell fails hands down (in the Locke Lectures) to capture the central theme of Hegel's *Bildung* and, as a consequence, fails to capture the nerve of what naturalism now requires. But I intend the verdict in a generous way. Because McDowell succeeds (by failing in his own venture) in drawing our attention to the flat impossibility of enlisting the full significance of Hegel's critique of Kant and pre-Kantian philosophy (reaching back to Aristotle), *if* the analytic movement itself fails (or we, that is, philosophers of any stripe, fail) to include in its (or our) conception of naturalism what we may reasonably term the "metaphysics" (or the meaning) of historicity and the difference between a biologized and a hybrid (or encultured) conception of "human nature." For we lose thereby the decisive contrast between the utterly different (in fact, incommensurable) conceptions of humankind's "second nature"—implicated in the paradigms offered in Aristotle and Hegel, now doubtfully conflated in McDowell's new synthesis.

McDowell is hardly alone in his speculation. But he may be the most visible contemporary analyst to have grasped the inherent limitations of the separate naturalisms of Aristotle, Hume, and Kant—hence, then, the limitations of any current analytic naturalism made to rely on such or similar resources—when (as McDowell believes) a relatively small adjustment (reconciling Kant and Aristotle) would be enough to overcome the decisive limitation he claims to have isolated in analytic philosophy itself.

But McDowell's way of solving the problem remains remarkably unhelpful. For one thing, to work, as McDowell prefers, within the framework of Kant's first *Critique* (with whatever additions may be drawn from the third *Critique* and the *Foundations of the Metaphysics of Morals*) goes no distance at all toward overcoming the so-called de jure solutions Kant favors, solutions that, as is well known, preclude any causal processes involving the combined work of the different primary faculties that contribute to knowledge and the effective application of practical reason (within Kant's system); hence, for another, a Kantian strategy never comes to terms with the usual requirements of contemporary naturalism (or Aristotle's kind of naturalism, for that matter), and Kant's faculties—understanding and reason in particular—are not, as such, easily admitted as naturalistic powers of the appropriate sort. Finally, since both Aristotle and Hegel are, in effect, opposed to Kant's kind of analysis, we cannot tell from McDowell's recommendations whether and how he means to integrate the contributions of all three in a way that strengthens the resources of analytic philosophy along naturalistic lines. I'm afraid much of what he says misses the mark.

It is also a fact that McDowell reads Hegel's notion of *Bildung* as tantamount to the Greek conception of *paideia* (as in Aristotle's conception of what we may now call *his* "ethical *Bildung*"), which McDowell then adds to his own improved reading of Kant's having located the causal order of a "disenchanted" (Humean) nature and the order of explanatory reasons available to Kantian moral agents within the boundaries of one and the same natural world. If you are willing to allow the extraordinary busyness of this—McDowell's—strategy (which is not mine at all, and which cannot possibly succeed), you see at once the surprising economy of relying on the close analysis of McDowell's option to gain a proper sense of analytic philosophy's fatal reluctance to admit the full conceptual resources of the sui generis space we call the human or encultured world. For it is precisely those resources (I've been suggesting) that, rightly joined, account for the distinctive "second nature" of the uniquely hybrid human mode of being that contemporary naturalism can no longer disallow, without providing compelling reasons for the continued limitation.

The point of all this is that the dawning of the conceptual novelty of human history and culture—well, for one thing, the very analysis of human language and the "enlanguaged" nature of human experience and thought and intelligence—begins to take form (as early as the late eighteenth century) only *after* the work of Aristotle, Hume, *and* Kant was thoroughly and canonically mastered. For all his courage and candor, McDowell, I'm afraid, simply collects the supposed advantages of Hegel's conception of *Bildung*—without honest toll—by way of grafting Aristotle's conception of *paideia* (or *Bildung*, if you wish) onto Kant's entirely separate (but similarly inadequate) marriage of theoretical and practical reason.

The whole affair is a house of cards—though skillfully constructed. It obviously draws its principal strength from resources that a fresh naturalism would inevitably have to eclipse. Its failure—which is decisive for my own brief—depends on two very telling shortcomings. For one thing, Aristotle treats ethical education (McDowell's sense of Aristotle's *Bildung*) in biologized terms alone—and, there, only perfunctorily (though Aristotle's biology is of course ampler in scope than ours); and, for another, Kant's transcendentalism *never* comes to terms with the analysis of actual knowledge of the world or effective intelligence in practical life, even in his own account: for Kant *never* gets beyond the notorious question of the transcendental "possibility" of knowledge and practical intelligence. That is, in fact, the decisive point of Hegel's critique of Kant,[3] which builds on the contributions of figures like Maimon, Herder, and Fichte. So McDowell's proposal cannot but be regressive, though it highlights, by its transparent retreat, what we genuinely still lack.

It's impossible to grasp the full force of the extraordinary turn in Western thought launched by Hegel (in his critique of Kant's *Critiques*) without grasping this double limitation. But McDowell plays into both sorts of weakness, which serves us, here, as a sort of general symptom of the self-impoverishing tendencies of contemporary analytic philosophy inclined toward scientism. There's the reason for my close attention to McDowell's adventurous strategy for recovering an adequate naturalism for our time. A bit of textual elucidation helps to clinch the argument: here, philosophy and its history come to the same thing. But there's more to the argument—and more that is invisible in the sense already broached.

I hesitate to plunge in here without providing more in the way of preparation for what needs to be said. But perhaps I'll not be misunderstood after all, if I draw a clearly circumscribed, perfectly obvious small clue from McDowell's reflection on naturalism (well, from his reflection on ethical naturalism, which is hardly the same thing), which nevertheless falls short of what I have in mind. It goes this way: in "Two Sorts of Naturalism" (1996), McDowell notes that in the *Nicomachean Ethics*, Aristotle "stipulates . . . that he is addressing only people in whom the value scheme he takes for granted has been properly ingrained" (as by "ethical upbringing").[4] There's the point! (McDowell offers nothing more expansive.) But *he cannot mean what he says*, unless he means to legitimate *Aristotle's Bildung* (if I may call it that) by way of *Hegel's* usage (which would rightly require introducing the modern distinction between biology and culture, *which Aristotle lacks* and Kant all but lacks—or opposes); or he means that Hegel's *Bildung* is essentially the same as the Greek *paideia* (which, of course, is false).

Failing here, McDowell (and the analytic avant-garde, newly attracted to the continentals) fail in a decisive and telling way. For, on the paradigm of the *Nicomachean Ethics*, Aristotle ventures no essential explanation of the *given* practices of Greek societies: he is only interested in how, rationally, we abstract and essentialize in normative ways what we take to be the executive values of this or that society; *his* "second nature" is no more than what is conventionally constructed *from* what is given, societally, whereas Hegel thinks of human "second nature" in terms of the enculturing conditions under which the human creature *becomes* a *geistlich* agent *for the first time*—whether ethically or cognitively (or in other ways).

Precisely because McDowell wants to enrich the Kantian vision so that *it* can be made to yield an account of the "natural" that would be home at once to both reasons and causes, he shortchanges Hegel, misses the irrelevance of Aristotle's *Ethics* (the same would have been true of the *Poetics*), and utterly fails to see that Kant himself faces an insuperable problem regarding the identification of the natural world! Disaster all around. But then, the solution that is needed stares you in the face: simply admit the natural emergence of the cultural world that Hegel speaks of; alternatively, read Hegel's *Phenomenology* as a thoroughly naturalistic account of the cognitive process of a culturally formed agent, whatever may strike you as Hegel's verbal extravagances.

According to McDowell, then, Aristotle conveys the sense (the sense *McDowell* champions) in which the ingrained spontaneity with which we learn to respond to ethical matters identifies (our) "second nature" entirely *within* the conceptual resources of (our) "first" nature. "Any actual second nature [McDowell says] is a cultural product, a formed state of practical reason . . . not something that dictates to one's nature *from outside*." He then adds: where we apply

> the rhetoric of ethical realism, second nature acts in a world in which it finds more than what is open to view from the [merely] dehumanized stance [that is, more than what it could possibly gain from the "disenchanted," "naturalistic," Humean-like world we treat as "viewed from nowhere"—as lacking human meaning altogether] that the natural sciences, rightly for their purposes, adopt. And there is nothing against bringing this richer reality under the rubric of nature too.[5]

Fine. But McDowell nowhere explicitly accounts for the concrete reality of the very cultural (or "enculturing") transformation of the human that makes "practical reason" and "ethical upbringing" *meaningful in the first place or at all*. Unless, that is, "second nature" is no more than a selective strand of a biologized ethic, which is noticeably less than what Hegel and (I would say) we require. The legitimation of ethical norms cannot be gained through any "enriched" naturalism by merely re-enchanting nature: *that* is no more than Aristotle's (*and* McDowell's) *and* (for altogether different reasons) Kant's fatal limitation. McDowell does not seem to grasp what's missing. He never rightly touches on the question whether, in re-enchanting nature (in a sense informed by Max Weber's analysis), the sui generis emergence of the cultural and historied world (which I am associating with Hegel's commanding critique of Kant) is implicated at all. The reason, as you may guess, is simply that, on *Hegel's* account, reason is itself a cultural artifact open to continual historical transformation; but that, precisely, is missing (in different ways and for different reasons) in both Kant and Aristotle.

There you begin to collect again the invisibilities I mentioned at the start of these remarks. In our time, there can be no adequate naturalism that does not explain the complex interpenetration of biology and culture in all versions of what we call the human condition. There's the pivot of the three-legged contest among pragmatists, analysts, and continentals.

Still, McDowell is entirely justified in thinking that there cannot be any discontinuity between our grasp of truth and explanation respecting physical nature *and* legitimated norms and reasons applied to human action. For the concept of what is "natural" or "naturalistic," as we now understand matters, requires provision for the different "natures" of what we distinguish as physical and cultural—not meaning by that to prejudge reduction's prospects, but rather to feature the importance of the distinction in all our inquiries, whether or not reductionism fails. For if reductionism fails (as I believe it must), then what falls *within* the bounds of naturalism may yet need to be metaphysically sorted, nonexclusively, in terms of "cultural" and "noncultural" properties.

I say McDowell is absolutely right about Aristotle's "ethical naturalism," identifying what makes it the splendid exemplar that it is. But the two naturalisms McDowell distinguishes through his reading of Aristotle and Kant are entirely *internal* to some deeper conception (of naturalism) on which they depend—which *McDowell nowhere examines* and without which even Aristotle's account remains a complete conceptual mystery. McDowell borrows the term *Bildung* from Hegel. But if he applies it to Aristotle's account of the conventions of "ethical upbringing," then he reads Aristotle in a way in which Aristotle couldn't have read his own work; and if he intends *Bildung* in the sense of Aristotle's notion of a paideutic extraction from, and idealization of, the biologized conventions of Greek life (*however they arise*), then he cannot have grasped the novelty of Hegel's usage. Aristotle and Hegel cannot be read as construing human "second nature" in the same sense: Aristotle means little more than the conventional first-order differences between one Mediterranean society and another (Greek or barbarian), without metaphysical implications of any transformative kind; whereas, as in the *Phenomenology*, Hegel means to feature the original transformation *of* the members of the human species as, *emergently*, ethically and cognitively competent agents.[6] This is, of course, also the central topic of that attenuated Hegelian offshoot that we characteristically name pragmatism.

III.

McDowell never defines the metaphysical difference between physical nature ("disenchanted" nature) and human culture ("nature" perfused with and penetrated by encultured meanings and reasons). It's the second distinction (the one I have in mind) that makes the first feasible at all, that captures the modern quarrels regarding naturalism that are most pertinent in any resolution of the divisions among the principal philosophical movements of our time. McDowell distinguishes handily between science and morality, dubbing the capabilities required for the second as "second nature" relative to the first (or the first re-enchanted); whereas what's needed for our larger question is the distinction between physical nature and human culture itself—in order to test whether the pertinent differences that now pit pragmatists, analysts, and continentals against one another might not be tamed within the terms of a more promising naturalism—which, featuring historicity and enculturation, might outflank the intractable claims and charges that obscure a possible (deeper) compatibility that we must now get clear about.

Let me be as straightforward as possible. I've just identified—obliquely, it's true—the last (shall I say) decisive invisibility that forms the best sketch of naturalism's current problematic. Treat that as a sixth distinction that captures the full challenge of the previous five. Here, thinking in tandem with McDowell, but also in opposition to his largely textual advice, we can hardly doubt that the main thrust of the philosophical revolution that spans Kant's and Hegel's innovations (and what they have yielded in our own time) features findings such as these: that there are no privileged cognitive faculties of any kind; that science and knowledge are themselves critical constructions of some kind relative to what, presuppositionlessly, but affected in ways that are admittedly prejudiced and horizoned nevertheless, *is* admittedly *given*, reportorially, in public experience; that all such data are subject to the forces of historicized formation and interpretation; that transcendental or a priori reflections on the conditions of knowledge are inescapably a posteriori posits about what, relative to the perceived success of our sciences, appear, changeably, to be our best guesses about the sources, conditions, and methods of science itself; that there is no principled way to segregate the so-called subjective and objective sides of cognitive competence.

If you accept these and similar truisms—I take them to be truisms, but they will certainly be opposed by those who oppose the conception of naturalism that I favor—then you surely glimpse my sixth invisibility. I mean the truism that perception and experience, as well as thought, *are,* in the very sense in which the human condition (the human mode of being, if you wish, the nature of what it is to be a person or self or agent or subject) *is* "second-natured," hybrid, artifactual (involving the union of biology and culture)—*are* also, let me repeat—sui generis, transformed by enculturing forces, inextricably *penetrated* by language, history, theory, belief, tradition, practice, idiosyncrasy, prejudice, and the like, uniquely emergent, described and explained in profoundly incommensurable but perfectly manageable ways. My best evidence that this is true rests with the phenomenon of speech itself. I take it that we are creatures so altered by our "second nature" that *we actually hear speech spontaneously and understandingly*: we do not first hear sound, which we somehow reliably interpret to be meaningful speech!

If you think carefully about this datum (and its obvious analogues) under the condition of the flux of history, then you may wish to consider theorems like these: for one, that the data on which all inquiry rests cannot but be phenomenological rather than merely phenomenal—in a sense akin to the minimal theme of Hegel's *Phenomenology* rather than (say) Husserl's *Ideas*, or, for that matter, Hume's *Treatise*; and, for another, that the foundational standing of the physical sciences is itself a constructive, alterable artifact of admitting the "second-natured" nature of human experience and what we take to be the human condition. In short, my sixth invisibility implicates the assumption that every science is a human science: so that even the picture of a "disenchanted" nature, which McDowell draws from Hume and Kant, is the result of an already idealized, antecedent abstraction from the more labile work of the incipient inquiries of any science.

This clinches the sense in which McDowell plainly puts the cart before the horse: every pertinent naturalism in our time will have to turn to deeper puzzles than McDowell admits. And yet, at the moment of its introduction, McDowell's formula seemed to promise an entirely fresh command of the naturalism question drawn from resources most favorably received by the best analytic philosophies of the day. The trouble is that McDowell might have generated his solution already in Kant's time, well before philosophy began to conjure with the radical resources of emergent history and culture; his reference to contemporary analytic philosophy hardly makes a difference. Hegel, I suggest, facilitates our entry into the enriched resources that we now require, if we are ever to overcome the double impoverishment of Aristotle's biologism and Hume's and Kant's tolerance of a "disenchanted" nature. Pragmatism is merely the opportunistic beneficiary of the Hegelian influence that courses through Peirce and Dewey. Accordingly, it also needs a better discipline.

About "acquiring a second nature," McDowell says (in *Mind and World*), "I cannot think of a good short English expression for this, but it is what figures in German philosophy as *Bildung*."[7] But this, precisely, stops short of the deeper theme of *Bildung* or second nature that McDowell now needs and that we must explore further. You cannot fail to see that McDowell is aware of the problem, since, on the very next page of his text, after remarking that "we need to recapture the Aristotelian idea that a normal mature human being is a rational animal, but without losing the Kantian idea that rationality operates freely in its own sphere," he explicitly says: "Modern naturalism is forgetful of second nature."[8] Of course, he's right; but it's not the sense of what he actually delivers. *That* sense (the *second* sense of "second nature," as it were) cannot be drawn from Aristotle or Hume *or* Kant or from the "modern naturalism" that McDowell discounts ("disenchanted" nature)—*or*, indeed, from his own improved naturalism. It requires our turning to Hegel's decisive innovations (even if not to Hegel's own extravagant system). I take McDowell to be signaling such a need, though he nowhere crosses the metaphysical divide.[9]

To put the matter crudely: if McDowell cannot or dares not go further in pursuing the analyst's account of naturalism, then, since it's perfectly fair to say he's taken as bold a step as any strong analyst has in our time (anyone who has not simply gone over to Husserl or Heidegger), analytic philosophy regularly deprives itself of the conceptual resources of historicity and the enculturing processes that *first yield our second nature*—which McDowell's theory of ethical naturalism presupposes (to ensure its own coherence) and which the pragmatists and continentals have never ignored. Where, then, do ethical norms come from? What accounts for their validity? What explains their compatibility with naturalism?

You have only to remember that Wilfrid Sellars (whom McDowell admires but finds it necessary to improve on) had already supposed that we could (if we wished) simply *add* the norms and rational functions assigned to persons (the language of reasons, meanings, explanation, and justification) to the language of disenchanted science (the language of causes) to capture (in effect) all that McDowell might require.[10] Of course, Sellars's maneuver also fails utterly: persons are *already* "hybrid" entities in the sense I've been hinting at, *if they speak a language*: ethical values are *natural*—second-natured—*for them* and *for them alone*!

It's hard to believe that Sellars ever meant *his* "addition" to be taken seriously. McDowell has his own improvement ready at hand: "The right contrast for the space of reasons," he says, "is not the space of causes, but [echoing Kant] the realm of law." It's true, he adds, "that a *merely* causal relation [which nature 'as the realm of law' already exceeds] cannot do duty for a justificatory relation"; but "it is also disputable that the idea of causal connections is restricted to thinking that is *not* framed by the space of reasons. . . .The contrast leaves it possible for an area of discourse to be in the logical space of causal relations to objects without thereby being shown not to be in the logical space of reasons [for 'reasons might *be* causes']."[11] Of course!

But all this skirts the essential issue. What finally *is* the domain of nature that could coherently include and join (disenchanted or re-enchanted) causes and (justificatory) reasons without yielding to such problematic extremes as reductionism, dualism, transcendentalism, or the mere tinkering of a philosophical *bricoleur*?[12] What is the world of *reasons*? McDowell never answers, except in Aristotle's and Kant's profoundly question-begging ways. It was only when the very validity of Kant's transcendentalism revealed a lacuna that it could never fill that the corrective power of admitting the constructive forces of history and culture transformed the whole of "modern" modern philosophy. We have hardly probed its consequences to this day—and yet that was more than two hundred years ago.

Let me add, in the briefest possible way, a word about what our altered naturalism augurs for philosophy's future. Of course it signals a middle way between reductionism and extranaturalism; but that *is* already the emerging contest of Eurocentric philosophy. More profoundly still, I think it will mean marginalizing all of the distinctive marks of the original confidence of Kantian transcendentalism and, of course, of its analogues in Aristotle and the bizarre excrescences of the post-Humean and post-Kantian world down to our own day: in particular, the stalemating or elimination of universalism, ontological necessities, systematicity, and the real and conceptual closure of the world. All of these notions dominated the inventiveness of the German idealist world more than fifty years beyond Kant and on into the American variant of idealism, at least in Peirce and, more sparely, in Dewey—though it was surely doomed from the start. The same themes appear, at least as targets of opportunity, in the recovery of a leaner empiricism informed by those same German excesses (as, in different ways, in Quine and Rorty and McDowell).

That surge may be over now; the new current may well favor the metaphysics of change and history. But the decisive focus of all these matters rests (in my opinion) with the right analysis of predicative generality under the conditions of the flux of cultural history. At any rate, I see no better clue before us. The only viable answer (I'm convinced) lies in the prospects of a *naturalistic account of the hybrid nature of a human person.*[13]

It's possible that I've used McDowell unfairly. But the *Bildung* theme of his *Mind and World* seems to promise a breakthrough (not yet delivered) on the part of Anglo-American analytic philosophy in the direction of recovering Hegel at least, which is essential to rightly understanding the full force of McDowell's reclamation of Aristotle's ethical naturalism *and*, through that, the beckoning rapprochement that larger currents within Eurocentric philosophy now find irresistible. Analytic philosophy without Hegel (or, better, without the metaphysical distinction between nature and culture) cannot generate a naturalism bolder than Sellars's dualism! There's the limitation of McDowell's intended "re-enchantment" of nature.

The truth about McDowell's strategy is stranger than I've admitted. I've pulled my punches. The facts are much less hospitable than I've made them out to be. Because, although Kant is not a dualist of Sellars's sort—Sellars is (*at times*) an extreme partisan of "disenchanted" nature, as when he contrasts the "manifest image" and the "scientific image"—Kant *is* a hopeless dualist of an a-priorist sort when it comes to reconciling the transcendental "possibility" of natural science and the transcendental "possibility" of moral agency. That is to say, McDowell simply takes advantage of the odd (the all but extraneous) fact that Kant holds that the powers of transcendental reason are perfectly capable of accounting at one and the same time for the "possibility" of both! There is absolutely nothing in the *Foundations of the Metaphysics of Morals*, for instance, or in the first *Critique*, that affords the least basis for recovering either Aristotle's biologized account of *Bildung* (or *paideia*) or Hegel's *geistlich* account of the "second-natured" *Bildung* of the human self.

That alone confirms, hands down, the complete irrelevance of

McDowell's reminder (in the passage cited earlier from "Two Sorts of Naturalism") that, in Kant's account, the explanations of natural causes and of the acts of responsible agents are easily brought within the same space of transcendental reason! That was Kant's plan all along. But Kant never demonstrated—he couldn't—that the account he offers bears on *any* questions of actual history or actual cultural formation or contingent change: he was unable to show how his analysis of the "possibility" of science and morality had anything to do with the analysis of *actual* science and morality. There's the mortal weakness of Kant's entire system. There is no way to reach Hegel's innovations from Kant's philosophy. There is, therefore, no way McDowell could (by the strategy he elects) have enlarged the conceptual resources of naturalism to include the sui generis distinctions he rightly believes analytic philosophy has deprived itself of. McDowell fails to grasp the full meaning of what a disenchanted world disallows. It's as if philosophy had become little more than a clinical symptom.

NOTES

1. See, for instance, the interesting discussion in Edo Pivčević, *The Reason Why: A Theory of Philosophical Explanation* (Zagreb, Croatia: Kruzak, 2007), chap. 8—and, implicitly, through the entire book.

2. See Immanuel Kant, preface to the second edition, *The Critique of Pure Reason*, trans. Paul Guyer and Allen W. Wood (Cambridge: Cambridge University Press, 1998); and Steven Weinberg, *Dreams of a Final Theory: The Scientific Search for the Ultimate Laws of Nature* (New York: Random House, 1996). See also my *Unraveling of Scientism: American Philosophy at the End of the Twentieth Century* (Ithaca, NY: Cornell University Press, 2003), chap. 1; and Jaegwon Kim, *Physicalism, or Something Close Enough* (Princeton, NJ: Princeton University Press, 2007).

3. John McDowell, "Two Sorts of Naturalism," in *Mind, Value and Reality* (Cambridge, MA: Harvard University Press, 1998), pp. 195–96, 197. McDowell is referring to the *Nicomachean Ethics*, 1.4.1095b-6 (which he cites).

4. I have explored this matter in "The Point of Hegel's Dissatisfaction with Kant," unpublished.

5. McDowell, "Two Sorts of Naturalism," pp. 192–94 (italics added).

6. See G. W. F. Hegel, *Phenomenology of Spirit*, trans. A. V. Miller (Oxford: Clarendon Press, 1972).

7. John McDowell, *Mind and World* (Cambridge, MA: Harvard University Press, 1994), lecture IV, p. 84.

8. Ibid., p. 85.

9. The only other reference in those of McDowell's publications with which I am familiar that seems to lean, ever so tentatively, in the direction I'm suggesting, appears in John McDowell, "In Defense of Modesty," in *Meaning, Knowledge and Reality* (Cambridge, MA: Harvard University Press, 1998), which briefly links Herder's and Hegel's general views on Enlightenment thought, in a running critique of Michael Dummett's theory of meaning.

10. See Wilfrid Sellars, "Philosophy and the Scientific Image of Man," in *Science, Perception and Reality* (London: Routledge and Kegan Paul, 1963).

11. McDowell, *Mind and World*, p. 71n.

12. See ibid., p. 5 n4: "In much of the rest of these lectures, [McDowell says,] I shall be concerned to cast doubt on Sellars's idea that placing something in the logical space of reasons is, as such, to be contrasted with giving an empirical description of it." I agree with McDowell here. But McDowell's words presuppose a deeper account that he nowhere supplies.

13. I take the chapters that form part IV of McDowell's *Mind, Value and Reality* as confirming just how distant the doctrine of *Bildung* is from McDowell's account of naturalism, apart from his use of it (in his special sense) in explicating Aristotle's ethical naturalism.

For a discussion of the internal relationship between Bildung and the disenchantment/re-enchantment question, see *Reading McDowell: On Mind and World*, ed. Nicholas H. Smith (London: Routledge, 2002), chapters by Richard J. Bernstein, Robert B. Pippin, Rudiger Bübner, and J. M. Bernstein. All of these, I find, appreciate the incipient new departure McDowell intends to pursue; and all (in different ways) see (as well) the sense in which "nature" (inclusive nature) and "second nature" are insufficiently developed (as yet) to meet the requirements of a "naturalistic" justification of ethical values (thus construed) as well as of perceptual and explanatory judgments pertinent to the work of the sciences. See also McDowell's remark, in the preface to *Mind and World*: "I would like to conceive this work . . . as a prolegomenon to a reading of [Hegel's] Phenomenology" (p. ix). I take this to be a promissory note.

See also John McDowell, "Having the World in View: Sellars and Intentionality," the Woodbridge Lectures 1997, *Journal of Philosophy* 45 (1998): 490.

3.

Advantages and Limits of Naturalism

Mario Bunge

N aturalism is the view that the universe and nature are the same, so that there is nothing supernatural. We may distinguish two kinds of naturalism: naïve and sophisticated. Naïve naturalists hold that everything desirable "comes naturally," that is, is part of human nature, innate, or hard wired in the brain. Thus fairness would be "in the genes," and rationality and science would be just extensions of common sense.

Although naïve naturalism itself may "come naturally," it is false and self-destructive. It is false because artificiality is known to be distinctively human: even the most primitive hunter-gatherers fashion or use tools of various kinds, invent social conventions, and organize themselves into unnatural social systems. And naïve naturalism is self-defeating because it may be used to justify religion, the law of the land, and other social constructions: remember the search for the God gene, the natural law doctrine, and the claim that slavery, or else capitalism, is the natural social order.

Sophisticated naturalism is something else: it is just a reminder that, for all our sophistication, humans are animals, and consequently should attend to our biological needs, and anchor the various disciplines to biology: in particular, we should naturalize social science, ethics, and epistemology. In turn, sophisticated naturalism comes in two main varieties: vitalism (such as Nietzsche's) and pragmatism (such as Peirce's, James's, and Dewey's).

Whereas the vitalists reject reason and science altogether, the pragmatists wish to make full use of science and technology in order to improve the human condition. This explains the well-known connection between vitalism and fascism (through the Blood and Soil doctrine) and the pragmatism-democracy connection. The trouble with pragmatism, though, is that, by holding that disinterested inquiry is a waste of time, it neglects or even discards basic science, which not only enriches our lives but is the ultimate source of technology.

Whether crude or refined, naturalism opposes spiritualism in all its guises, from religion to idealist philosophy. And sophisticated naturalism promotes the scientific exploration of nature but neglects mathematics and attempts to force social inquiry into the naturalist box—witness sociobiology and its offspring, evolutionary psychology. In short, naturalism promotes inquiry but only up to a point. I hasten to note that naturalism is limited not because it excludes the mental, which it does not, but because it denies the specificity and irreducibility of the social.

Hence the plan of this chapter: a quick review of spiritualism, followed by a glimpse at the realizations of naturalism, ending with the suggestion that scientific materialism includes whatever is valuable in naturalism while transcending its limitations.

1. SPIRITUALISM

The traditional worldviews revolved around imaginary beings: they attempted to understand facts in terms of fictions, and the reputedly lower in terms of the allegedly higher. Recall the following outstanding examples. Plato claimed that concrete things are but the shadows of ideas. John the Evangelist thought that "[i]n the beginning was the Word, and the Word was with God, and the Word was God" (John 1); Aristotle fantasized that planets move because they are pushed by angels; and Hegel argued that the magnet is the materialization of the argument (*Schluss*). It is still widely believed that we are alive ("animated") as long as we have souls (*animae*) and die when these leave us; that bodies cannot think because the word *body* is synonymous with the word "corpse" (the thesis of a paper read at the 1988 World Congress of Philosophy in Brighton); that seeing cannot be a process because the English grammar treats the verb *to see* as standing for a point event (Gilbert Ryle); that mental processes cannot be neural because the brain-mind association is not logically necessary—whence people in alternative worlds might not need brains to think (Saul Kripke); and that the conceptually possible worlds are no less real than ours.

Every philosophical school or religion is characterized by the stand it takes with regard to the nature of reality and its knowledge. Thus, the neopositivists prescribed that we should always employ the "formal mode" rather than the "material mode": we must say "the word X means Y," not "X is Y" or "X does Y"; Heidegger maintained that "the word is the house of being," which Derrida translated as "there is nothing outside the text"; Charles Taylor famously wrote that social facts "are texts or like texts." And, of course, all religions have claimed to explain the worldly in otherworldly terms. In short, according to magical thinking, "the higher" trumps "the lower" both in time and in power, hence in explanatory power as well. Theology would explain metaphysics, which in turn would explain physics.

By contrast, scientific thinking takes the real existence of the external world for granted: it is realist or objectivist. And the sociologies of science, technology, and religion attempt to explain in social terms the emergence and fortunes of their subjects. Moreover, the science-oriented worldviews are free from disembodied souls, world spirits, and other fictions: they are also tacitly naturalist or materialist in some sense—without, however, necessarily denying the existence and power of the mental.

Nor do naturalists and materialists reject spirituality, although they redefine it. Indeed, whereas in traditional cultures spirituality was identified with religiosity, in modern cultures spirituality consists in cultivating or appreciating the basic sciences, the humanities, and the arts. This includes learning theorems, reading philosophy, history, or poetry, admiring Notre Dame or the Sydney Opera House, and being overwhelmed by Beethoven. Spirituality also includes toppling false icons, such as Hegel, Nietzsche, and Heidegger.

2. NATURALISM

Naturalism is the worldview according to which every existent is natural, and none are spiritual or supernatural. Put it negatively: there is nothing outside nature (see, e.g., Krikorian 1944; Ryder 1994; Kanitscheider 1996). Many materialists call themselves "naturalists," some to avoid being mistaken for greedy hunters after material goods, and others to dodge the accusation of being "crass materialists" or, worse, "soft on Marxism." Thus, naturalism is often only timid materialism. But just as often it is a reckless form of nothing-but-ism or radical reductionism, which focuses on the ultimate components of things, with disregard for their structure and modus operandi or mechanism—as is particularly obvious in the case of sociobiology.

But the terms *natural* and *naturalism* are ambiguous, so that their use gives rise to equivocations. In fact, naturalism refers to somewhat different though related doctrines in the philosophy of religion, value theory, ethics, ontology, epistemology, and the philosophy of the social sciences. Let us recall briefly these different meanings, in order to clarify some recent philosophical controversies.

In relation to religion, naturalism usually involves the rejection of supernaturalism. The ancient Greek Stoics, Spinoza, and Einstein may be regarded as religious naturalists for having identified God with nature. But the organized religions were never fooled by this tactic: they smelled in it disguised atheism. At other times, naturalism has stood for the attempt to derive religious beliefs from pure reason rather than revelation ("natural religion"). In still other cases it has characterized the search for, and interpretation of, the footprints allegedly left by God when creating the world ("natural theology"). The doctrine of intelligent design, favored by most contemporary American Republicans, is the latest attempt in this direction. However, let us confine our discussion in this section to philosophical naturalism.

A number of components or branches of philosophical naturalism should be distinguished (see, e.g., Koppelberg 1999; Mahner 2007a). Let us sketch and briefly analyze the following varieties, starting with the root.

In *metaphysical naturalism*, the universe and nature coincide, so that the supernatural is just a fiction. This ontology comes in two strengths: radical and moderate. Radical naturalism denies the existence of the mental or spiritual and, a fortiori, that of consciousness and free will—which is why it is often called "eliminative." For example, the eminent neuroscientist Rodolfo Llinás (2001, p. 128) has claimed that the self is a construct that "exists only as a calculated entity," namely, "a complicated eigen (self) vector"—but he did not disclose the corresponding operator or matrix, as a consequence of which his assertion is puzzling. In any event, the reader is likely to resent the claim that she is just a mathematical object and, as such, incapable of doing anything of her own free will.

Many eliminative naturalists regard the brain basically as a computer and, as such, devoid of disinterested curiosity, self-knowledge (consciousness), initiative, and free will (e.g., Paul Churchland 1984; Patricia Churchland and Sejnowski 1993). Consequently they do not explain creativity—the ability to come up with radically new ideas. Moderate naturalists, by contrast, admit creative minds. And some of them—in particular, Donald Hebb (1980), the father of contemporary cognitive neuroscience—have even acknowledged free will. But, unlike scientific materialists, the naturalists of both varieties underrate the influence of the social context, and consequently they ignore developmental and social psychology, which account for the differences between the cognitive abilities of moderns and primitives (Mithen 1993) and the educated and the uneducated (see Vygotsky 1978), as well as between identical twins reared apart.

Incidentally, the free will hypothesis started as a theological fantasy that was a convenient means to blame humans for what might be taken as God's perversity. (This is how Augustine used free will to combat Manichaeism.) But morally justified punishment presupposes self-consciousness, the ability to tell wrong from right, and free will. This is why in advanced nations, nonhuman animals, very young children, and the mentally handicapped, and in recent years victims of injuries to the frontal lobe as well, are exempted from the rigors of criminal law. To my knowledge, eliminative naturalists have not tackled this problem. So, one does not know whether they should hold that no one should be blamed for his crimes, or that there can

be no extenuating circumstances, in both cases because consciousness and free will are illusory.

Logical naturalism comes in two versions: strong and weak. The
former says that logic is general ontology: that it contains the most
general laws of all objects, real and imaginary. This view, first suggested by Aristotle and killed by Nagel (1956), is false, for the laws of
science are material-specific, whereas logic is topic-neutral. What is
true is that logic *refers* to anything even though it *describes* nothing
extralogical (see Bunge 1974). Indeed, the predicates in predicate
logic, just like the sets in set theory, are arbitrary, which is why logic
refers to anything. But formal logic does not contain the concept of
change, which defines that of matter. Presumably this is why Hegel
([1812] 1929) thought that formal logic is subjective, whereas his
own "logic" (metaphysics) pivoted around the notion of becoming.

The weak version of logical naturalism holds that the laws of logic
are laws of thought, and as such they are psychological (or neuroscientific) laws. This view, also known as psychologism, is false, as
shown by the fact that most "natural" (spontaneous, untutored)
thinking is invalid (see, e.g., Johnson-Laird and Wason 1977). These
are some of the most common fallacies: (a) confusing "some" with
"all," or "a" with "the"; (b) identifying necessity with necessity and
sufficiency; (c) concluding A from "If A then B" and "B." The laws of
logic are actually rules, and as such artifacts. Moreover, there is no
single logic: in addition to the standard or classical logic, there are
many nonclassical logics (see, e.g., Haack 1996). Much the same
holds for the laws of pure mathematics: they are not natural or intuitive; if they were, they would not look mysterious to the vast
majority of people. This explains why logic and mathematics
emerged less than three millennia ago: they had to be invented, just
like bronze, money, writing, and the state. In short, logical naturalism is untenable. By contrast, materialists have something to say
about logic and mathematics: namely, that, just like plows and
poems, they are human creations rather than residing either in
mines or in Plato's lofty realm of ideas.

Semantic naturalism says that meaning and truth, the two foci of
philosophical semantics, should be accounted for in a naturalistic
fashion. For instance, Franz Brentano (1960) accounted for refer-

ence—a component of meaning—in terms of "intentionality." In fact, he claimed that the peculiarity of mental phenomena is their reference to an object other than the said phenomena. (And some of his followers, such as John Searle, have adopted his confusion between intention, a psychological category, and reference, a semantic one.) In a similar psychologistic vein, Quine (1973) attempted to explain reference by the way children and foreigners learn to master a word, "attesting to the presence of an object." But learning how to use a word is irrelevant to knowledge of the object that the word names. For example, one does not learn economics by investigating the way children acquire the concepts of good, price, market, and the like. Besides, a psychological account of reference cannot help us find out, say, whether or not quantum mechanics refers to observers rather than to physical things. In short, naturalism does not supply a theory of meaning, any more than it can explain the origin of legal codes—which is why the expression "natural law" is a contradiction in terms.

There are two kinds of semantic proposition: linguistic conventions, such as "Let f designate an arbitrary reference frame," and semantic assumptions, like "Function f represents property P." Like all conventions, the former are arbitrary and therefore freely replaceable. By contrast, semantic assumptions are testable and therefore subject to error and eventual rectification. For example, there are rival hypotheses with regard to the operator that represent correctly the velocity of a quantum-mechanical thing (Bunge 2003). In any case, whether conventional or hypothetical, semantic stipulations do not grow on trees: they are just as unnatural as legal codes.

As for truth, Nietzsche, a notorious naturalist of the vitalist variety, regarded truth as only a tool in the struggle for life: He neither *defined* the concept of truth nor proposed truth *criteria* or conditions. Worse, Nietzsche exalted lies, in particular, Plato's "noble lie," as an even more potent weapon than truth in the superman's struggle for supremacy. This is why he has been the hero of uncounted reactionaries, among them Hitler, Heidegger, and Leo Strauss.

Epistemological naturalism holds that cognition is a natural process and, as such, the subject of scientific research: that Plato's

Realm of Ideas is fictitious, and so is the idea of knowledge in itself, that is, without a knowing subject. Cognitive psychology is of course implementing the naturalist program in epistemology. But it has no obvious normative force.

Methodological naturalism prescribes that the design, construction, and operation of measuring instruments should be so as to exclude the possibility that they might be interfered with by unnatural entities, such as ghosts, Descartes' malicious imp, and the experimenter's soul. In other words, no spiritual entity shall interpose itself between the observer and the observed thing. The reason is that, if instrument readings could be accounted for in other ways, they would inform us about thing-spirit compounds rather than about "normal" (natural or social) things. This does not show that naturalism is dogmatic: it only shows that naturalism is a precondition of scientific knowledge (see Mahner 2007b). However, naturalism is insufficient, for it does not preclude the interference of nonsupernatural immaterial agencies, such as Descartes' mischievous spirit, and paranormal abilities, such as telekinesis. I submit that only materialism can eliminate such fantasies, for it holds that mental processes are brain processes and, as such, undetachable from the body.

3. PHYSICALISM AND BIOLOGISM

Physicalism is the thesis that everything is physical, and that nothing is supraphysical, let alone supernatural. Like all *isms*, physicalism comes in at least two varieties: hard and soft. Hard physicalism holds that there are only physical entities, whereas soft physicalism prescribes that we use only the language of physics and, in particular, that we describe everything in spatio-temporal terms. Thus, hard physicalism is identical with what is ordinarily called "crass" (or "vulgar") "materialism." By contrast, soft physicalism is often subjectivism in scientific disguise, namely, phenomenalism.

Phenomenalism declares that there are only phenomena, that is, appearances. The logical positivists—in particular, the members of the Vienna Circle—were the heirs to Mach, who followed Comte, who in turn owed much to Kant's subjectivist idealism, which had been invented by Berkeley. In his first *Critique*, Kant (1787) held that the world is a pile of phenomena (appearances) rather than a collection of things existing in themselves; that, although all things exist in space and time, space and time are forms of intuition rather than traits of the real world; and that "God is a mere idea." Thus Kant was a timid naturalist—a position that could satisfy neither materialists nor idealists. The same applies to Hume, his precursor, although, unlike Kant, Hume believed in the independent existence of the external world. But Hume denied the possibility of knowing anything other than phenomena (appearances)—and this at a time when physicists and chemists were studying nonphenomenal facts such as planetary orbits, imperceptible gases, and invisible chemical reactions.

A century later the great experimental physicist and physiological psychologist Ernst Mach ([1900]1914) elaborated Berkeley's, Hume's, and Kant's phenomenalism. He stated unambiguously the thesis that the building blocks of the universe are sensations. Obviously, this claim is naturalistic but also unscientific, because it is anthropocentric. A possible root of this claim—apart from its historical origin in Berkeley—is the confusion of reference with evidence (Bunge 1967). Thus, a piece of empirical evidence for the hypothesis that this lump of material is radioactive is hearing the clicks made by a Geiger counter placed in its vicinity. In my youth one could buy for a dime a tiny sample of radioactive material mounted on a screen that would be seen to sparkle in the dark. But of course one did not identify radioactivity with the perception of such tiny brief flashes: this was just evidence for the presence of the said material.

Neurath (1981), one of the pillars of the Vienna Circle, advanced what may be called *linguistic physicalism*. This is the empiricist thesis that, in the last instance, all the scientific statements are reducible to "protocol sentences," which in turn are of the same kind as "Otto, at place X and time Y, perceived Z." By collecting all such empirically "basic statements" one obtains the most general physics, the unified science, or physicalism, which is but "a tissue of laws that express spatiotemporal connections" (Neurath 1981, 1:414). Regrettably Neurath, a sociologist trained as a mathematician, did not know that the basic laws of physics, such as Maxwell's equations, did not contain any reference to test procedures, for the same reason that Reference ≠ Evidence.

Energetism is the now forgotten variety of physicalism according to which everything, from bodies to values, is made of energy. Its creator, the eminent physical chemist Wilhelm Ostwald (1902, p. 373), regarded matter as "a secondary appearance that occurs as the coexistence of certain kinds of energy." And he thought that, because energy is neither matter nor idea, energetism was the alternative to both materialism and idealism. (He dedicated his book to Ernst Mach, who could not have approved of it because for Ostwald energy trumps sensation.) But of course there is no such thing as energy in itself: energy is a property of concrete (material) things, indeed their peculiarity. That this is so is shown when you inspect any physical formula containing the concept of energy, such as the most famous of all: E(closed system) = constant, and E(body of mass m) = mc^2. No energy bearers, which are material things, no energy.

We shall examine next a far more restricted version of naturalism, namely, biologism.

Biologism comes in two versions: strong and weak. Strong biologism is the ancient animist view that everything in the world is alive (or "animated"). This worldview was common in ancient India, and it was partly shared by Plato, who in his *Timaeus* held that the Earth is an animal. However, this particular belief of Plato's did not contaminate his remaining works, which were thoroughly rationalist, whereas consistent vitalists, such as Nietzsche and Bergson, are irrationalists, in particular, intuitionists.

Weak biologism holds that everything human is understandable only in purely biological terms, without recourse to sociological concepts. A number of modern doctrines fall under biologism: Nietzsche's vitalism, psychoanalysis, social Darwinism, the Nazi cult of race and instinct, sociobiology, and current evolutionary psychology. In his *Genealogy of Morals* (1887), as well as in some of the aphorisms collected in *Will to Power,* Nietzsche demanded the "naturalization" of all human knowledge, in particular, that of ethics. He realized that standard morality thwarts our instincts, which he wished to free. Nietzsche rejected all the "unnatural" limitations to egoism, in particular, the "will to power": let the stronger prevail, let the "law of the jungle" rule. Hence Nietzsche's contempt for compassion and cooperation, democracy and socialism. Unsurprisingly, Nietzsche was Hitler's favorite pseudophilosopher—an admiration Hitler shared with Heidegger. True, Nietzsche was also admired by anarchists and other nonconformists, but only for his iconoclasm and pamphleteering. Nietzsche was superficial, inconsistent, and vitriolic enough to win the admiration of half-educated rebels.

Fast, radical social changes, such as urbanization, industrialization, militarization, alphabetization, and democratization, refute biologism, for they are not etched in the genome and they do not result from biological alterations. On the contrary, they cause changes in nutrition, metabolism, hygiene, and modes of thinking. For example, the emergence of cities favored the spread and lethality of plagues; the decline of the Maya civilization was followed by a decrease in stature; the "discovery" and looting of America decimated the indigenous populations because it spread Western germs among them; social inequality induces stress and the accompanying pathologies—and so on. On the positive side, suffice it to recall the health benefits of sanitation, the reduction in the length of the workday, female emancipation, and progressive social legislation. In short, social organization has a strong biological impact. This is why advancing the biosocial sciences and technologies is far more important than attempting to reduce the social sciences to biology (Bunge 2003).

4. NATURALIZED ETHICS, LAW, AND TECHNOLOGY

Ethical naturalism is the project of reducing moral norms to the natural sciences, in particular, human biology (Edel 1944). This project has failed and is bound to fail again for two reasons, one methodological and the other factual. The former is that ethics deals with rules of behavior, and as such it is a social technology, not a branch of natural history. And social technologies, unlike social crafts, are expected to make deliberate use of scientific laws. Now, a scientific law, if applicable at all, is technologically ambivalent, for it countenances two distinct and even mutually opposed technological rules or prescriptions (Bunge 1967). Indeed, a law L involving a means M and a goal or consequence G of practical interest has the following form:

Law: If antecedent *M* occurs, consequence *G* follows (or is likely to follow). [1]

A law of this form suggests two mutually dual technological rules:

Rule 1: To attain *G*, put *M* into effect. [2a]

Rule 2: To avoid *G*, prevent *M* from happening. [2b]

Note that, whereas the above law schema is value free, the two rules based on it (though not deduced from it) are value laden. Moreover, the choice between seeking *G* and avoiding *G*, hence between applying 2a and using 2b, will involve moral deliberations if the consequence *G* is likely to affect individuals other than the actor. Hence the naturalization project involves a logical circle: the attempt to derive any moral norm from science involves moral norms.

The factual obstacle to the naturalization project is that all morals belong to a tradition and exist in some social context. That is, moral norms are invented and applied by human actors with definite interests and in definite social circumstances. Change either actor or circumstance, and a different set of moral deliberations is likely to be involved. This is why morals differ from one society to the next, and why they have changed through history (see, e.g., Westermarck 1906–1908). For instance, a secular humanist is likely to regard much of the Bible as highly immoral, for it condones genocide (in particular ethnic "cleansing"); punishment of the sinner's progeny; stoning of the unbeliever, the adulteress, and the homosexual; slavery; harsh gender discrimination; and other atrocities. In conclusion, morality cannot be naturalized because it is a chapter of the social maintenance manual. But it can be "materialized," in the sense that it can and must be regarded as a feature of the social coexistence of material agents (persons) in material systems of the social kind. We shall return to this point.

Still, Darwin and some of his successors claimed that morality, in particular altruism, is a product of biological evolution. Moreover, many evolutionary biologists and psychologists have embraced William Hamilton's rule, according to which altruistic behavior occurs spontaneously in all species when a certain condition is met.

This condition is that the cost c of the altruistic behavior is less than its benefit b discounted by the coefficient r of genetic relatedness between actor and beneficiary: $c < rb$. Some interesting confirmatory cases have been cited. But in humans, social relatedness trumps biological relatedness; for example, we are likely to help genetically unrelated spouses and friends more often than we help our genetic relatives. And chimpanzees, our closest evolutionary relatives, fit the main postulate of standard economics, that we are all basically selfish (Jensen, Call, and Tomasello 2007). This finding confirms the hypothesis that fairness is uniquely human (Fehr and Fischbacher 2003). It would seem that nature alone does not account for human nature: only a combination of biological evolution with social evolution may explain the emergence, reform, and repeal of moral norms.

What holds for ethics also holds, mutatis mutandis, for the law—which is why laws differ from one society to the next. That is, there is no such thing as natural law: all legal codes are artificial. And, like all artifacts, they are bound to be imperfect, but also perfectible through research and debate. Unfortunately the contemporary debate over natural law has been distorted by the legal positivists, whose arguments, in their eagerness to defend the status quo and the corresponding legal order, have led to the belief that one must choose between the two schools, natural law and legal positivism, and that the former is just a vestige of tradition, whereas science is on the side of the "might makes right" school. Actually no such choice is mandatory, because there is a *tertium quid*, namely, legal realism. This school holds that the law is more than a tool of social control: it can also be a tool of social progress, in particular an adjunct of any policies aiming at attaining social justice (see Pound [1924] 1954; Bunge 1998).

What holds for social technology, in particular ethics and the law, also holds for the other branches of engineering: they too are artificial activities centered on the design of artifacts. What is also true, if paradoxical, is that artificiality is of the essence of human nature: humans, however primitive, use or even invent and fashion artifacts of many kinds, from tools and weapons to institutions and words. Only the artifacts made by nonhuman animals, such as honeybees, beavers, crows, and weaverbirds, are natural, in the sense that the corresponding animals make them without first making any drawings and with no need for formal schooling. Human artifacts, and their corresponding crafts and technologies, are just as unnatural as poems, songs, rules of etiquette, legal codes, religions, and scientific theories. Since naturalism cannot account for the artificial, it misses what distinguishes humans from other animals, no less. Hence it is not fit for human consumption.

5. NATURALISM'S THREE MUSKETEERS

The writings of the mechanist or "vulgar" materialists Ludwig Büchner, Jacob Moleschott, and Karl Vogt were hugely popular in the second half of the nineteenth century. Büchner, a physician, was by far the most original and influential of the three. His *Force and Matter* (1855) circulated in several languages throughout Europe and remained in print for half a century. True, the annexation of biology, psychology, and social science remained at the programmatic stage; but the spiritualist cosmology was severely wounded in almost all domains.

A century later, another troika fired the enthusiasm of the naturalists: this troika was composed of Richard Dawkins (e.g., 1976), Steven Pinker (e.g., 1997, 2003), and Daniel Dennett (e.g., 1995). These popular writers enjoy an advantage over their predecessors: they preach from the academic lectern. Regrettably, as will be argued, the naturalism of these Three Musketeers involves much bad science of their own making, as a consequence of which they have actually weakened the naturalist cause.

To begin with, all three writers in question have propagated innatism, whose central dogma is "Nature trumps nurture"—or, in modern parlance, "Genome is destiny." This doctrine is in turn based on an extravagant version of genetics, according to which the DNA molecule is "selfish," or intent on spreading its own kind as far and wide as possible; it will also be self-sufficient, in particular, self-duplicating, as well as the subject and unit of natural selection; by contrast, the very existence of the whole organism will be "paradoxical," since its only function will be to serve as the means for the transmission of genetic material from one generation (of organisms!) to the next.

These views are at variance with biochemistry and biology. Indeed, DNA is rather inert and is divided by enzymes. The whole organism, not the genome, is subject to natural selection, and therefore is the unit of evolution. The reason is that natural selection is about survival and reproduction, which only organisms can perform. One's precious genes would not be transmitted to the next generation if one were to die before reproducing. Furthermore, unlike the passive gene, the organism reacts back on its environment: it takes part in the construction of its own habitat.

Second, the writers in question share the widespread misconception that natural selection preserves all adaptations and eliminates all dysfunctional traits. Although natural selection is indeed a wonderful adaptation mechanism, it is far too slow to completely eliminate such dysfunctional things as toenails (which benefit only podiatrists) and debilitating disorders such as depression (which benefit only psychiatrists)—even though Nesse and Williams (1994) have seen it as adaptive for leading the patient to giving up hopeless struggles.

Third, another original if wrong contribution of our self-appointed "brights" is the idea that evolution has been programmed by "evolutionary algorithms" (Dennett 1995). But of course a process cannot be at the same time natural and guided by algorithms, for these are artifacts. Moreover, every algorithm is designed to produce an outcome of a prescribed kind, whereas speciation is hardly predictable—except of course in the deliberate creation of hybrids such as the tangelo.

Moreover, as Stephen Jay Gould and Richard Lewontin have rightly insisted, evolution is characterized by contingency—by non-biological external circumstances, such as geological and climatic catastrophes. And, as François Jacob has suggested, the evolutionary process looks less the work of a designer than the work of an opportunistic tinker who works with whatever odds and ends he finds in his toolbox. That is, molecules and organs change functions as opportunity allows. For instance, sponges, which are extremely primitive organisms with very few neurons, contain neurotransmitters, which in humans play prominent roles; and humans' suprarenal glands, which in a well-designed human body would be inside the brain, straddle the lowly kidneys.

Fourth, the three self-appointed champions of Darwin admire and propagate the fantasies of the so-called evolutionary psychologists (see, e.g., Buss 2004). In particular, these writers share the belief that the human mind was basically adapted to "the Pleistocene environment," in a period that started about 1.6 million years ago. So, according to this belief, we would basically be living fossils: we would walk the mean streets of Miami, and some of us the safe Harvard Yard, or even the surface of the moon, endowed with the same prehistoric brains. Nothing, not even the Neolithic, Industrial, or French revolutions, could possibly alter human nature, which has remained unchanged for at least fifty thousand years. Evolutionary psychology, indeed! (See the criticisms of Buller 2005, and Cochran and Harpending 2009.)

Finally, both Pinker and Dennett, along with Hilary Putnam, Patricia Smith Churchland, and many other philosophers, have championed the computer metaphor of the brain. True, at first sight this view looks naturalistic because it dispenses with the immaterial soul. But computers are not exactly natural. Worse, unlike live human brains, they are limited to performing algorithmic operations. They lack spontaneity, creativity, and the ability to feel emotions. Indeed, computers have to be programmed; there can be no programs for coming up with original ideas; and an emotional computer would be unreliable.

In sum, the cause of naturalism has not been well served by the Three Musketeers, for muskets are outmoded.

6. NEURO THIS AND NEURO THAT

Neuroscience has displaced physics as the sexiest science, and it is successfully completing the naturalization of psychology that Hippocrates and Galen began in antiquity. Indeed, cognitive and affective neuroscience have replaced at the same time behaviorism, which was scientific but extremely narrow, and psychoanalysis, which was very broad but pseudoscientific. Fortunately, cognitive neuroscience has not eliminated social psychology but has merged with it. Indeed, traditional social psychology, which was born in the 1930s, is currently being enriched with cognitive neuroscience to produce social cognitive neuroscience.

It was perhaps unavoidable that the success of the naturalization program in capturing the mental would inspire what may be dubbed *neuroimperialism*—the attempt to explain every bit of behavior in neuroscientific terms. Indeed, in recent years we have witnessed the birth of neuroeconomics, neurolaw, neuroethics, neuromarketing, and neuropoetics. How much of this is legitimate science or technology, and how much empty promise? Let us see.

Neuroeconomics is the study of the economic behavior of individuals in the light of cognitive and affective neuroscience. This emergent science has shown certain differences between planned and impulsive buying: whereas the former is guided by the prefrontal cortex, the latter is under the strong influence of the limbic system—as was to be expected. Results of this type are interesting but limited, because they concern individuals rather than firms, and because laboratory results are a poor guide to real-life behavior.

Neurolaw is the neuroscientific study of what jurists call *mens rea*, the criminal mind. It has been known for decades that juvenile offending peaks at about the age of seventeen, because this is when youths form new attachments, beyond the control of home and school, and when their brains become awash in testosterone, while their prefrontal cortices are still immature. But neurolaw cannot explain why the crime rate is far greater in the United States than in neighboring Canada, which in turn has a higher rate than Western Europe and Japan. Nor can neurolaw explain what drives persistent offending, that is, adult crime. These limitations of neurolaw are due to the fact that crime, unlike poetry or mathematics, is identical with antisocial behavior, and understanding such behavior calls for an exploration of the social environment (see, e.g., Wikström and Sampson 2006).

Neuroethics is the study of the way the brain internalizes moral norms, as well as the study of the pathological causes for the failure of such moral enculturation. The classical case is of course that of Phineas

Gage, who lost his moral conscience as a consequence of a severe injury to his frontal lobe. But this was a very exceptional case: in the vast majority of cases, immoral behavior results from either incomplete socialization or social pathology rather than from neural deficiency.

How about the seven deadly sins: could neuroscience explain anger, greed, sloth, and the rest, as suggested by a recent program on the History Channel? This is extremely unlikely, for two reasons. One of them is that every list of sins is culturally determined. For example, aggression, enslavement, theft, and social insensitivity do not occur in the Christian list of sins. And the worst aggressions, the military ones, are not committed in anger; likewise, thieves are not motivated by anger or greed: most of them steal because they have no other way to feed their families. In this case, focusing on the brain as the source of evil amounts to diverting attention from the structural sources of social ills.

The reason neuroscience alone cannot cope with social problems is that it explores what goes on inside people's brains, not among them: only the social and biosocial sciences are equipped to deal with social relations. Therefore the neuroscientific approach to all kinds of human behavior should be welcomed with caution, for every person is a member of several social circles or systems, which constrain behavior in some respects while stimulating it in others. Thus, while it is true that stock market transactions are influenced by fear and greed, these emotions are generated by macrosocial facts, such as social unrest, war, unemployment, and industrial innovation. Naturalism must be expanded to make room for the economy, politics, and culture. This expansion is called emergent materialism (Bunge 1979, 1981).

7. CLOSING REMARKS

The great merit of naturalism is that it rejects magical thinking, in particular, supernaturalism. But naturalism is limited, for it denies the emergence of qualitative novelty, and consequently the qualitative distinctions among levels of organization—physical, biological, and social, among others. In particular, naturalism does not account for the specificities of the social and the technological. According to naturalism, human nature is immutable, and therefore social reform is ineffectual or worse, as Pinker (2003, p. 294) has claimed. Thus, ironically, naturalism, which was progressive at the time of the Enlightenment, can now be invoked in favor of conservatism. This alone suggests that naturalism should be expanded to encompass the artificial and the social.

REFERENCES

Brentano, Franz. 1960 [1874]. "The Distinction between Mental and Physical Phenomena." In *Realism and the Background of Phenomenology*, edited by Roderick M. Chisholm, 39–61. Glencoe, IL: Free Press.

Buller, David J. 2005. *Adapting Minds: Evolutionary Psychology and the Persistent Quest for Human Nature*. Cambridge, MA: MIT Press.

Bunge, Mario. 1967. *Scientific Research*. 2 vols. New York: Springer. Rev. ed., New Brunswick, NJ: Transaction, 1998.

———. 1974. "The Relations of Logic and Semantics to Ontology." *Journal of Philosophical Logic* 3: 195–210.

———. 1979. *Treatise on Basic Philosophy*. Vol. 4, *A World of Systems*. Dordrecht, Netherlands: Reidel.

———. 1981. *Scientific Materialism*. Dordrecht, Netherlands: Reidel.

———. 1998. *Social Science under Debate*. Toronto: University of Toronto Press.

———. 2003. *Emergence and Convergence*. Toronto: University of Toronto Press.

Buss, David M. 2004. *Evolutionary Psychology: The New Science of the Mind*. 2nd ed. Boston: Pearson.

Churchland, Patricia Smith, and Terrence J. Sejnowski. 1993. *The Computational Brain*. Cambridge, MA: MIT Press.

Churchland, Paul M. 1984. *Matter and Consciousness: A Contemporary Introduction to the Philosophy of Mind*. Cambridge, MA: MIT Press.

Cochran, Gregory, and Thomas Harpending. 2009. *The 10,000 Year Explosion: How Civilization Accelerated Human Evolution*. New York: Basic Books.

Dawkins, Richard. 1976. *The Selfish Gene*. Oxford: Oxford University Press.

Dennett, Daniel. 1995. *Darwin's Dangerous Idea*. New York: Simon & Schuster.

Edel, Abraham. 1944. *Naturalism and Ethical Theory*. In Krikorian, ed. 1944: 65–95.

Fehr, Ernst, and Urs Fischbacher. 2003. "The Nature of Human Altruism." *Nature* 425: 785–91.

Haack, Susan. 1996. *Deviant Logic, Fuzzy Logic*. Chicago: University of Chicago Press.

Hebb, Donald O. 1980. *Essay on Mind*. Hilsdale, NJ: Erlbaum.

Hegel, Friedrich. [1812] 1929. *Science of Logic*. 2 vols. London: George Allen & Unwin.

Jensen, Keith, Joseph Call, and Michael Tomasello. 2007. "Chimpanzees Are Rational Maximizers." *Science* 318: 107–109.

Johnson-Laird, P. N., and P. C. Wason, eds. 1977. *Thinking: Readings in Cognitive Science*. Cambridge: Cambridge University Press.

Kanitscheider, Bernulf. 1996. *Im Innern der Natur: Philosophie und moderne Physik*. Darmstadt: Wissenschaftliche Buchgesellschaft.

Kant, Immanuel. 1787. *Kritik der reinen Vernunft*. 2nd ed. Hamburg: Felix Meiner.

Koppelberg, Dirk. 1999. "Naturalismus/Naturalisierung." In *Enzyklopädie Philosophie*, vol. 1, edited by H. J. Sandkühler, 904–14. Hamburg: Felix Meiner.

Krikorian, Yervant V., ed. 1944. *Naturalism and the Human Spirit*. New York: Columbia University Press.

Llinás, Rodolfo R. 2001. *i of the Vortex: From Neurons to Self*. Cambridge, MA: MIT Press.

Mach, Ernst. [1900] 1914. *The Analysis of Sensations and the Relation of the Physical to the Psychical*. Chicago, IL: Open Court.

Mahner, Martin. 2007a. "Kann man als metaphysischer Naturalist zugleich erkenntistheoretischer Naturalist sein?" In *Naturalismus: Positionen, Perspektiven, Probleme*, edited by T. Sukopp and G. Vollmer, 115–36. Tübingen: Mohr Siebeck.

———. 2007b. "Unverezichtbarkeit und Reichweite des ontologischen Naturalismus." In *Zufall Mensch?* edited by L. Klinnert, 77–90. Darmstadt, Germany: Wissenschaftliche Buchgesellschaft.

Mithen, Steven. 1996. *The Prehistory of the Mind*. London: Thames & Hudson.

Nagel, Ernest. 1956. *Logic without Metaphysics*. Glencoe, IL: Free Press.

Nesse, Randolph M., and George C. Williams. 1994. *Why We Get Sick*. New York: Times Books Random House.

Neurath, Otto. 1981. *Gesammelte philosophische und methodologische Schriften*. 2 vols. Edited by R. Haller and H. Rutte. Vienna: Hölder-Pichler-Tempsky.

Ostwald, Wilhelm. 1902. *Vorlesungen über Naturphilosophie*. Leipzig: Veit & Comp.

Pinker, Steven. 1997. *How the Mind Works*. New York: Norton.

———. 2003. *The Blank Slate: The Modern Denial of Human Nature*. New York: Penguin Books.

Pound, Roscoe. [1924] 1954. *An Introduction to the Philosophy of Law*. Rev. ed. New Haven, CT: Yale University Press.

Quine, W. V. 1973. *The Roots of Reference*. La Salle, IL: Open Court.

Ryder, John, ed. 1994. *American Philosophical Naturalism in the Twentieth Century*. Amherst, NY: Prometheus Books.

Vygotsky, L[ev] S[emyonovich]. 1978. *Mind in Society: The Development of Higher Psychological Processes*. Cambridge, MA: Harvard University Press.

Westermarck, Edward. 1906–1908. *The Origin and Development of Moral Ideas*. 2 vols. London: Macmillan.

Wikström, Per-Olof H., and Robert J. Sampson, eds. 2006. *The Explanation of Crime: Context, Mechanisms, and Development*. Cambridge: Cambridge University Press.

4.

Primitive Naturalism

John Lachs

Experience, even of a primitive sort, even the experience of primitive, untutored people, reveals a world continuous with our bodies. The hunted beast is vulnerable to our weapons; when it turns in anger, however, we are the ones endangered. The symmetry of causal influence, known to all as mutual endangerment, serves as the foundation and curse of animal life; we seek food and are food, in turn. This is the primitive naturalism of ordinary people who know, unreflectively, that they live in the same world as is populated by everybody and everything.

This world may have surprising regions, accessible only through special openings, such as the mouths of caves, or as a result of special events, such as death. Mysterious holes in the sides of mountains can open our eyes to a magical world of crystals and rivers, which is soon understood to be a part, a very special part, of the ordinary world. Similarly, death may reveal to us a fabled province of happy people given to singing the praises of God, or else a dark realm marked by screams of pain. These regions are also parts of the ordinary world, even though they can be reached only on condition that we die, just as Columbus could visit the West Indies only on condition that he leave Spain behind.

Primitive naturalism, which is the inarticulate conviction of all, is amply confirmed by our actions. We live in a single spatio-temporal world that is largely regular in its habits and hence somewhat predictable in its behavior. Beings that may seem supernatural—elves, spirits, guardian angels, and leprechauns—are all parts of this world; if they exist at all, they exist here and now or somewhere else at some other point in time, always ready to engage in mischief or protective action. Even if mental events are different from what takes place in the brain, they belong in this world and obey its laws. They exist at a time and for a while; they exercise influence over such portions of the world as the human body; and, since Locke is right that when we travel we don't leave our minds behind, they are clearly associated with certain regions of space.

Is there anything that does not belong in the natural world? God does if He listens to prayers, rewards the righteous, and punishes the wicked. So also do ghosts, poltergeists, and the Virgin Mary, who ascended to heaven and lives there with her son. Possibilities expand this world immeasurably, though they are not existing powers. Numbers pertain to the world as applicable abstractions, as do hypotheses and relevant errors. Ordinary people have few ontological problems; they know where to turn to deal with entities of virtually any sort.

Such a naturalism is undermined by those who wish to raise one part or another of this crowded world to prominence. They may want to call special attention to God and His angels, control mystical powers, or stress the prerogatives of mind. In doing so, they think they establish grand dualisms or display the ontological priority of one world-region over all the rest. In reality, however, they overlook the fact that in making the supposedly independent regions relevant to ours, they strip them of prerogatives and render them continuous with the mundane. So long as any being has a purchase on space and time and stands with what exists in them in causal relations, it cannot escape being a part of the single world in which we all live.

Philosophers who associate naturalism with the universe as described by science tend to forget about this more primitive, pervasive, and inclusive version of the view. Naturalism is not the position that there is a single world populated by entities that are the proper objects of science, but the unuttered conviction that the world is one and all its parts have access to all the others. The job of science is to determine the constituent regions of the world and to learn the nature of their populations. The Russian cosmonaut who returned from space informing us that there is no God, for he had been "up there" and saw only darkness, was not altogether foolish. He was right that if there is a God, we should be able to find Him, or at least feel His influence. But he may well have looked in the wrong place or failed to perform the proper rituals to invoke the presence of God.

Primitive naturalism makes all issues of existence empirical questions and provides reassurance that a being whose presence and influence cannot be ascertained need not be counted among the existing. The connection of the sciences to this view is primarily through their efficacy in resolving empirical problems. They can trace the source of hidden influences and more often than not provide definitive answers to the question of what exists and what does not. If deviation from the expected path of Neptune suggests a previously unknown object, astronomers can calculate the location of that body and identify it on their telescopes. Other specialists with the relevant expertise can determine whether there are quarks and muons, reproduction across species, and gold deposits under the sea. The evidence for the existence of ghosts and telepathy and for the efficacy of faith healing and prayer must be examined by the best available methods, which typically are—but may not always be—scientific ones.

The conditions for obtaining empirical evidence may, of course, be deadly. Anthropologists have been cooked and eaten by their subjects, and the astronomer who tries to determine the temperature of the sun by carrying a thermometer to it is vaporized long before arrival. Similarly, some areas of the world may exist behind trapdoors, permitting the investigator to enter but never to return. Black holes may function in this way, along with death as a condition of studying the afterlife. Once we realize this, we may be satisfied with never trying to enter, or else employ, these limitations as spurs to inventiveness. The important fact is that what we want to explore lies open to our efforts even if we must be cautious and clever in how we investigate it; however difficult and dangerous it may be to get to some parts of the world, they can in principle be reached.

What we think of as mystical powers and miraculous events are no less natural than the most mundane forces and happenings. Lack of imagination and the desire for security make us believe that the sequences of the world are always regular and hold no surprises. In fact, the opposite of this is the case: even the most common of ordinary things, the weather, can be astonishing. Extraordinary forces and events surround us, due not to the intrusion of supernatural beings but to the natural operation of the restless world. If shamans know how to cure diseases by words and dance, and if the cures are not accidental, then they must have found a shortcut to the relevant mechanisms of nature. If some people know how to raise the dead by calling on them to rise, the sensible response is to learn the right words so we may be able to do it as well and to believe that some verbal rituals are more effective than resuscitation by pumping the chest or administering chemicals. And it is no miracle if only some people can do it and the rest of us can never learn: no one else can write music the way Mozart did, and only one person could paint like Mondrian.

Much has been made of the ineluctable privacy of minds and feelings. And indeed, my cousin who tends to bore me to tears has no idea of what I think of him. But the impenetrability is not intrinsic, or else I could dispense with making sure that my drooping eyelids and painful urge to yawn do not betray my secret. If the world is continuous with my body and envelops it, thoughts and feelings must find their places in the orders of space and time. Some think that naturalism is an inadequate view because feelings of anger and sensations of red cannot be discovered in specific areas of the brain. But the expectation that everything must be like mailboxes and Christmas trees, located in unique places with sharp spatial boundaries, is groundless. Radio waves spread everywhere and lack definitive borders; actions such as calling a friend in New Jersey are not located in a single place; and summer heat can suffuse an entire continent.

Philosophy suffers from an impoverished selection of examples; sometimes it operates with a single model and is quick to create dualisms when not everything fits that mold. But there is no need to invent arcane substances and a private world. When I get excited at a football game, I know exactly where my feelings are; they were admitted to the stadium with me and on my ticket. Worries about the existence of other minds and about our ability to communicate with them appear to be the specialty of loners too much in love with themselves to notice the movements of the world. The rest of us know how to get in touch with other people to monitor their feelings, to learn their thoughts and to annoy them. I could not drive home if I were unable to gauge the intentions of others on the road, and I would never kiss anyone if I thought they lacked feeling or experienced it as a stabbing pain. Success in our physical and social operations provides ample support for the one-world thesis of primitive naturalism.

The primitive naturalism I have described is the tacit belief and operational guide of everyone. We think and when we act we suppose that the world is a single place, all of whose inhabitants are, potentially at least, within our causal reach. Philosophically sophisticated versions of naturalism are derivatives of this mind-set and of such experiential enactments. Is there anything that could disconfirm our silent belief that the world is a continuous field? Only repeated frustration of our plans due to the failure of actions to be efficacious could convince us that reality is, in structure at least, not an even playing field, and this conviction would dawn on us slowly.

If, for example, one day we manage to cross the Potomac on Memorial Bridge but the next, inexplicably and irremediably, we cannot, our faith in the one-world hypothesis may suffer damage. Imagine that the bridge is there, we can walk, no one is holding us back, and yet, as in a dream, we make no headway in getting to the other side. A few days later, we get across without trouble, but then the nightmare scenario repeats itself. We would of course invent a hundred naturalistic explanations for our failure and propose an equal number of remedies. But what if none of the explanations accounted for the irregularity and none of the remedies accomplished what we want? We would over time come to view ourselves as caged beasts, feeling our power yet witnessing our impotence. Since we can imagine many such disconfirming instances, primitive naturalism is not a view to whose truth we are committed no matter what. It lives or dies, as we do, by the success of our actions.

A point worth stressing is that primitive naturalists believe, first and foremost, in the efficacy of action in a field of agency continuous with our bodies and only derivatively in the regularity of the world. So what would concern them about Memorial Bridge–type experiences is not that they subvert the accustomed sequences of nature and even less that what goes on is difficult or impossible to understand. The problem as they see it is that we cannot do what we intend, that even well-executed actions bear no fruit. The idea that the order of nature has changed serves only as an explanation of this failure, and the desire to grasp why and how it has done so is part of the attempt to reestablish our power. Primitive naturalists are not theoreticians. They do not believe in the primacy of action in theory but by enacting it. Their interest in understanding and in the regularity of nature is practical to the core: they want to be able to achieve concrete results.

The claim that ordinary people unreflectively embrace primitive naturalism raises the question of how it is possible for them to be unaware of their commitment. If what I have said so far is anywhere near right, even people who take religious texts literally believe that the world is a unified system of interacting forces. Why, then, do they profess to believe in supernatural agencies, thinking of heaven and hell as discontinuous with the mundane realm? Would they not be aghast if presented with the idea that the natural and the supernatural form a single universe with identifiable doors or transfer points?

In fact, unreflective people are much clearer about what they believe than philosophers make them out to be. They know perfectly well that the realms religion describes are appendages to the world of the everyday; if they were not, heaven would hold no reward and hell no threat. There is an analogy between misbehaving students being sent to the principal for punishment and nasty adults finding themselves on the way to the nether regions. Religious people believe such things unproblematically and they get the ontology right: the natural and what is claimed to be supernatural are equally real elements of the one world in which we live. God is, for such people, a force that can strike you down and a person with whom conversation is possible.

The confusion about the status of the supernatural comes not from people who believe in it but from those who do not. Nonbelievers think that since the world they know contains neither heaven nor hell, believers must have transcendent realms in mind. Yet that is not an accurate depiction of the religious perspective. God-centered people live amid signs and meanings in a world whose "supernatural" regions complement the mundane and rectify its moral failings. But though outcomes in the supernatural realm are just, and hence different from the way things work here, the causal mechanisms bringing them about are identical: companionship and love provide heavenly satisfaction and the fires of hell bring unremitting pain.

Disagreements between religiously and scientifically inclined people concern not the unity or continuity of the world but the inventory of its elements. The former assert and the latter deny the existence of beings such as God and of places such as heaven and hell. Everyone except rationalist philosophers agrees that such matters must be decided by methods that are empirical in a broad sense of the word, that is, by positioning ourselves in the way required to get or fail to obtain certain experiences. Individuals committed to Enlightenment values tend to think that forms of consciousness serving as evidence for the existence of religiously significant entities cannot be obtained. Their opponents charge them with insensitivity to divine signs and impatience in not wanting to wait for evidence that may be presented upon death. When called on to reflect, religious people have no trouble realizing that they are primitive naturalists, even though enlightened spirits want to disallow their claim to naturalism altogether.

A central job of philosophy is to uncover the basic structure of human beliefs. I do not mean, of course, that philosophers are to study the opinions of sundry individuals. They need, instead, to pay attention to the beliefs enacted again and again in daily life, such as the active convictions that food nourishes and that what is lost does not go out of existence. Primitive naturalism is one such deep-seated and frequently verified belief, as is the realism that asserts the mind-independent existence of objects surrounding us. Such an examination of the general beliefs on which people are willing to act keeps philosophy safe from frenzied speculation and the irrelevance of clever moves and hairsplitting distinctions.

I know of only one thinker who has argued that philosophy can make headway by attending to the action-oriented general beliefs of people. George Santayana proposed to establish a philosophy of "animal faith," consisting of the excavation and critical examination of the beliefs behind what people confidently do. This, he thought, would reveal to us "the shrewd orthodoxy" of the human mind and undermine the contrived problems of professional philosophy. The identification of primitive naturalism as a shared belief we continually enact is a step in the direction of developing the tenets of animal faith. Although various other beliefs implicated in action are also in need of study, this one stands out as a central view that honest philosophies must explore, acknowledge, and adopt.

To be sure, there is dishonesty in action, as when we pretend to be friends with someone we despise. In fundamental matters, however, actions reliably reveal people's beliefs. We cannot pretend for long to get by without food or disguise our habit of situating our bodies with a careful view to other objects, such as trucks that hurtle by. We can say that the trucks are ancient chariots or comets sent by God; such descriptions—picturesque and perhaps symbolic—can usefully call attention to certain features of the objects. But considering what we do, we cannot deny that such things occupy spaces continuous with those inhabited by us and that we believe they have both helpful and harmful causal properties.

Dissembling in philosophy, by contrast, is easy and attractive. We can pretend to doubt everything, maintain that space and time are illusions, invent substances, or announce the discovery of human world–creative categories. All the while, of course, we sincerely believe that our books reach other human beings, take time to lecture in distant cities, find ourselves satisfied with the possession of ordinary objects, and accept the world pretty much as it presents itself, without our contribution. The call for honesty in philosophy is a plea to have our actions serve as the test of our convictions and to give no professional credence to what we cannot enact, that is, to bring our philosophical lives into line with our lives as agents in the world. Honoring the call does not close the chapter on philosophy in the intellectual history of our species. To the contrary, it places the field on a sound footing by setting it a new and clearly achievable task.

The idea that belief is, among other things, a tendency to act has been with us since the days of Plato. Oddly, however, the connected truth that action is or reveals a tendency to believe has escaped the notice of philosophers. Calling attention to it and laying bare the beliefs implicit in ordinary action can eliminate insincere and implausible theoretical views. It can also establish at last the primacy of action in philosophy. A great many thinkers have avowed their commitment to this primacy. Kant, for example, announced that reason cannot gain satisfaction in its theoretical employment; only in the sphere of action can it be fulfilled. Yet his reason takes no instruction from activity as we know it in this world. Kant develops, instead, his own idea of what action, properly conceived, should be. So it is not empirical acts that acquire primacy in his system but only the idea of action, or action as it is thought in philosophy. The distinguished thinkers emerging from Kant and reinterpreting his ideas have not succeeded in establishing more than the primacy of practice *in theory*, that is, of the *idea* of practice; they have not surrendered themselves to the examination of real-world action and the implications it holds for the theories we should embrace in philosophy.

Primitive naturalism is an important part of the philosophy that explores the generic beliefs suffusing action in a space-time world. In fact, it is the central tenet of the philosophical system derived from "empirical confidence." Although Santayana was the first to develop them, it is important to note that this view of the task of philosophy and this notion of naturalism are independent of the ontology he attached to them. His categories of essence, matter, truth, and spirit or mind have merits of their own, but they neither imply nor are implied by primitive naturalism. This means that the weaknesses of the ontology and the current unpopularity of such conceptual structures leave primitive naturalism untouched.

There are at least two reasons for the separation of primitive naturalism and its connected philosophy of animal faith from the ontology of different "realms of being." The first is that though Santayana attempts to make them a seamless whole, they are nevertheless quite distinct, the former gaining expression in *Scepticism and Animal Faith* and the latter appearing only in the later books, collectively entitled *Realms of Being*. The second and more urgent reason for detaching primitive naturalism from ontology is that the ultimate issue worth exploring is not the truth, adequacy, or usefulness of Santayana's system of thought but his proposals for how we might understand naturalism and, more generally, how we can develop a method by which philosophical thinking might profitably be conducted.

Our age is one in which philosophy has, once again, lost its way. Some believe critical thought can sweep clean the Aegean stables of mistaken religious, popular, and scientific opinions. Others despair of the ability of philosophy to accomplish anything at all, with the possible exception of its own burial. Still others attempt to employ outlandish methods to come, not surprisingly, to outlandish conclusions. At such a time of crisis, modesty and good sense are hard to come by and desperately needed. Examining human actions for the time-tested beliefs they reveal is a promising way to conduct philosophical inquiry. Primitive naturalism as the first fruit of this method reestablishes the social usefulness of philosophy and points in the direction of sensible and lasting results.

PART TWO:
CAN PRAGMATISM ASSIST NATURALISM?

5.

Pragmatic Natures

Sandra B. Rosenthal

To say that pragmatism is naturalism can lead to more confusion than clarification, for there are many forms of naturalism. Moreover, pragmatic naturalism itself is a multitiered structure that focuses on nature in more than one sense. The following discussion will explore the threefold sense of nature that is operative in pragmatic naturalism, and trace its significance for a systematic worldview and for the many issues and paradoxes that arise at the levels of both philosophy and common sense as the findings of science and the deliverances of sense compete, conflict, or collide. And, perhaps the best place to begin is with the pragmatic understanding of science,[1] for the relation between pragmatism and scientific method has been the source of much misunderstanding in past examinations of pragmatism, which have attempted at times to assimilate it to various sorts of reductionisms. Such renderings were perhaps nurtured by the general fact that the method of gaining knowledge that was the backbone of the emergence of modern science was confounded with the results of the first "lasting" modern scientific view—the Newtonian mechanistic universe. A particular philosophical interpretation of nature as described by science led to a worldview that gave rise either to dualistic causal accounts of knowledge in terms of correlations between mental contents and material qualities or to the reductionist account in terms of stimulus-response, with the complete rejection of mentalistic terms.

A deep-seated philosophical tendency completely rejected by pragmatism is the acceptance of the framework of Cartesian dualism. Humans, for the pragmatist, are within nature, not outside of nature and causally linked to it. They do not, through introspection, arrive at something "inside" that has been caused by something "outside." In brief, not only Cartesian dualism, but also the entire philosophical baggage with which it became linked, is rejected by pragmatism. Such an assertion, however, when interpreted in the light of the modern period, can be glibly read as a type of reductionism. If humans are a part of nature, then they are reducible to nature. The model for understanding their relation to nature, since it is not that of mental contents causally linked to physical particles, must be the behavioristic model of stimulus-response. In brief, the phenomenon of humans and their behavior must be reducible to a level that is no longer human. This alternative, however, is definitively rejected by pragmatism. Pragmatism is naturalism in that humans are within nature, but nature is not the mechanistic universe of the Newtonian worldview. The assertion that it is has confused lived experience with the "experience" that results when one takes a naively realistic view that allows the abstractions of a particular science to become the building blocks of reality.

Though the reductionistic interpretation of pragmatic doctrines has happily and rapidly waned, the focus on causal analysis in one of its several forms as the keystone of naturalism and of scientific method has not. Recent claims that epistemology should be naturalized go hand in hand with a causal theory of justification in terms of causal processes that produce psychological belief-states that are true. Further, this type of analysis is held to be patterned after scientific inquiry and theory construction. Epistemology thereby becomes dependent upon scientific inquiry, and scientific inquiry, like naturalism, centers around doctrines of causal analysis.

However, this understanding of scientific method has still not rid itself of the confusion of scientific method with scientific content to which pragmatic naturalism so strongly objects.[2] While claiming that the position is patterned after the method of scientific inquiry, adherents of this view are in fact using the contents of particular sciences as materials for attempting either to understand or to build an epistemological theory. Indeed, causal connections are always expressed as relations among particular types of objects or events, and the nature of the events or objects being connected enters into the very understanding of the nature of the causal relationship sustained. This focus on scientific method still not purified of content represents a lingering influence of modern worldview thought and is contrary to the pragmatic focus.

But, when the pragmatic focus on method is rightly viewed as a focus on pure method, this is too often taken to imply that it neither entails nor emanates from broad metaphysical and epistemological issues. However, though the pragmatic focus on scientific method is a focus on pure method in the sense that it is a focus on scientific method as opposed to content, the method itself has far-ranging philosophical implications. What, then, does classical American pragmatism find when it examines scientific methodology by focusing on the lived experience of scientists rather than on the objectivities they put forth as their findings or the type of content that tends to occupy their interest; on the history of modern science rather than on its assertions; and on the formation of scientific meanings rather than on a formalized deductive model?

First, the beginning phase of scientific method exemplifies noetic creativity. A focus on such creativity will reveal several essential features of scientific method that permeate the structure of a distinctively pragmatic world vision. Such scientific creativity arises out of the matrix of ordinary experience and in turn refers back to this everyday, ordinary "lived" experience. The objects of systematic scientific creativity gain their fullness of meaning from, and in turn fuse their own meaning into, the matrix of ordinary experience. Though the contents of an abstract scientific theory may be far removed from the qualitative aspects of primary experience, such contents are not the found structures of some "ultimate reality" but rather creative abstractions, the very possibility of which requires and is founded upon the lived qualitative experience of the scientist.[3] However, the return to the context of everyday or "lived" experience is never a brute returning, for as Dewey succinctly observes, "We cannot achieve recovery of primitive naiveté" but we can obtain "a cultivated naiveté of eye, ear, and thought, one that can be acquired only through the discipline of severe thought."[4] Such a return to everyday primary experience is approached through the systematic categories of scientific thought by which the richness of experience is fused with new meaning. Thus, the technical knowing of second-level reflective experience and the "having" of perceptual experience each gain in meaning through the other.

This creativity implies a radical rejection of the passive spectator view of knowledge and an introduction of the active, creative agent, who through meanings helps structure the objects of knowledge and who thus cannot be separated from the known world. The creation of scientific meanings requires free creative play that goes beyond what is directly observed. Without such creativity there is no scientific world and there are no scientific objects. As James acutely notes of scientific method, there is a big difference between verification, as the cause of the preservation of scientific conceptions, and creativity, which is the cause of the production of these conceptions.[5] Dewey summarizes this noetic creativity in discussing the significance of Heisenberg's principle of indeterminacy. As he states, "What is known is seen to be a product in which the act of observation plays a necessary role. Knowing is seen to be a participant in what is finally known."[6] As he further points out, "either the position or the velocity may be fixed at will,"[7] depending upon the context within which one begins. Thus both perception and the meaningful backdrop within which it occurs are shot through with the intentional unity between knower and known, and the way the electron situation is seen depends upon the goal-driven activity of the scientist who utilizes one frame of reference rather than another. Using this characteristic of the model of scientific methodology in understanding everyday experience, Dewey can observe, "What, then, is awareness found to be? The following answer . . . represents a general trend of scientific inquiry. . . . Awareness, even in its most perplexed and confused state, that of maximum doubt and precariousness of subject-matter, means things entering, via the particular thing known as organism, into a peculiar condition of differential— or additive—change."[8]

Such dynamics lead to a second general characteristic of the model of scientific method. There is directed or purposive activity, which is guided by the possibilities of experience contained within the meaning structures that have been created. Such a creative structuring of experience brings objects into an organizational focus from the backdrop of an indeterminate situation and, as constitutive of modes of response, yields directed, teleological, or goal-oriented activity. The system of meanings both sets the context for the activity and limits the directions that such activity takes, for such meaning structures are constituted by the possibilities of acting toward a situation. Thus, James remarks that conceptions are "teleological weapons of the mind," or instruments developed for goal-oriented ends.[9]

A third general characteristic, the adequacy of such meaning structures in grasping what is there or in allowing what is there to reveal itself in a significant way, must be tested by consequences in experience. Only if the experiences anticipated by the possibilities of experience contained within the meaning structures are progressively fulfilled—though of course never completely and finally fulfilled—can truth be claimed for the assertions that are made. And, as Charles Peirce so rightly notes of even the most rudimentary commonsense perception, "There is no span of time so short as not to contain . . . something for the confirmation of which we are waiting."[10] Thus, initial feelings of assurance, initial insights, initial common assent, or any other origins of a hypothesis do not determine its truth. Rather, to be counted as true, a claim must stand the test of consequences in experience. Thus, Peirce stresses that scientific method is the only method of fixing belief, for it is the only method by which beliefs must be tested and corrected by what experience presents.[11] In brief, scientific method, as representing a self-corrective rather than a building-block model of knowledge, is the only way of determining the truth of a belief. Our creative meaning organizations, though developed through our value-driven goals and purposes, must be judged by their ability to turn a potentially problematic or indeterminate situation into a resolved or meaningfully experienced one, and if they fail to do so they must be revised.

Here it is important to clarify the point of the comparison of scientific method with the dynamics of everyday experience. This is in no way an attempt to assert that perceptual experience is really a highly intellectual affair. The opposite is more the case. Scientific objects are highly sophisticated and intellectualized tools for dealing with experience at a "second level," but they are not the product of any isolated intellect. Rather, the total biological organism in its behavioral response to the world is involved in the very ordering of any level of awareness, and scientific knowledge partakes of the character of even the most rudimentary aspects of organism-environment interaction. Further, the scientific purpose of manipulation of the environment and the use of scientific concepts as an instrument of such manipulative control are not technological maneuvers into which human activity is to be absorbed. Again, the opposite is more the case. All human activity, even at its most rudimentary level, is activity guided by direction and noetically transformative of its environment. As such it is instrumental, and the abstractly manipulative and instrumental purposes attributed to science have their roots at the foundation of the very possibility of human experience in general. Moreover, human activity and the concepts that guide it are permeated by a value-laden, value-driven dimension, and this dimension pervades the activity of the scientist, just as it pervades all human activity.

All experience is experimental, not in the sense that it is guided by sophisticated levels of thought but in the sense that the very structure of human behavior, both as a way of knowing and as a way of being, embodies the features revealed in the examination of scientific method. It is not that human experience, in any of its facets, is a lower or inferior form of scientific endeavor, but rather that scientific endeavor, as experimental inquiry, is a more explicit embodiment of the dynamics operative at all levels of experience; hence, the ingredients are easier to distinguish. The pursuit of scientific knowledge is an endeavor throughout which the essential characters of any knowing are "writ large," and it partakes of the character of the most primal modes of activity by which humans participate in creatively structuring their world.

Pragmatism, in focusing on scientific methodology, is providing an experientially based description of the lived-through activity of scientists that yields the emergence of their objects. In so doing, it is focusing on the explicit, "enlarged" version of the conditions by which any object of awareness can emerge within experience, from the most rudimentary contents of awareness within lived experience to the most sophisticated objects of scientific knowledge. In providing a description of the lived experience within which the objects of science emerge, pragmatism is uncovering the essential aspects of the emergence of any objects of awareness. In brief, an examination of scientific method provides the features necessary for understanding the very possibility of its existence as emerging from rudimentary experience. If this interplay is not understood, then the result is the paradoxical criticisms that are often leveled against pragmatism: on the one hand that it is too "intellectualist" because all experience is experimental, and on the other hand that it is too "subjectivist" because of its emphasis on the rudimentary, "felt" aspect of experience.

When one turns to everyday experience, one comes to see that though humans emerge from nature as a unique part of nature that has the ability to know and to relate in other unique ways, nature, as humans encounter it within their worldly experience, is partially constituted by a system of meanings. Only through meanings does that from which humans have arisen reveal itself to them. Such meanings are characterized in terms of possibilities of experience rooted in habits of response. Unfortunately, the pragmatic focus on the biological context of meaning as habit has tended to lead to far-reaching misinterpretations of the position that was intended. The pragmatic focus, in its richness, does not lie in opposition to a view of human awareness as incorporating a field of meanings partially constitutive of "the world that is there"[12] as the horizon of meaningful encounter; rather, when properly understood, it reveals the purposive activity out of which awareness of meanings emerges.

For all pragmatists, the irreducibly meaningful behavior of the human organism in interaction with its natural environment is the foundation of the noetic unity by which humans are bound to their world. Human behavior is meaningful behavior, and it is in behavior that meaning is rooted. There is an inseparable relationship between the human biological organism bound to a natural environment and the perceiver who constitutes a world. There is an interactional unity at a primordial behavioral level that is the context from which a unity at the conscious level emerges. From the context of organic activity and behavioral environment, there emerge irreducible meanings that allow objects to come to conscious awareness. Such meanings are irreducible to physical causal conditions or to psychological acts and processes; yet they emerge from the biological, when the biological is properly understood,[13] for the content of human perception is inseparable from the structure of human behavior within its natural setting. Thus, Dewey and Mead alike emphasize that meanings can be expressed both in terms of the ongoing conduct of the biological organism immersed in a natural universe and in terms of the phenomenological description of what appears;[14] while James can emphasize that "the world of living realities . . . is thus anchored in the ego considered as an active and emotional term."[15] As Peirce cryptically expresses this type of relationship, "Desire creates classes."[16]

The significance of habits, dispositions, or tendencies is that they are immediately experienced and pervade the very tone and structure of immediately grasped content, thus incorporating an intentional human-world relationship that can be phenomenologically grasped from within. Such an understanding of the rootedness of meanings in the context of a natural organism engrossed in a natural environment must be understood neither as biological nor as psychological descriptions but as foundational, as an ontological description of the necessary conditions for the distinctively human experience of a perceived world.

The commonsense world and the scientific world result from two diverse ways in which the richness of the natural universe is approached by us in our interpretive activity, utilizing the method of scientific experimentalism. They do not each get hold of different realities; nor does one get hold of what is "really real" to the exclusion of the other. Rather, they arise as different ways of understanding the natural universe in which we live, as different areas of interest, serving different purposes. The nature onto which our concrete experience opens is not captured by the contents of science, for its richness overflows such abstractions. The perceived world of everyday experience grounds the abstract inferences and experimental developments of physical science, which, through its use of the tool of mathematics, leaves behind, for its own valid purposes, the very sense of concrete experience that grounds its endeavors. The things and events within nature as they arise within the world of science cannot be confounded with the natural universe in its ontological fullness. To speak of a slab of concrete reality is not to indicate the ordered content of some particular mathematical system but rather to indicate the ongoing unfolding of the concrete universe that ultimately grounds the possibility of, and renders "peculiar" to common sense, the contents of the abstract world of science. If the explanatory net of science is substituted for the temporally grounded features of an indefinitely rich universe or becomes in any way the absolute model for understanding it, then the roadblock constituted by the problems and dilemmas that have haunted the philosophical tradition will remain impassable.

The various abstract worlds of the various disciplines, each utilizing its specialized tools of abstraction, are diverse, limited approaches to the concrete matrix of the intertwined relational webs within which individuals operate. What is needed is a recognition that each area of interest is highlighting a dimension of a unified, concretely rich complexity from which each draws its ultimate intelligibility and vitality. The problem is not to figure out how to unite ontologically discrete facts studied by different disciplines. Rather, the problem is to distinguish various dimensions of the concrete matrix of relational webs in which human experience is enmeshed.

Distinguishing these dimensions is necessary for purposes of intellectual clarity and advancement of understanding and is accomplished through the dynamics of experimental method. If the problem and solution are viewed in this way, then there will be no temptation to view the resultant "products" in ways that distort both the indefinitely rich, concrete natural universe they are intended to clarify and the creative process by which these products are obtained. If such distortion is allowed to happen, then these products can too easily be seen either as self-enclosed relativistic environments immune from criticism from "outside" or as a direct grasp of "what is" in its pristine purity.

This is especially the case when one operates within more abstract environments with the specific experimental tool of mathematical quantification and the "rigor" this allows. One tends to forget that this tool, in the very process of quantifying, leaves behind all of the richness of nature that cannot be caught by a quantitative net. The use of the tool of quantification predetermines the type of content that is apprehended as being inherently mathematizable, while in turn the exclusively mathematizable type of content apprehended reinforces the belief that it alone provides the truth about nature.

But nature as described by science is the creative product of a second level, abstract, reflective restructuring of the nature revealed in everyday experience, not a substitute for it. As G. H. Mead stresses, in rejecting such a realistic interpretation of science and the reductionism to which it gives rise, "The ultimate touchstone of reality is a piece of experience found in an unanalyzed world. . . . We can never retreat behind immediate experience to analyze elements that constitute the ultimate reality of all immediate experience, for whatever breath of reality these elements possess has been breathed into them by some unanalyzed experience."[17] In Dewey's terms, the refined products of scientific inquiry "inherit their full content of meaning" within the context of everyday experience.[18] C. I. Lewis's agreement with such a position is evinced in his claim that any "truth about nature" must refer back to "what is presented in sense."[19] The position intended is perhaps most succinctly expressed in Peirce's claim that the foundationally "real world is the world of sensible experience."[20]

The nature and function of language, for the pragmatist, must be understood within the above context of naturalism and perspectivalism. The notion that if language is to relate to reality it must be able to capture a series of independently existing fully structured facts, and that if it cannot do so it bears no relation to reality at all, is itself a remnant of the alternatives offered by the spectator theory of knowledge and the atomism of the modern period. For the pragmatist, the compulsiveness of the world enters experience within the interpretive net we have cast upon it for delineating facts, for breaking its continuities, for rendering precise its vagueness. Pragmatism does not reject the linkage of language and the world but rather rethinks the nature of this linkage. It does not reject the idea of reality's constraints on our language structures but rather rethinks the nature of these constraints as a nature that is not that of correspondence. Language does not deny the presence of reality within experience, nor does it mirror this reality, but rather it opens us on to reality's presence as mediated by meanings, for language is emergent from and intertwined with ongoing praxis in a "dense" universe. We do not *think to* a reality to which language or conceptual structures correspond; rather we *live through* a reality with which we are intertwined, and in which the intertwining with it constitutes experience. Our primal interactive embeddedness in the world is something than can never be adequately objectified.

The structure of the mute world of active engagement with the other is one of ongoing interpretive activity such that the possibilities of language are already given in it. Pragmatism thus explains the origins and function of language by examining its role in the social process. Our fundamental logical laws of thought are themselves abstractions from the concrete matrix of behavioral interactions.[21] Languge is a type of gesture that is intimately incorporated into concrete experience, is inseparably intertwined with thought, and, as lived, incorporates both settled tradition and present creativity. Language cannot be divorced from temporally grounded human praxis in a "dense" universe. For pragmatism, language is indeed a tool, but it is a tool for providing a perspectival grasp of the natural world in which we are embedded. Language is a tool born of our primal bond with nature and it mediates our experience in and of nature; it does not cut us off from nature's real properties; it does not stand between us and nature; and, if the tool is well formed, it is not something that distorts nature. Dewey, in agreeing that language is a tool, stresses that any tool "is a thing in which a connection, a sequential bond with nature is embodied. It possesses an objective relation as its own defining property. . . . A tool denotes a perception and acknowledgment of sequential bonds in nature."[22]

Our primal, perspectival interactive openness onto the ontologically dense universe is also an openness onto the experience of concrete value qualities as real emergent features of human existence. Within the above framework for understanding human experience, humans and their environment—organic and inorganic—take on an inherently relational aspect. The properties attributed to the environment belong to it in the context of that interaction, and it is within such an interactional context that experience and its qualities function; what we have is interaction as an indivisible whole. And, these interactive contexts are rich with ontologically real value-laden qualities that span the range of the richness of human existence in its fullness. The occurrence of the immediate experience characterized by value is a qualitative dimension of a situation within nature, on an equal footing with the experiencing of other qualitative aspects of nature.

Value situations, like all situations, are open to revision and require the general method of experimental inquiry in order to progress from a problematic situation to a meaningfully integrated one. Ongoing dialogue and debate about experimental reconstruction of problematic situations, and about resultant new norms and ideals that develop as working hypotheses out of such concrete situations, must ultimately be rooted in the creative utilization of an attunement to the valuings of humans and their ongoing flourishing, or there is nothing for the debate to be about. Moral awareness permeates experience, and all experience is value laden to some degree. Human experience as anticipatory is also ultimately consummatory, and thus experimental method as operative in the process of living must serve the qualitative fullness of human interests, leading to the aesthetic-moral enrichment of human existence.

Pragmatism's understanding of value qualities as naturally occurring, irreducible contextual, environmental emergents, and of normative claims as experimental hypotheses about ways of enriching and expanding the value-relevant dimension of concrete human existence, denies the tradition of a narrow empiricism that holds to a limited view of what can be experienced empirically and a quasi-reductionist ontology that holds to a limited view of what kinds of qualities can exist in nature; both of these traditions are ultimately founded in the modernist acceptance, either explicitly or implicitly, of the ontological ultimacy of the scientific description of nature. Moreover, value qualities are contextually emergent facts, and so-called brute facts are value laden through the contexts in which they emerge. Pragmatism clearly undercuts the fact-value distinction.

Humans have a plurality of values emerging from their organic embeddedness in a natural and social world. Dialogue between diverse groups or diverse sociocultural environments cannot be achieved through the dogmatic imposition of abstract principles or inculcated traditions. Rather, what is needed is a deepening to a more fundamental level of human rapport that strives to get beneath the confines of particular environments to the demands of the human condition qua human in its desire to flourish. And the deepening process of reason can regain touch with the concrete richness of the experience of value as it emerges from humans who are fundamentally alike, confronting a common reality that they must render not only manageable and intelligible but also enriching of concrete human existence, through the diverse interpretive nets offered by diverse cultural histories. This deepening of reason can liberate us from the confines of tradition and rules, and this liberation is also the liberation of real possibilities that these traditions and rules have partially hidden from view; it is not a liberation from the ontological richness of the past and the possibilities it offers the present, but a liberation from a constrictive access to them. Pragmatism does not destroy reason but brings it down to earth, so to speak. Rationality is not fundamentally abstract, discursive, and calculative but concrete and imaginative.

In the area of value as in other areas of human inquiry, what is involved is not a linguistic or cultural self-enclosed relativism but an ontologically grounded open perspectivalism that accommodates a diversity of perspectives but not any and every perspective. The incommensurable, historically contingent value systems have arisen out of the directly felt value textures of experience as these emerge in our concrete interactive contexts. And while differing environments yield differing practices and beliefs, and while there may be a diversity of such relational webs that allow for the flourishing of human existence, there may also be those that mutilate it. We create and utilize norms or ideals in the moral situation, but which ones work is dependent upon the emergent but real domain of conflicting immediately experienced valuings that need integrating and harmonizing. This position of course rules out absolutism in ethics. But what must be stressed is that it equally rules out subjectivism and relativism, for normative hypotheses are rooted in, and ultimately judged by, the conditions and demands of human living and the desire for meaningful, enriching lives. In a similar vein, this position undercuts the various ethics of rule application and inculcated tradition in favor of a moral creativity in decision making that focuses on contextual reconstruction of problematic situations in a process of ongoing moral growth.

In addition to the nature manifest in our everyday worldly experience and the nature of science that emerges via second-level abstractions from such experience, there is yet another sense of nature operative within pragmatic thought and pervasive throughout the previous discussion. This third sense of nature has not yet been made the object of explicit focus, and doing so brings us to the pragmatic understanding of the nature and function of metaphysical speculation. This sense is captured in Mead's concern with nature as that which we never totally encompass in our perception or theories, "which is independent of all the worlds of perception and scientific theory, that would explain all of them and yet would not transcend them in the sense of being of a nature which could not appear in perception or scientific theory, and would be independent of observation and perception and thought, and would itself include these."[23] The purpose of knowledge, it has been seen, is to allow us to engage this reality, which is not beyond the reach of experience, which *may be* unknown in many ways, but which is eminently know*able*, though always via a perspectival net by which we render intelligible its indeterminate richness.

Though what nature in this sense can consistently be held to be is partially determined by the range of meaningfully projected possibilities within which it can emerge within experience as a perceived world of unified interrelationships, yet, it is independent of our meanings and the possibilities they allow. Within such a context, Lewis compares worldly facts to a landscape. "A landscape is a terrain, but a terrain as seeable by an eye. And a fact is a state of affairs, but a state of affairs as knowable by a mind."[24] Peirce notes of worldly facts that instead of being "a slice of nature," they are abstracted from it, for "any fact is inseparably combined with an infinite swarm of circumstances, which make no part of the fact itself."[25] Peirce captures the status of nature as both dependent and independent, in his claim that "Nature, in connection with a picture, copy, or diagram does not necessarily denote an object not fashioned by man, but merely the object represented as something existing apart from the representation."[26] Indeed, Mill was led astray in his analysis of the uniformity of nature, according to Peirce, precisely because he failed to recognize the distinction between nature as independent of mind's organizing activities and the mind relatedness of worldly nature.[27]

Pragmatists as metaphysicians are led, in accordance with the experimental model of gaining knowledge, to a "speculative, interpretive description," via a speculative extrapolation from experience, of what independent reality must be like in its character as independent to give rise to the primordial level of experience and to "answer to" the meanings by which it reveals itself to us. And, it should be well noted here that there is a vast difference between the illicit reification by past philosophies of common sense or scientific meanings and the speculative extrapolation from within experience of the pervasive tones and textures of the thick nature that enters into all experience. The categories of metaphysics provide the illumination by which traits of "what is there" can come into focus. Such categories represent the persistent attempt to illuminate and articulate, through a creative scheme or explanatory structure, the textures present within all experience. Thus James and Peirce distinguish between the content of science and the content of a naturalistic metaphysics,[28] and as Peirce clarifies, the latter incorporates the "kind of phenomena with which everyman's experience is so saturated that he usually pays no attention to them."[29]

Peirce characterizes such a concretely rich nature independent of mind's organizing activities as one that "swims in indeterminacy"[30] because of its indefinite richness. And this indefinite richness is characterized by all the pragmatists in terms of activity or process, for one of the basic pervasive tones or textures of all experience is the experience of temporal flow. The vision of a "thick," "dense," processive natural universe not of our making, and of an indefinite richness of potentialities for ordering within it, is gained by a sophisticated elaboration of, or extrapolation from, the reference to the primitive experience of anticipatory potentialities and unactualized possibilities as this occurs through the actual functioning of concrete living meaning as anticipatory activity in the flow of time.

Such a processive universe, which reveals itself in the pervasive textures of experiencing, is the home of the whole of the sensory, with its richness and spontaneity; the home of the brute otherness of the independently real with which I interact and to which I respond; the home of the continuities and regularities that pervade by commerce with it and allow me to anticipate the type of presence to be contained within the approaching moment. Thus all the pragmatists, through their respective terminologies, converge toward a process metaphysics of nature that can be characterized in terms of the categories of qualitative richness, diversity, spontaneity, possibility; interaction, over-againstness, shock, presentness; dispositional tendencies, potentialities, and lawful modes of behavior. These categories are understood and interrelated in terms of the ways in which a thick, natural, processive universe functions.

This emerging metaphysics thus envisions a universe in which humans are at home and with which their activities are continuous; a universe in which their lived qualitative experience can grasp real emergent qualitative features of reality and in which their creative meanings, embodying dispositionally generated noetic potentialities, can grasp the real dynamic tendencies of reality to produce operations of a certain type with a certain regularity. A universe, in short, which is both grasped by and reflected within the pervasive textures at the heart of all experience and at the foundation of all meaning.

The categorial contents of such a naturalist metaphysics are in no way intended as a grasp of being in some spectator vision. But they are also not merely hypothetically supposed at the beginning without our having some experiential awareness of them. The second-level reflections of philosophy must be grounded in lived experience and be constantly fed by this experience. Such an open system is explanation rooted in and answerable to lived experience, not the direct grasp of "being in itself." Though rooted in the lived level, it is never completely adequate to the lived level. It is open to change and development, just as all claims are open to change and development. Pragmatism gives rise to a new understanding of metaphysical system as an open system or explanatory structure, and to a view of explanation rooted in, rather than opposed to, a history of evolving change.

Here it may be objected that the view of metaphysical system as perspectively and temporally rooted in a processive, natural universe involves relativism and historicism, both for metaphysical claims and for knowledge in general, of which it is a kind. However, such objections again sever experience from its creative, interactive unity with, and openness upon, that which is independently there. The unity denies the arbitrariness of antifoundationalism, antirealism, relativism, a historicism of present happenstance, and the demise of metaphysics. The temporally founded creativity denies the absoluteness of foundationalism, realism, objectivism, the absolute grasp, and a metaphysics of pure presence. Instead of the stultifying self-enclosement of a relativism in terms of arbitrary conceptual schemes, this pragmatic view houses an open perspectivalism in which perspectives open onto the natural universe as the common concrete ground of their possibility.

Instead of a historicism of present happenstance, it involves a temporalism in which historical rootedness is at once natural ontological rootedness, and in which perspectives emerge within the context of a past that presents itself in the richness of the potentialities and possibilities of a processive present oriented toward a novel and indefinite future. Like all knowledge claims, the metaphysical claims of pragmatic philosophy are fallibilistic, perspectival, and temporal, but nonetheless ontologically grounded in the richness of the natural universe.

It has been seen, then, that in the pragmatic rethinking of the human-nature relation in the return to lived experience, three different senses of nature thus come into focus. First, there is nature as that "thick," dense, independently real that is the foundation for all that is and for all the ways of being, including the uniquely human having of a world as the horizon of meaningful activity. Second, there is nature as our worldly environment, as it emerges within the contours of our world, as it emerges as a network of relations of things used in everyday purposive activity. Finally, there is nature as an object of science, which we theoretically abstract from our everyday natural environment as a second-level reflection upon it. Neither the richness of nature as that from which all, including humans, spring nor the richness of nature as the human everyday worldly environment can be confounded with or reduced to the abstract character of the events and objects in the world of science.

It has been seen, further, that the first sense of nature is not something "other than" the latter two; rather, the latter two are diverse ways in which this nature enters the openness of human horizons of activity. Thus it founds the latter two. And only because independent nature enters into human purposive activity as the everyday worldly environment can nature as the object of the abstractive focus of the scientific endeavor begin to emerge.

We do not know the natural universe in its pristine purity independently of the interpretations we bring to it, but the natural universe is always that which we experience, providing the given or presented dimension within experience. Our lived perceptual world and the independently real natural universe are not two spatially, temporally, or experientially different realities; rather, our everyday worldly environment is the result of the way the natural universe enters into our interpretive experience, into the horizons of our everyday active engagement with it. And the various worlds of various abstract levels of reflection arise from within this concrete everyday world of lived perceptual experience as various explanatory nets cast upon it.

This complex contemporary naturalism, operative in pragmatic thought, undercuts all levels of illicit reifications, and in so doing it provides the path for freeing thinking from premature ontological assertions, allowing it to explore the experience of the dynamics of natural attunement as the ultimate inspiration for philosophy. The path to the natural universe in its concrete fullness is not gained through conceptual clarity but by attunement to the pulse of existence. Only by getting beneath the false reifications of the products of selective activity that give rise to the various levels of the various types of worlds can human existence become attuned to the rich textures of its natural embeddedness. Attunement to the concrete richness of this natural embeddedness can prove itself to be at the same time both a more demanding and a more tolerant master than any of the diverse second-level articulations to which it gives rise.

NOTES

1. This point and several others to be discussed throughout the chapter are examined and supported in some depth in my *Speculative Pragmatism* (Amherst: University of Massachusetts Press, 1986; paperback edition Peru, IL: Open Court, 1990).

2. This stress on pure method is not intended to deny that pragmatism is influenced in its philosophical claims by the findings of various sciences. Indeed, it pays careful attention to these findings. However, the model of scientific method, as pure method, to which pragmatic philosophy is inextricably linked, is one thing. Its attention to various findings of various sciences achieved by the general method is something quite different. These two issues should not be conflated.

3. G. H. Mead, "The Definition of the Psychical," in *Mead, Selected Writings*, ed. A. J. Reck (New York: Bobbs-Merrill, 1964), p. 34; G. H. Mead, *The Philosophy of the Act* (Chicago: University of Chicago Press, 1938), p. 32; John Dewey, *Experience and Nature, The Later Works*, vol. 1, ed. Jo Ann Boydston (Carbondale: Southern Illinois University Press, 1981), p. 37.

4. Dewey, *Experience and Nature*, p. 40.

5. William James, *The Principles of Psychology*, 2 vols., in *The Works of William James*, ed. Frederick Burkhardt (Cambridge, MA: Harvard University Press, 1981), 2:1232–34.

6. John Dewey, *The Quest for Certainty, The Later Works*, vol. 4, ed. Jo Ann Boydston (Carbondale: Southern Illinois University Press, 1984), p. 163.

7. Ibid., p. 165.

8. John Dewey, "Does Reality Possess Practical Character?" in *The Middle Works*, vol. 4, ed. Jo Ann Boydston (Carbondale: Southern Illinois University Press, 1977), pp. 137–38. See also Charles Peirce, *Collected Papers*, vols. 1–6, ed. Charles Hartshorne and Paul Weiss (Cambridge, MA: Belknap Press of Harvard University, 1931–35), 5.181; and vols. 7–8, ed. Arthur Burks (Cambridge, MA: Harvard University Press, 1958) (vols. 1–8 are hereafter cited using the conventional two-part notation); G. H. Mead, *The Philosophy of the Act*, ed. Charles Morris (Chicago: University of Chicago Press, 1938), p. 25.

9. James, *The Principles of Psychology*, 2:961.

10. Peirce, *Collected Papers*, 7.675.

11. Ibid., 5.384.

12. This is Mead's terminology, but such a concept is to be found operating in the positions of all the classical American pragmatists. Mead's

"world that is there" is "there" in relation to the organizing activity of humans, for "there is no absolute world of things." Mead, *The Philosophy of the Act*, p. 331.

13. It must be emphasized that purposive biological activity, as the foundation of meaning, cannot be understood in terms of scientific contents or scientific categories.

14. Dewey, *The Quest for Certainty*, p. 142; John Dewey, "The Experimental Theory of Knowledge," in *The Middle Works*, vol. 3, ed. Jo Ann Boydston (Carbondale: Southern Illinois University Press, 1977), pp. 114–15; Mead, *The Philosophy of the Act*, pp. 115–16.

15. James, *The Principles of Psychology*, 2:926.

16. Peirce, *Collected Papers*, 1.205.

17. Mead, *The Philosophy of the Act*, p. 32.

18. Dewey, *Experience and Nature*, p. 37.

19. C. I. Lewis, *Mind and the World Order* (New York: Dover Publications, 1929), appendix A, p. 399.

20. Peirce, *Collected Papers*, 3.527.

21. Dewey, *Later Works*, vol. 12, p. 385; Lewis, *Mind and the World Order*, pp. 210–13.

22. Dewey, *Experience and Nature*, p. 101.

23. Mead, *The Philosophy of the Act*, pp. 277–78.

24. Lewis, "Replies to My Critics," in *The Philosophy of C. I. Lewis*, ed. P. A. Schilpp, Library of Living Philosophers (La Salle, IL: Open Court, 1968), p. 660.

25. *Microfilm Edition of the Peirce Papers*, Harvard University Library, section 647, p. 8.

26. Peirce, *Collected Papers*, 3.420.

27. Ibid., 6.67.

28. James, *Principles of Psychology*, 2:671; Peirce, *Collected Papers*, 1.282; 6.2.

29. Peirce, *Collected Papers*, 6.2.

30. Ibid., 1.171–1.72.

6.

The Value of Pragmatic Naturalism

John Ryder

It has been said that we are more or less all naturalists now, though I am sure that it is not true.[1] Philosophers are, though, comfortable enough with many of the defining characteristics of naturalism that it *seems* as if we can now all be described as naturalists. This is the case with those of us who work within the more or less broad parameters of the pragmatism and naturalism in the American tradition. Such pragmatists and such naturalists tend to take it for granted that they also belong in each other's camp. I realize that there are those who would describe themselves as naturalists or pragmatists who come at these perspectives from philosophic sources outside the American tradition, and that the affinity between pragmatism and naturalism may or may not be so automatic to such people. But for those who would identify themselves with the pragmatism of Peirce, James, or Dewey, or with the naturalism of Woodbridge, Dewey, and the Columbia tradition, the association of pragmatism and naturalism seems to be, well, natural.

Several years ago I had the occasion to write a piece that I called "The Reconciliation of Pragmatism and Naturalism," a title that surprised people for whom the affinity is natural and not in need of reconciliation.[2] The point I made there is that the two are not the same, which is why people like George Santayana, John Herman Randall Jr., or Justus Buchler could do naturalist philosophy but maintain a distance from pragmatism, while people like Richard Rorty could do pragmatist philosophy while maintaining a distance from virtually all the technical philosophy of the sort that characterizes American and other forms of naturalism. In the end, however, the two can be and frequently are reconciled, and it is quite possible to speak coherently about pragmatic naturalism. However, because there remains too quick an inclination mistakenly to identify the two, it is also too easy not to appreciate what is valuable about a pragmatic naturalism more carefully thought through. These remarks will address that question, that is, the question of the value of pragmatic naturalism.

Once pragmatism and naturalism have been reconciled, which I assume has been successfully done, we then need to specify what pragmatic naturalism is and what its virtues are. The first of its traits, which it shares in general outline with other forms of naturalism, is that nature is broadly and richly enough conceived that there is no philosophical need to posit anything outside nature. The usual candidate for the designation "nonnatural" is the "supernatural," so we are in effect saying here that philosophical inquiry can and should be undertaken without having recourse to a supernatural. We need to be clear about what this does *not* mean. First, it does not mean that naturalism necessarily does without a concept of the divine. Personally I do not see, and never have seen, the point of a naturalist theology, but others do see the point, and there is nothing about the naturalist conception of nature that necessarily precludes a meaningful theology. Of course the effort of Santayana to liberate the aesthetic and other traits of traditional spirituality from the supernatural is well known, as is Dewey's attempt to free the language and ethical aspirations of traditional religion from their supernatural home.[3] But others have attempted something that looks more like theology, though in a consciously naturalistic philosophical context. John Herman Randall Jr. is one of the more outstanding contributors in this respect, and more recently Robert Corrington has attempted his own version of a naturalist theology, in his case relying on a more or less Buchlerian, ordinal ontology.[4]

This point suggests two additional observations about what treating nature as the comprehensive category does *not* mean, namely, (a) that nature is equivalent to the material world, and (b) that scientific inquiry is the only method that can produce knowledge of nature. With respect to matter, I would if pressed want to argue for a form of materialism, but like Santayana, I would also say that it seems to me patently false to say at the same time that nature is all there is and that nature is equivalent to the sum total of matter, that is, that only matter exists. The experience of all of us is replete with the nonmaterial, from the products of imagination to meanings and emotions. The sort of materialism I would want to defend would involve the claim that matter is the ontological sine qua non of everything else, but matter is not due to that any "more real" than other existences, and certainly not exclusively real. Pragmatic naturalism is not reductively materialistic.[5]

Nor is pragmatic naturalism friendly to the claim that all knowledge derives from the methods of the natural sciences. On the one hand, none of us seriously doubt the epistemological value of the sciences, regardless of how we might describe the scientific method. If we did seriously doubt it, we would not get into a car, drive across a bridge, or for that matter even get up in the morning. Our lives from moment to moment rely on the principles of engineering, and the principles of engineering are impossible without the results of basic science. But that is not to say that every activity we undertake or everything we think we know is the direct result of the natural sciences and the engineering they enable.

It has been suggested that naturalism should go beyond its interest in the natural sciences and begin to take more seriously the social sciences. I would endorse this call, but I would go further and say that naturalism, if it is to take seriously the breadth of experience and of nature itself, also needs to look much more closely at the humanities and the arts. Literature, music, poetry, the visual arts, theater, even philosophy can reveal to us knowledge and understanding of no less significance than that derived from the sciences, natural and social. I am convinced that a careful reading of Dostoyevsky can provide us with as much understanding of human motivations as any careful psychological study. In any case, Dostoyevsky's insights are at least part of the story of human behavior, in fact, to such an extent that they offer us something scientific studies do not and cannot reveal. Something similar can be said about any great work of literature, music, art, or philosophy. I have not the slightest doubt, for example, that my understanding of myself, or life, or the world, is enhanced by listening to nearly anything Franz Schubert wrote. Schubert does not do that for everyone, but then neither does Einstein, Skinner, or Quine, which says nothing about the epistemological value of the results of their work. Science, to use a pragmatist metaphor, is one tool in the pursuit of knowledge. It is a critically important tool, but it is not the only one; nor is it in all respects and situations the most important, valuable, or useful one. Not all aspects of nature are amenable to the methods of science. Some require the poet, the composer, the painter, or the philosopher.

Part of the problem traditionally is that we are too quick to assume that anything of cognitive significance must come to us in the form of bits of data or information. But we do not simply assimilate the world; we manipulate it as well. Sometimes our manipulations assert something, sometimes they display or exhibit something, and sometimes they consist of action. None of these three ways of interacting with the world, or three ways of judging, to use that word in a certain technical sense, has a monopoly on cognitive significance. Thus the exhibitive manipulation that constitutes a painting, to select one example from many possible examples, selects aspects of nature and combines them in ways that, ideally, we have not seen before. In doing so, it brings into focus traits or characteristics of nature that "speak" something new to us. This is why the visual arts, music, literature, and poetry can be and often are cognitive. We do in fact learn something from novel and insightful ways of manipulating form and color, or sounds, or words, no less than we do by manipulating objects and processes in the natural sciences. An adequate pragmatic naturalism understands this.[6]

So the category of nature is sufficient to our purposes, nature itself is wider than the physical world, and the natural sciences are not the only source of knowledge. Furthermore, pragmatic naturalism takes a relational view of nature. Dewey, who is the paradigmatic case of a pragmatic naturalist, fairly explicitly, if not systematically, employed a relational understanding of nature throughout his work. A "situation," in his technical sense of the term, whether a problematic situation or not, is not merely a collection of discrete, unrelated entities. It is, rather, a complex in which the constituents mutually determine one another's traits. It was Justus Buchler who developed in considerable categorial detail a relational naturalist ontology, though he did so without any wish to have it construed as pragmatic. The basic ontological idea is that all "things," that is, anything whatsoever, are constituted by constituents and their relations, and that no constituent, no matter how deeply or broadly one looks, or how thoroughly one analyzes, is atomic. Or to put the point positively, every thing, or entity, or complex, is constituted by its constituents and their relations, including the constituents themselves. Furthermore, constituents are not identical to parts in any normal sense. The history of a complex may be among its relevant constituents, for example, as may its social or physical context. All complexes are relationally constituted, whatever the detailed relations may be for any given entity.[7]

The reason why relationality of this kind is crucial to pragmatic naturalism is that it is what allows the reconciliation of the differing philosophical approaches of pragmatism and naturalism. Neither Dewey nor Buchler put it quite this way, though Randall did: one of the critical differences between the two is that pragmatism privileges experience while naturalism privileges nature. This disconnect would be fatal to any effort to reconcile them unless it is possible to show that experience and the rest of nature are related to one another in such a way that the world can be understood as the interconnection of experience and the rest of nature without reducing either to the other. A relational ontology allows us to do precisely this by making it possible to say that complexes of nature, whether themselves experienced or not, are constitutive of experience, and that experience is constitutive of the complexes of nature to which it is related. Thus the two are integrated without experience being defined away and without nature being inappropriately subjectivized. Dewey, Randall, and Buchler all understood this.

The final definitional point is that, for pragmatic naturalism, philosophical ideas are justified by their success. This of course is not a novel point with respect to pragmatism, but it is less commonly applied in naturalist circles. Nonetheless, even the more technical philosophical aspects of pragmatic naturalism, by which I mean its naturalist side, cannot be justified by reason alone. Let us take the claim that "nature is to be understood relationally" as an example.

There is no amount of argument or analysis that will force or even enable us to say that this claim is true and that its alternatives, for example, that "nature is to be understood atomistically," are false. The best that argument can do is to demonstrate that it is logically possible, or reasonable, or maybe even desirable, to hold that nature is to be understood relationally. Even if I were the most clever philosopher since Aristotle, and even if I were able to demonstrate rationally to the satisfaction of everyone in the room the appropriateness of the proposition that nature is to be understood relationally, sooner or later some even less clever philosopher would come up with a counterargument, or an objection, or a rational alternative. You may want to point out that this is in fact what has happened and continues to happen to every philosophical proposition made, and I would agree with you. I would go so far as to say that philosophers have misconstrued our enterprise by understanding it by analogy with mathematics, wherein propositions can be proven. But even if you do not want to go as far as that, it is nonetheless appropriate for us to regard pragmatic naturalism as subject to pragmatic valuation. It is appropriate, for example, for us to accept and put to work the proposition that nature is to be understood relationally, if we can render the proposition consistent and meaningful, and if by putting it to work we are able to do things we are not able to do otherwise, and create relatively few new problems along the way. The same principle of valuation should be taken to apply to other aspects of pragmatic naturalism as well, and of course to the many issues and problems that philosophy can appropriately address.

So to sum up the definitional side of pragmatic naturalism: it is a relational philosophy; it is a philosophy for which nature is a category sufficient for all things; it holds that nature consists of more than material objects; it proceeds as if natural science is one of a larger number of sources of knowledge; and it is a philosophical perspective that expects to be evaluated by its usefulness and value in philosophical and other contexts. We may now consider the question of what value it does in fact have. Each of the specific virtues of pragmatic naturalism highlighted is related to one or another of the defining characteristics just described.

First, pragmatic naturalism avoids the many artificial dualisms that have driven philosophy into too many dead ends. Whenever he had the opportunity, Dewey bemoaned the many bifurcations that have characterized philosophy in the Western world over the centuries, and he quite rightly thought that we would do well to get past them. Despite his efforts, and those of many other people, philosophy seems to have accommodated itself to, even continues to thrive on, those same dualisms: mind and body; belief and knowledge; self and world; individual and society; and so forth. One might reasonably wonder why these dichotomies have the strength and longevity that they do, and I think the answer is simple. They continue to attract our attention and often to drive our thinking because, in each case, both sides of the dichotomy have a compelling claim on our attention. Whatever our reasonable philosophical and scientific efforts, and even contortions, to explain human being in material terms, there remain aspects of our experience that continue to drive us to appeal to mind of some kind. And though the Berkeleyan idealist and the Buddhist may insist on the insignificance and even illusory character of body, the rest of us cannot live without it. One could go on to make similar observations about the terms of the other dualisms mentioned above. In each case, the terms taken alone are plausible enough, but when juxtaposed to one another as mutually exclusive alternatives they make trouble. But why is that, that is, why does the juxtaposition of mind and body become a technical "problem" around the discussion of which philosophers have made entire careers? The answer, I think, and this applies to all the dualisms mentioned and no doubt to others as well, is that we have continuously misunderstood what they are. Mind and body are a problem for each other only if we insist that each is a substance and that the two are substances of radically different kinds, or that there is no way to understand how they interact. Such misunderstandings force us to define one or the other away, or reach for metaphors, such as the contemporary inclination to understand mind as either a computer or as a piece of software, that are dubious at best and perhaps detrimental.

There is no need within a pragmatic naturalist framework to distinguish mind and body, or belief and knowledge, or self and the world, or the individual and society, in such a way that each becomes a problem for the other. For one thing, a relational ontology allows us to make the distinctions that mind and body suggest without assuming that in essence each is entirely different from the other. On the contrary, given a relational approach, we are driven to say that mind or anyway mental complexes are in any number of ways constitutive of bodies, and bodies are constitutive of mind and mental events. There is nothing stranger in saying this than there is in saying that eating ice cream makes me happy. Furthermore, if we are prepared to say that the value of ideas is in the work they do, then we never need to ask the questions that constitute the "mind/body problem" in the first place. Or if we find that we do, then the terms, the concepts, and whatever relations we posit for them will stand or fall on the adequacy of what they accomplish for us. Philosophy, in what we can call the Humpty-Dumpty Fallacy, has unnecessarily and artificially shattered a fairly coherent world into many pieces and cannot seem to get it back together without creating monsters. One value of pragmatic naturalism is that it does not compel us to push Humpty-Dumpty off the wall in the first place.

A second value of pragmatic naturalism is that it allows us to accept the realism of our experience, contra many postmodernisms. Among the many tragedies of philosophy in recent decades is that many philosophers (whom I will here call, perhaps inappropriately, postmodernists) who emphasize experience or the human subject tend to fear objectivity because they suspect that it ignores the human perspective. The result of the all-too-frequent fear of or hostility to objectivity has been a denial of its very possibility. The tragedy of this is that philosophers, scientists, and others who continue to insist that there are traits of nature that do not depend on us tend to ignore the postmodernists, and vice versa. In some sense this is not necessarily a problem, because the two sets of scholars are often working on different issues and questions. But in many ways, each could benefit from the insights of the other, and they too often fail to do so.

This, however, is a problem we can avoid. There are two factors that contribute to the difficulty: (1) the more or less constructivist view that knowledge and inquiry are always perspectival, and (2) the mistaken though common assumption that if x is not absolute then x is not objective. The pragmatist side of pragmatic naturalism would endorse the claim that knowledge and inquiry are always perspectival because they are always undertaken for a reason, that is, to do something, and that therefore knowledge is never absolute. Similarly, the naturalist side of pragmatic naturalism is likely to acknowledge that whatever place human beings and our experience have in nature, there remain aspects or traits of nature that are what they are entirely independent of human interaction with them. This is to say that in at least some respects, human perspective is irrelevant to the traits of nature, which means there are traits of nature that are objective.

This complication can be dealt with if we carefully sort out how perspective, objectivity, and absoluteness are connected with one another. The good news is that the relational ontology of pragmatic naturalism allows us to do precisely that, and in such a way that we can understand that the absence of absolute knowledge does not preclude objectivity, either epistemological or ontological.[8] For example, when I see the door at the side of the room I see it from a point of view, from a perspective, but the door is no less objectively there and not somewhere else. Traditionally, this commonsensical observation has led to a bifurcation between the world as it is in itself, that is, the door with its objective traits, and the world as it is experienced, that is, the door from my particular angle of vision.

Though Kant contributed tremendously to the development of European intellectual life, this particular Kantian move has been pernicious, and it continues to seep into our way of thinking about this problem: if our epistemology is perspectival but our ontology is objectivist, there must be a gap between them. But this is a non sequitur. Perspective is inconsistent with absoluteness, such that if our perception of the door is perspectival it cannot be absolute. This is, in the end, the reason why knowledge is always contextual. This is a problem for objectivity only if to be objective is to be absolute. If, however, we are willing to separate the two, then there is nothing puzzling about the fact that the traits of the door, that is, its location, size, and so forth, really are the traits of the door and that we encounter the door from some angle and in some context. We can see that there is no problem here once we realize that given a relational ontology, the objective traits of the door are themselves relationally constituted, regardless of the door's relation to us as perceivers. Every aspect of the natural complex that is the door—its location, size, shape, weight, material properties, functions, color, and so forth—is itself in a complex set of relations with the other constituents of the door and with the broader relational contexts in which the door finds itself. There is, in other words, absolutely nothing absolute about the door in the first place. It, like every other complex of nature, is thoroughly relational, and the relation to us as perceivers is one more relation that contributes to the traits of the door. The entire relational web of door and its perception is decidedly not absolute, but it is all nonetheless objective in that the relations are what they are and not something else, including our perspectival perception and knowledge of the door. This being the case, we can see that the relational ontology of pragmatic naturalism enables us to retain the realism of ordinary experience even while appreciating the many insights of recent constructivist philosophy.

A third value of pragmatic naturalism is that it allows us to avoid the reductionism common to much of contemporary philosophy. As we noted above, philosophers have too routinely allowed nature to be carved up into competing categories, that is, mind and body, self and society, individual and complex, and so on, even while knowing that the dichotomies thus created are themselves problems that must be addressed. One of the ways philosophers have traditionally tried to deal with the inadequacy of their many dualisms and dichotomies is to reduce one side to the other: mind being dissolved into body, the biological into the physical and chemical, the social into the individual. The problem with such reductionism, besides the technical difficulties of trying, for example, to describe all mental events in purely physical or neurochemical terms, is that the conception of nature and of our experience that results is no more plausible than the dichotomies that the reductions are intended to mend. A memory may be delightful, but a neurochemical process cannot be delightful. So even if neurochemical processes of certain kinds are necessary conditions of a memory, the two are not identical. A philosophical analysis that attempts to make one of them disappear into the other is no more acceptable than the philosophical analysis that initially turned them into absolutely distinct categories.

It was suggested earlier that one of the virtues of pragmatic naturalism is that it does not compel us to push Humpty-Dumpty off the wall, that is, we are not compelled to slice nature into irreconcilable pieces. The same characteristics of pragmatic naturalism that make this possible also allow us to accept the multiplicity of nature without any need to dissolve some of it into the rest. Each complex of nature possesses the traits that define it as the complex it is and not another. Precisely how it is related to other complexes is critical to understanding its traits. If a specific memory can only arise in certain neurochemical conditions, then that memory's relations to those specific neurochemical processes are among its traits and defining characteristics. Such a relational understanding of memory and neurochemistry makes it possible for us to recognize and acknowledge the diversity in nature while at the same time accounting for the close, and in many cases necessary, relations among them. In this respect, pragmatic naturalism is following in the footsteps of some of its intellectual ancestors. Spinoza, for example, though without the relational dimension, also painted a picture of nature with, as he put it, infinite attributes. There is a rich tradition in the history of philosophy, of which Spinoza is only one example, of careful attempts to avoid reductionism. Pragmatic naturalism is the contemporary expression of that tradition.

This point allows us to suggest a fourth value of pragmatic naturalism, which is that it permits us to acknowledge the multiple facets not only of nature in general but also of our experience and creativity, specifically art, music, poetry, literature, theater, and so on. Several of the points that have so far been made speak to the advantages of naturalism over other philosophical approaches. This fourth value speaks to the value of pragmatic naturalism over other varieties of naturalism that focus, sometimes exclusively, on the natural sciences. By insisting on the monopoly of science in the production of knowledge, too many naturalists are forced to deny, overlook, or suppress the experience any reasonably sophisticated person has when attending a concert, viewing an exhibition, reading a novel, or watching a play.

The point was made earlier that there is something cognitively significant about the arts, something well understood by those who work in the arts. The Adagio of Schubert's C Major Quintet helps us understand the human condition more deeply; Monet reveals various

dimensions of the Parliament Building on the Thames and its relation to different kinds of light; Picasso's *Guernica* speaks volumes
about war and its effects on civilian populations; and throughout his
vast production, Shakespeare brings into focus human strengths and
frailties. These are not simply nice sounds, pretty pictures, and
clever words, though sometimes they are all of these. They are judgments rendered, with the greatest skill and insight in the manipulation of sound, rhythm, form, color, and language, on aspects of
nature and our experience. They bring into focus dimensions of
nature, traits of our world, that are otherwise either unavailable to us
or available less dramatically. None of these insights is produced by
science, though in many ways, once the insights are made by great
composers, painters, and writers, science can augment them. But if
we insist on science as the sole source of knowledge and understanding, we will miss the insights of the arts and thereby do violence
to our experience. By encouraging a philosophical approach that
fully and enthusiastically incorporates the creative arts and humanities as cognitively significant activities, pragmatic naturalism gives
us naturalism together with the full riches of our experience.

A fifth value of pragmatic naturalism is that it avoids the logical
pretensions of much of historical and contemporary philosophy.
Despite our reliance on deduction, the fact is that philosophers have
proven very little to one another, and virtually nothing that lasts very
long. If the goal of philosophy is to arrive at deductively demonstrated proofs, then our discipline is a dreadful failure. But that is not
the goal of philosophy, or anyway it need not be. The importance of
deduction and inference is not to enable us to prove anything but to
provide tools that are useful in arriving at consistent positions that
have some acceptable degree of plausibility. Such positions will then
stand or fall to the extent that they do the work we want them to do.
And they will last only until they cease to do that work, or until the
work is no longer needed, or until another position is developed that
does it better. Something like what Thomas Kuhn said about developments in the natural sciences is applicable to philosophy. Philosophy changes over time, and from place to place, not because we
progressively build on the results of prior proofs but because new
approaches are introduced with enough plausibility that they cap-

ture our imaginations, or because old problems about which we once argued are no longer of moment, or because new problems emerge for which older methods are ill adapted.

This does not mean that argument is inappropriate in philosophy. It would be rather self-defeating to argue against argument. The point, rather, is that there are several different sorts of argumentation, and that it is unnecessary, indeed unwise, to insist that deductive argument is the only proper form of reasoning in which philosophers should engage. For one thing, there is, as we all know, inductive argument as well, and for another there is, alongside deductive and inductive reasoning, pragmatic reasoning. One can argue, as I am doing throughout this chapter, for the plausibility, or reasonableness, or even desirability, of a particular idea or intellectual commitment. Plausibility, reasonableness, and desirability are of course not the end of the story. Proposition p may be plausible or reasonable yet turn out on the strength of other evidence to be false; and proposition q may be desirable in some ways but not others, or to a greater or lesser extent in different contexts. So plausibility, reasonableness, and desirability are not simple and clear-cut principles of valuation of an idea or proposition. They are, nonetheless, plausible, reasonable, and desirable.

Is this reasoning circular? Well, yes, but so much the worse for deductive validity in this case. Pragmatic naturalism does not pretend to approach the world from an unshakable foundation. Pragmatic reasoning begins wherever it is, assumes whatever the situation compels it to assume, and goes from there. Philosophy does not have the luxury of beginning at the beginning. If intellectual bootstrapping of this sort is circular, then so be it. Dealing with the philosophical dimensions of our experience, of nature, is not mathematics, and philosophers do our own enterprise a disservice by pretending that it is. The upshot of this attempt to expand philosophical methodology beyond deductive argument is to make the point that one of the values or virtues of pragmatic naturalism is that it is a way of understanding philosophical inquiry such that it retains its rigor and significance without continuing to pretend to be something it is not, will never be, and need not even desire to be.

The last of the values of pragmatic naturalism to which I would like to point has to do with social, in fact political, life: pragmatic naturalism enables us to avoid ideology. Let us consider as an example international relations and foreign affairs. In this area, nothing is more dangerous than ideology, by which I mean a tenacious commitment to one's concepts, perspectives, and ideas regardless of evidence and experience. Ideologies, both religious and political, have been responsible for more suffering and evil than we can note here. Recent experience with the ideology of fundamentalist Islam as well as that of neoconservative imperial aspirations offers only the most current examples of the destructiveness of ideology, no matter the end to which it is put.

Pragmatic naturalism, by virtue of its experimentalism and fallibilism, is a corrective to ideology, and its intellectual tradition is sufficiently sophisticated and broad in application to provide a rich mine from which we can draw. In 1916, in *Democracy and Education*, Dewey gave an initial definition of "democracy" that included the necessity of cultivating common interests with members of one's own community and with those across borders. This characteristic of a democratic society gives us a way to reconceive international relations and foreign policy. If a democratic nation should be expected to pursue and cultivate interests with those abroad, then its foreign policy cannot be based solely, as foreign policy traditionally has been, on "national interest," at least not as long as national interest is determined without a serious consideration of the interests of other nations.

The implications of this shift would be enormous, especially by contrast with traditional realist and liberal approaches to international relations, not to mention the recently influential neoconservative approach. For one thing, it implies the sacrifice of some degree of national sovereignty. For another, traditional approaches to foreign policy and international relations assume some set of commitments—for example, democracy, free trade, revolution, human rights, power, or religion—in the interests of which a national government would then conduct its policy. One of the shortcomings of all of the traditional approaches is that they are conducive to the development of an ideological commitment to whichever values they endorse. It becomes politically difficult or impossible to compromise, and one's overall values become not virtuous ends but weapons with which to bludgeon other nations. It may be appropriate in other spheres of life for our values to dominate our decisions and actions, but not in foreign policy. The reason is that in foreign policy one is by definition dealing with other nations. If the other nations also hold tenaciously to their fundamental values, foreign policy becomes not diplomacy but simply war by other means.

A pragmatic naturalist foreign policy, by contrast, must by definition derive the interests of its government and nation in collaboration with the nations with which it interacts. In that case it is much less likely that an overarching ideological commitment can short-circuit the pursuit of the democratic ends of the cultivation of shared interests. Conditions may or may not be right at any given time for the expansion of the values of democracy, or human rights, or whatever other set of social values one holds most dear, but even if they are not, a foreign policy based on the pursuit of shared interests will encourage rather than impede communication, and that is surely a virtue in both secure and dangerous times.[9]

It is worth pointing out that the relationality of pragmatic naturalism also supports this approach, by contrast especially with the assumptions of traditional realism. The discipline of international relations dates the origins of its subject matter to the creation of the modern nation-state, specifically with the Treaty of Westphalia in 1648. Like so much else that was born in the seventeenth century and matured in the eighteenth, conceptions of the modern nation-state assumed the atomism that was common to baroque-era physics, mathematics, psychology, economics, epistemology, metaphysics, and music. Nation-states were understood as discrete entities, each of which possessed its characteristics and defining traits independently of the others and interacted with the others more or less like balls on a billiard table. In such an environment, one that informed Hobbes's "war of all against all," as well as the more tempered versions of such liberals as Locke, the role of diplomacy and foreign policy was to manage the interactions of the balls as they rolled around the table. At worst one wanted to minimize the damage created by the occasional collision of balls, and at best one might manage the course around the other balls in such a way as to benefit oneself. At bottom, this is still how contemporary realism sees the world of international relations, and these are the results it hopes for in foreign policy.

If, however, the international world is not baroque in this sense, that is, if we understand nation-states not as "atoms in a void" but as having their characteristics and defining traits constituted in their relations with one another, then the foreign policy picture changes accordingly. It no longer seems natural for nations to interact based on self-defined national interests. If the very traits and nature of nations are formed in their relations with one another, then it only makes sense to conceive of interests as developing within that same relational network. In other words, in an international environment that is relationally understood, the pursuit of common interests becomes the more obvious course for any nation's foreign policy to take. Pragmatic naturalism, then, has the added value of encouraging, and providing the resources for, a revised approach to international relations and foreign policy that could well contribute to the solution of many of the more difficult problems facing all nations.

One could go on in this vein for some time and delineate other values and virtues of a pragmatic naturalism defined as we have defined it here. There are other points one could make with respect to both technical and applied philosophical inquiry and analysis. It is for all these reasons that pragmatic naturalism seems to me to be a useful, indeed wise, philosophical direction for now and for the future.

NOTES

1. See, for example, Barry Stroud, "The Charm of Naturalism," *Proceedings and Addresses of the American Philosophical Association* 70 (November 1996).

2. John Ryder, "Reconciling Pragmatism and Naturalism," in *Pragmatic Naturalism and Realism*, ed. John R. Shook (Amherst, NY: Prometheus Books, 2003), pp. 55–77.

3. George Santayana, "Ultimate Religion," in *American Philosophic Naturalism in the Twentieth Century*, ed. John Ryder (Amherst, NY: Prometheus Books, 1994), pp. 466–76; John Dewey, *A Common Faith, The Later Works*, vol. 9 (Carbondale: Southern Illinois University Press, 1986).

The Dewey work is also excerpted in Ryder, *American Philosophic Naturalism in the Twentieth Century*.

4. John Herman Randall Jr., *The Meaning of Religion for Man* (New York: Harper Torchbooks, 1968). See also Willard E, Arnett, "Are the Arts and Religion Cognitive?" in *Naturalism and Historical Understanding: Essays on the Philosophy of John Herman Randall, Jr.*, ed. John P. Anton (Albany: State University of New York Press, 1967); Robert S. Corrington, *Nature and Spirit: An Essay in Ecstatic Naturalism* (New York: Fordham University Press, 1992), and *Ecstatic Naturalism* (Bloomington: Indiana University Press, 1994).

5. See John Ryder, "Ordinality and Materialism," in *Nature's Perspectives: Prospects for Ordinal Metaphysics*, ed. Armen Marsoobian, Kathleen Wallace, and Robert S. Corrington (Albany: State University of New York Press, 1991), pp. 201–20.

6. For a more developed articulation of this conception of judgment, see Justus Buchler, *Nature and Judgment* (New York: Columbia University Press, 1955).

7. See Justus Buchler, *Metaphysics of Natural Complexes* (New York: Columbia University Press, 1966); also second, expanded edition, ed. Kathleen Wallace and Armen Marsoobian, with Robert S. Corrington (Albany: State University of New York Press, 1990).

8. For a more detailed elaboration of this point, see Ryder, "Reconciling Pragmatism and Naturalism."

9. See John Ryder, "American Philosophy and Foreign Policy," in *Self and Society*, ed. Sandor Kremer and John Ryder, Central European Pragmatist Forum, vol. 4 (Amsterdam: Rodopi Press, 2009).

7.

Wayward Naturalism: Saving Dewey from Himself

Isaac Levi

The most important contribution that the classical figures in the tradition of American pragmatism made is to the elaboration of models of problem-solving inquiry. That, at any rate, is the way I have understood matters ever since I appreciated the extent to which, for Dewey, the creation of works of art is understood to be a species of inquiry. For many authors, however, the emphasis on developing models of inquiry to be found especially in Peirce and Dewey has seemed less significant than the naturalism that Peirce, James, and Dewey all professed in one way or another.

Proposing a model of problem-solving inquiry includes proposing an account of how inquirers ought to change their beliefs and their values and to fix on policies in order to respond to the problems confronting them. Inquiry is concerned with justified changes in points of view.

The high priest of naturalism, John Dewey, seems to have disagreed. Inquiry according to Dewey "is the controlled or directed transformation of an indeterminate situation into one that is so determinate in its constituent distinctions and relations as to convert the elements of the original situation into a unified whole" (*Later Works,* vol. 12 [hereafter LW 12], p. 108). I prefer Peirce's assertion that the aim of inquiry is the removal of doubt. This is not merely a predilection for one style of formulation over another. Inquiry according to Peirce seeks a transformation of an initial state of doubt to a state in which the doubt is removed. This suggests that the transformation is the replacement of one *state of belief* by another (or more generally of *one point of view* by another, if it is important to take into account attitudes other than full belief, such as states of probability judgment and value judgment).

Dewey explicitly resisted formulations of this kind. An indeterminate situation, according to Dewey, is one that is doubtful:

> It is the *situation* that has these traits. We are doubtful because the situation is inherently doubtful. Personal states of doubt that are not evoked by and are not relative to some existential situation are pathological; when they are extreme they constitute the mania of doubting. Consequently, situations that are disturbed and troubled, confused or obscure, cannot be straightened out, cleared up and put in order by manipulation of our personal states of mind. The attempt to settle them by such manipulations involves what psychiatrists call "withdrawal from reality." Such an attempt is pathological as far as it goes, and when it goes it is the source of some form of actual insanity. The habit of disposing of the doubtful as if it belonged only to *us* rather than to the existential situation in which we are caught and implicated is an inheritance of subjectivist psychology. (LW 12, pp. 109–10)

Dewey was concerned to distinguish problem-solving inquiry from techniques for the removal of doubt by some form of therapy, such as taking a pill or undergoing hypnosis. To make this distinction, he argued that the doubts addressed by the inquirer should not be the inquirer's doubts. Instead, the doubt addressed should be the doubtfulness of the *situation* in which the inquirer is located. The situation is an interaction between the agent and the environment. It is, according to Dewey, an entirely natural process.

I am, for my part, a rather wayward naturalist. My hostility to supernaturalism has always been strong. Its intensity has been reinforced in recent years by the embarrassment, shame, and disgust one must endure at witnessing the excesses of supernaturalism fostered by President George W. Bush of the United States and his minions. Commerce with overtly supernatural explanations of physical, biological, mental, and social processes is dangerous not only for the intellectual health of our society but for its political well-being as well.

The supernaturalisms fostered by religion are not the only superstitions that need to be combated. There are other insidious superstitions packed into the contemporary trafficking in notions of dispositions, propensities, abilities, chances, causes defended, and situations, in many cases in the name of naturalism.

Modern science seeks to liberate us from appealing to occult powers and propensities in the systematic understanding, prediction, and control of the subject matter to be explained, predicted, and controlled. Occult powers are objectionable but not because they appeal to what is unobservable. Whether we can acquire information directly and without inference or must extrapolate via some form of inductive expansion depends, in great measure, upon the information we already have. An appeal to the supernatural or theological is objectionable because it fails to explain, is useless for prediction, and fails to contribute to the promotion of our purposes.

Yet, inquirers often invoke and students of science condone or defend the practice of appealing to dispositions, propensities, chances, causation, nomological necessity, ability, and the like in efforts at explanation and understanding, and they sometimes do so in the name of a kind of naturalism. These practices are sometimes successful. But they often indulge in an appeal to the occult that modern science ought to be committed to avoid.

I do not insist that the practice of invoking these modal notions is always misguided. But some effort should be made to identify when such appeals are benign and even useful and to distinguish these occasions from practices that lead us into forms of modal superstition that are to be condemned along with the excesses of both theoretical and practical theology.

Sidney Morgenbesser and I proposed an account of dispositions that sought to account for the difference between the legitimate and illegitimate uses of dispositions (Levi and Morgenbesser 1964). In subsequent publications, I proposed extending this account to apply to abilities, and to attributions of chances and other statistical properties (Levi 1967, 1980a, 2003). Although I have not elaborated a case for using the same approach to address notions of causation, I am inclined to think that the placeholder view can be extended to apply to causal notions as well.

Morgenbesser and I focused on the view that beliefs are dispositions to linguistic and verbal behavior that had been suggested by ideas put forth by Bain, Peirce, and Braithwaite among many others. Attributions of dispositions—say, a disposition to respond in manner R to a stimulus or input of type S—are intended to provide what appear to be covering laws for use in explaining why some object or system behaved in manner R. The covering law explanation states that the object x is subject to an input of type S and has a disposition to R in response to input S. The covering law states that whatever has the disposition and is subject to the stimulus S responds in manner R.

The disposition appears as what might be called a theoretical primitive: x has the disposition to R when S'd. This primitive is associated with an axiom—the reduction sentence in Carnap's sense. Davidson famously objected to the idea of embracing infinitely many primitive predicates, on the grounds that they could not be learned. It is obvious that one could not learn the truth conditions for these predicates via Tarski's theory. But one could learn to identify a Carnapian reduction sentence for each such predicate according to an effective routine.

It may be objected that the covering law explanation just provided is too trivial or circular to be an explanation. The covering law, after all, serves as an axiom characterizing the disposition predicate and is, for this reason, disqualified as an explanatory premise. I grant the triviality. Circularity is avoided by using the covering law explanation as a stopgap measure while waiting for more satisfactory explanations that are forthcoming when the disposition term or the basis that may or may not replace it is better integrated into a well-articulated and explanatorily satisfactory theoretical framework. The function of the constituent disposition predicates is thus to raise problems for subsequent explanation-seeking inquiry and give direction to such inquiry. If and when the disposition terms are replaced or transformed into bona fide theoretical terms in an adequate theory, these terms cease to be placeholders. They can then serve as constituents of shorthand summaries of the successful explanations then available.

Even if, as is often the case, attribution of dispositions is thus problem raising, there is no objection to holding that dispositions are true or false of the systems to which they are applied. As long as the need for further inquiry is recognized before explanation by disposition can be considered satisfactory, inquirers may judge the truth of disposition attributions as earnestly and as seriously as can be. Yet attributions of dispositions should not be countenanced as fully satisfactory constituents of explanations.

Disposition predicates understood in this way are thus works in progress beginning as problem-raising dispositions and sometimes becoming nonproblematic theoretical terms.

In *Gambling with Truth* (Levi 1967) and in *The Enterprise of Knowledge* (Levi 1980a), I elaborated on the idea that attributions of abilities and chances may also be treated as problem-raising placeholders or works in progress pending the successful completion of programs of explanation-seeking inquiry. As intimated above, I think the same can be said of attributions of causal dependency of various kinds.

The placeholder view stands in stark contrast to views like those of Jon Elster (1983, 1989, 1999), who is willing to allow disposition (ability, chance, etc.) predicates to play the role of theoretical terms even when they fail to satisfy completely the requirements of explanatory adequacy.[1] My complaint is not that Elster refuses to endorse my placeholder view as a bit of conceptual analysis. It is rather an objection to the complacency concerning the need for further inquiry once dispositions, abilities, and so forth are in place, whether or not they are integrated into more comprehensive explanatory structures. Such views make it easy for students of psychology and the social sciences to think they are constructing explanatory accounts that do not require elaboration through additional inquiry. Morgenbesser and I called the disposition predicates in such explanatory accounts "mystery raising." To embrace theories in which such accounts are central is to endorse supernaturalism in a straightforward way.

Advocates of the placeholder view reject supernaturalism. In doing so they exhibit a certain wayward naturalism. They allow the usefulness of disposition predicates in nonsupernatural explanations as long as they are placeholders for explanatorily adequate terms in well-integrated theories. But they rail against those who think that explanations by disposition are perfectly acceptable as they are, even when such reduction within the framework of such well-integrated theories is not forthcoming. Disposition predicates that are treated in this manner are as occult and supernatural as dormitive virtue was supposed to be.

Those opposed to supernaturalism have long confronted supernatural explanation with superior explanations that appeal to physics, biology, and the other natural sciences. And many aspects of individual and social human behavior have been explained by appealing to natural science. But many philosophers think that explanations of human behavior by appealing to beliefs, desires, values, and the like can yield adequate explanations or at least sketches of explanations that may then be naturalized. In my judgment, much of the work along this line invokes supernaturalist ideas in a manner that self-styled naturalists ought to avoid.

Explanations that use beliefs, desires, and other attitudes in explanations declare these attitudes to be dispositions to behavior and insist that they conform to the requirements of naturalism. But such explanatory endeavors have had little success in replacing the disposition predicates by notions better integrated into physical and biological theory. Elster is right about this. And the reassurance of Elster that all is well nonetheless is, to my way of thinking, a revival of forms of supernaturalism reminiscent of scholasticism.

Perhaps there are good prospects for naturalizing the attitudes when the contentful aspects of the mental and the social can be ignored. But activities of believing, evaluating, inquiring, deliberating, and deciding are resistant to naturalization. I do not mean to suggest that the contentful aspects of the mental and the social are in principle irreducible to physical or biological properties or processes. Attitudes like believing, desiring, valuing, and so forth, may entertainably be treated as theoretical entities without incoherence. They could be the end result of inquiry that converts belief as a belief-disposition into a theoretical state or process. But the theoretical terms characterizing them require some sort of explication through the theoretical frameworks within which they are embedded. These attitudes are, indeed, embedded in such frameworks provided by models of rational belief, desire, and valuation. The theories have many of the trappings of excellent explanatory theories. They lack one qualification. They are false and known to be so by all of us.

Thus, according to standards of minimal rationality, it is axiomatic of X's rational full beliefs that if X fully believes that whenever X fully believes that h at time t, X fully believes all the logical consequences of h. It is axiomatic of X's probability judgments at time t that they obey the calculus of probabilities. It is axiomatic of X's preferences that preference be transitive. No flesh-and-blood agent does or can satisfy these requirements. No such agent satisfies them "by and large," if I understand what this Davidsonian quantifier means. Thus the attitudes of full belief, probabilistic belief, and preference cannot be characterized by a true explanatory theory of rational full belief, probabilistic belief, preference, and so on, and there is no alternative theory—say, of boundedly rational full belief or the like, to replace it.

This is not to say that that postulates of rationality fail to provide a theoretical structure for these attitudes. But this structure is either dismissible as false and the concepts explicated by the structure judged useless, or the structure should be understood differently. I prefer to explore the latter path. Doing so alludes to another way in which my devotion to naturalism is wayward.

I suggest considering the axioms of rational belief to be a standard of rational health to be emulated by all agents to the extent that they are able to do so.[2] When they fail to do so, they acknowledge that they should make efforts to correct their failings, cost and ability permitting. When cost and ability do not permit, they should encourage efforts to find ways and means to overcome the obstacles.

Rather than invoking the idea of a standard of rational health where the rationally healthy agent satisfies the axioms of rationality, I have often invoked the view that states of full belief, probabilistic belief, value judgment, and so forth should be understood to be states of doxastic, probabilistic, and value commitment. An agent X who fully believes that h at time t is in some state K of doxastic commitment, which I call a state of full belief. Being in that state of full belief has the potential state of full belief that h as a consequence. For X to be in that state K of full belief is for X to be committed to full belief that all potential states of full belief that are consequences of K are true. Fulfilling such doxastic commitments calls for having appropriate dispositions and manifesting them when the occasion arises. X may fail to fulfill the commitment. X's doxastic performance may fall short of X's doxastic commitment. Indeed, given X's limited computational capacity, memory, and emotional stability, failure to fulfill these requirements is inevitable. In this sense, X fails to fully believe the logical consequences of what X fully believes. But at the same time, X does in the commitment sense fully believe all the logical consequences of X's full beliefs.

The principles of minimal rationality remain "constitutive" of the attitudes in the sense that the success or failure of agents in fulfilling their commitments is characterized in terms of these principles. Attitudes like full belief, probabilistic belief, preference, and the like are true or false of agents in the sense in which it is true or false that an agent is committed to a network of undertakings. On the other hand, even if X is committed to full belief that h, it is in general a fact that X fails to behave in a way that manifests fulfillment of that commitment perfectly. X may fully believe that h in the commitment sense without fully believing that h in the performance sense. There is no contradiction but only ambiguity.

To be sure, X ought to fully believe that h in the performance sense given that X fully believes that h in the commitment sense. But this prescriptive judgment carries no factual content additional to what is carried by the judgment that X fully believes that h in the commitment sense.

That prescriptive value judgments are expressions of attitudes that lack truth values is widely taken to be agreeable to naturalists— or at least some naturalists. However, since belief in the commitment sense has prescriptive ramifications and yet, on my view, is a question of fact, it may seem as though my expressivism is betrayed. I think not. Whether X undertakes some obligation or other is a question of fact. The judgment that X ought to fulfill the obligation is a question of value.

In one sense, X fully believes that h and another not. Agent X may genuinely fully believe that h, in the sense that X is committed to being absolutely certain that h and its deductive consequences are true, to ruling out the logical possibility that h and its logical consequences are false, to lacking a real and living doubt that they are false, to using *h* and its consequences as evidence, and yet fall far short of fulfilling this commitment. At the same time, X may (and undoubtedly will) fall short of satisfying these commitments). In this sense, X fails to believe that *h* or fails to believe that *h* in some respects while believing it in others.

According to both the rational health model and the commitment model, empirical and natural scientific investigations concerning the attitudes and deliberate behavior are most usefully concerned with investigating how well flesh-and-blood agents succeed in satisfying their commitments and what may be done to improve performance when they fail. From this perspective, psychology and the social studies are species of clinical or engineering studies that should be focused on improving efforts to be rational agents.

This stands in contrast to reactions to our lack of computational capacity, memory, and so forth that seek to dumb down the standards of rationality in order to render them implementable so that the "ought implies can" dictum may be satisfied.

The proposals I am making aim to obey the dictum without the dumbing down. The attitudes are, on this view, undertakings to conform perfectly to the standards of rationality. Like religious vows, these undertakings are made while recognizing the hopelessness of perfect implementation. If we follow the dumb down strategy, there is no incentive to improve performance beyond what the dumbed down standards of rationality require. According to the view taken here, if an opportunity to meet the standards better arises, it should be taken.

I am prepared to deploy the rational health model and the commitment model interchangeably.

Thus, perfect rational health entails perfect fulfillment of doxastic commitment. No one is healthy and no one fulfills such commitments perfectly. But rational agents can undertake to devise new technologies and create new opportunities to improve their performance when circumstances arise in which such performance is required. And such agents undertake, so I claim, to do so. They are committed to satisfying standards of rationality whenever costs and abilities permit, and when the resources for meeting the standards are not available, such agents remain committed to efforts to improve our ability to improve our capacities, that is, our capacities to be rationally healthier agents.

According to this approach, two kinds of changes in attitude may be distinguished: changes in commitment and changes in performances striving to implement these commitments. I contend that the sorts of changes that are instituted through inquiry outside of mathematics and logic are changes in commitment rather than performance. They are changes in point of view. In scientific inquiries, the changes in point of view are changes in states of full belief or doxastic commitment, and confirmational commitments that are constraints on the credal probability judgments that inquirers should deploy given the inquirers' states of full belief. There are also changes in value commitments when agents confront conflicts in the value commitments they initially have.

Some elements of Dewey's *Logic* are congenial with this position. According to Dewey, in any given inquiry, there are methodological and logical principles that serve as standards for evaluating the conduct of current inquiry. Logical and methodological principles do not differ in this respect. And both types of principles are subject to modification in the ongoing practice of inquiry.

> If there are such habits as are necessary to conduct every successful inferential inquiry, then the formulations that express them will be logical principles of all inquiries. In this statement "successful" means operative in a manner that tends in the long run, or in the continuity of inquiry, to yield results that are either confirmed in further inquiry or that are corrected by use of the same procedures. These guiding logical principles are not *premises* of inference or argument. They are conditions to be satisfied such that knowledge of them provides a principle of direction and of testing. They are formulations of ways of treating subject-matter that have been found to be so determinative of sound conclusions in the past that they are taken to regulate further inquiry until definite grounds are found for questioning them. While they are derived from examination of methods previously used in their connection with the kind of conclusion they have produced, they are operationally a priori with respect to further inquiry. (Dewey, LW 12, p. 21)

Dewey points to two features differentiating logical from other methodological principles. First, logical principles are "habits" or rules of inference necessary to the conduct of *every* successful inferential inquiry. The other beliefs and values of the inquiring agent are relevant in some but not all inquiries. Second, logical principles are postulational.

> To engage in inquiry is like entering into a contract. It commits the inquirer to observance of certain conditions. A stipulation is a statement of conditions that are agreed to in the conduct of some affair. The stipulations involved are at first implicit in the undertaking of inquiry. As they are formally acknowledged (formulated), they become logical forms of various degrees of generality. . . . Every demand is a request, but not every request is a postulate. For a postulate involves the assumption of responsibilities. The responsibilities that are assumed are stated in stipulations. They assume readiness to act in certain specified ways. On this account, postulates are not arbitrarily chosen. They present claims to be met in the sense in which a claim presents a title or has authority to receive due consideration. (LW 12, p. 24)

According to the postulational reading of logical principles, all those who engage in inquiry are *committed* to reason in conformity with logical principles. Adopting these leading hypotheses is not assenting to a priori truths. And although conformity with them has been found to be necessary to the conduct of every successful inquiry, adopting such principles is not assenting to a posteriori truths. Postulation of a logical principle is, as Dewey says, the assumption of a responsibility to adhere to the principle.

The postulational reading of logical principles does not reassure us, however, that the difference between logical and other methodological principles is a difference solely in the universality of the success of logical principles in the conduct of inquiry. Logical principles, or more generally principles of minimal rationality, may be revisable as Dewey insists, just as methodological principles are. However, their universality precludes their revisability according to the same principles that regulate the modification of the other results of inquiry including the methodological principles with restricted domains of applicability (Levi 1980a).

Commitment as I understand it involves postulates in Dewey's sense. But it involves more. Like Donald Davidson after him, Dewey acknowledges that we subscribe to logical and other principles of rationality; but beliefs and value judgments are dispositions or theoretical states. As we have already seen, thinking of points of view in this way is difficult to sustain. And, as it turns out, thinking of inquiry as concerned with changing points of view in this sense is deeply problematic. On my view, not only do we undertake commitments to logical or rationality postulates but to specific beliefs and value judgments. Full beliefs, probability judgments, value judgments, and other attitudes are not dispositions or theoretical states. They are commitments that agents undertake to fulfill.

Peirce (*Writings*, vol. 3 [hereafter WCP 3], chap. 60) famously considered various methods of "fixing" belief, including methods that cover the kinds that Dewey wished to disown in his account of inquiry. Peirce thought the method of tenacity, for example, was often very effective in removing doubts. He objected to it because he thought beliefs formed by means of the method would be undermined when others using the method of tenacity obtained conflicting views that could not be resolved using the same method.

Peirce's objections to the method of tenacity are vulnerable to Dewey's objections to taking inquiry as focusing on changing points of view. Suppose we could devise a pill that agents could take to alleviate the tensions arising when others disagree. Disagreement would not threaten the success of the method of tenacity. But Peirce did, nonetheless, make an important point. The success of an inquirer's efforts to remove doubt depends on his or her goals as well as the consequences of his or her efforts.

Although Peirce did say that removal of doubt is the sole end of inquiry, charity in interpretation suggests that we be careful in interpreting what he meant by "the sole end of inquiry." I think what he had in mind is that it is the sole feature common to the diverse goals of diverse inquirers. Peirce thought that inquiries that focused on the single dimension of removing doubt are threatened with self-defeat. He suggested "that a method may be found by which our beliefs may be caused by nothing human, but by some external permanency" (WCP 3, p. 253). The concern to remove doubt ought to be tempered by an interest in avoiding the importation of false belief. Peirce did not wish to claim that all inquirers seek to replace doubt by true belief. That claim would be false. He maintained, however, that the common features of the proximate aims of inquiries occasioned by doubt *ought to be* removal of doubt and avoidance of error. Taking a doubt-eliminating pill or pursuing some other therapy for eliminating doubt may be an excellent way to succeed if success is defined as relieving doubt without regard to other desiderata. It will be suboptimal if one is concerned to replace doubt by true belief.

Dewey also thought of inquiry as having goals. But Dewey did not seem to think that avoidance of false belief is a common desideratum of the proximate aims of well-conducted inquiries. So he could not avail himself of Peirce's approach. Instead, he held that in inquiry, we seek to change situations—not states of belief or points of view.

Dewey had another motive for emphasizing changes in situations. According to Dewey, a situation is a state or episode of a system consisting of an organism in its environment. In his famous paper on the reflex arc, Dewey posited the process of an organism in its environment that is in some sort of disequilibrium, in modifying the organism/environment situation (*Early Works*, vol. 5 [hereafter EW 5], pp. 96–110). If the process is successful, a new equilibrium is attained. Dewey took this type of modification to be a common feature of the processes to which organism/environment systems are subject, no matter how primitive or sophisticated the organism and the overall system might be. Appealing to this sort of "naturalistic continuity" between simple and complex systems of these sorts is integral to Dewey's naturalism. Problem-solving inquiry is deliberately or intentionally conducted activity where the inquiring agent in its environment (this being the situation) engages in removing some doubtful aspect of that situation.

Dewey appealed to structural similarities between the behaviors of nonhuman organisms when adjusting to their environments and the deliberate efforts of inquirers engaged in problem solving. This way of "naturalizing" intentional behavior continues to find adherents. For example, biologists and economists have often recognized structural affinities between applications of game theoretical structures to the transactions of lower animals with other such animals and their environments and the interactions of buyers and sellers in a market that can be characterized by the models of game theory.

There are no doubt formal similarities between the structure of economic applications of game theory and biological ones, and between models of scientific inquiry (and practical deliberation) and processes of selection. If these considerations are to support the naturalization of inquiry, the application of decision and game theory to human conduct must be explanatory and predictive.

I have already registered reservations with regard to the claim that that propositional attitudes are dispositions. If they are, they are more like mystery-raising occult powers than natural processes well integrated into natural science. We can escape this predicament by treating attitudes as theoretical terms for which principles of rationality are axiomatic foundations. As any aficionado of "bounded rationality" ought to recognize, the claim that standards of rational belief, evaluation, and choice are explanatory and predictive of the behavior of humans is false. Standards of rational full belief require rational agents to fully believe all the logical consequences of their full beliefs; to make judgments of probability that recognize as permissible the use of probability measures to determine expected values that satisfy the requirements of the calculus of probabilities; and to recognize as permissible the use of utility judgments representable by functions that obey the von Neumann–Morgenstern requirements. Although Dewey seems to have at least tacitly supported informal versions of expected utility theory, it is unclear how much of it he would have endorsed had he considered it explicitly. But even advocates of alternative standards for assessing rational behavior replace the standards with alternatives that no one can fully obey.

It may, perhaps, be pointed out that both primitive organisms and deliberating agents sometimes approximate the behavior of rational players in a game and, with a good degree of approximation, tend to "solve" problems confronting them in situations of stress and disequilibrium by instituting modifications that lead to new equilibria. This point cannot help to sustain the idea that simple organisms and human agents and the many species in between are all games players and problem solvers. The beliefs, evaluations, and choices of deliberating agents carry intentions. The simulations of these attitudes found in other organisms do not. The difference is that the attitudes of deliberating agents are commitments to satisfy the principles of rational belief, evaluation, and choice. And deliberating agents attempt to fulfill these commitments even though they often fail. Recall that Dewey himself says that in undertaking inquiries, agents are committed to obey requirements laid down in the logic of inquiry:

Dewey's acknowledgment of these commitments does not cohere well with his insistence that the attitudes that carry intentions in deliberately conducted inquiry are simulated by the dispositions to behavior of other organisms when involved in transactions with their environments.

Both human beings and members of other species extricate themselves from situations in manners that may be studied empirically. Models may be devised that provide explanations and predictions for their behaviors.

But it is misleading to construct explanatory and predictive models of the conduct of inquirers solving problems using propositional attitudes such as belief (judgment of truth), probability judgment, value judgment, judgment of serious possibility, and the like as is common in psychology and the social sciences. To do so involves an appeal to postulates of rationality as empirical laws regulating the conduct of inquirers. But human agents fail to satisfy the requirements for rational belief, rational probability judgment, rational valuation, and rational decision making. Using principles of rationality in models of health or ideal types will not help, because the failures of rationality are massive.

One might try to construct models using the so-called propositional attitudes but without invoking principles of rationality as explanatory laws. The intelligibility of judgments of truth, of probability, of value and what is to be done would then be in serious jeopardy. As theoretical terms, *belief*, *desire*, *valuing*, and so forth would require postulates to *replace* the principles of rationality. This is crucial because bridge laws connecting such theoretical terms with bodily and linguistic behavior are not as readily available as one would like, whether one uses principles of rationality or not. The individuation of attitudes by appealing to contents or meanings cannot be fleshed out in a fashion that would make such attitudes useful in explanation and prediction.

Theoretical models of human behavior relying on an appeal to the attitudes are hopeless for the purpose of explanation and prediction, except in contexts where the complexity of the calculations involved is not excessive and the agents are sober and healthy. If the psychology of the propositional attitudes has a useful application, it will be found elsewhere.

Insofar as postulates of rationality are "constitutive" of the attitudes, it is due to the understanding of the attitudes as commitments explicated in terms of the postulates of rationality. Thus, to claim that X believes that h in the commitment sense is to claim that X is in a state of full belief or doxastic commitment that has as a logical consequence the potential state of full belief (or doxastic proposition) that h. In that state, X has undertaken to believe that h in the sense of a doxastic performance (i.e., a disposition to bodily and linguistic behavior or the manifestations of such dispositions). If X fully believes that h in the commitment sense, X fully believes in the commitment sense all logical consequences of h and X's state of full belief.

The "logical postulates" or norms of rationality so understood should not then be thought of as regularities that the beliefs in the performance sense of deliberating agents "by and large" obey (whatever the quantifier "by and large" means). Consider the injunction to fully believe all the logical consequences of one's full beliefs. Flesh-and-blood agent X may recognize some logical consequences. But X will be incapable of recognizing many others. The failure to satisfy the injunction is massive. Thus, the principle of rationality prescribing that X should believe in the performance sense the logical consequences of his beliefs fails miserably as a predictor of behavior. And it performs no better as an explanatory law.

Instead of thinking, as Dewey does, of the inquirer's state—the state that is "transformed in inquiry"—as the inquirer's *situation*, I propose to think of it as a state of *commitment*. The state of commitment cannot be merely the inquirer's state of full belief or doxastic commitment if we are to do justice to Dewey's views. We need to include other attitudes besides full belief judgments of probability, value, and other attitudes. In short, the commitment is to a point of view—that is, to a network of full beliefs, uncertainties, and values that, if perfectly fulfilled, would meet perfect standards of logicality or rationality.

I have noted that there are passages in Dewey's remarks that are supportive of the view that logical postulates are constraints on the commitments of agents. But the texts cannot support such an interpretation unless one thinks that the norms of rationality that characterize commitments are empirically grounded regularities, as Dewey apparently did believe. This is the major false assumption that is a component in Dewey's approach to inquiry as well as in the grandiose claims by game theorists that their theory has applications both in biology and in economics.

Whatever the merits of Dewey's vision of simple organisms and species of increasing degrees of complexity as following a similar process of responding to trouble of the sort he described in his account of the reflex arc, I deny that it can be extended to provide an explanatory account of the conduct of problem-solving inquiry.

Yet, it would be a serious mistake to throw out the baby with the bathwater. Many of Dewey's insights may be retained by replacing Dewey's characterization of inquiry as concerned with transforming one situation (the indeterminate one) into another (the determinate one) with inquiry concerned with replacing one commitment to a point of view by another.

Notice that what are changed here are commitments and not the performances that fulfill the commitments—that is, the behaviors and dispositions that attempt to fulfill these commitments and succeed or fail to varying degrees. The distinction between beliefs, goals, values, and so forth taken as *commitments* undertaken and beliefs, goals, values, and so forth as *performances* that attempt to fulfill these commitments captures the difference between the states transformed through inquiry and those changed by therapy, training, and the use of prosthetic devices better than Dewey's contrast between situations and subjective states. Fits of doubt may be manipulated in ways that, as Dewey said, are pathological even if release from the fits is successfully achieved. The agent who suffers from fits of doubt even when committed to an answer that removes such doubt is suffering from a pathology. In such cases, relief does not come from more inquiry (none is necessary) but from some form of therapy or training. Sometimes the use of devices that facilitate computation will help. The removal of doubt in such cases is not the product of inquiry. In inquiry, one removes doubt understood as a commitment to suspension of judgment. Changing such commitments involves an undertaking. And one should not undertake such changes without justification.

Thus, replacing a commitment to a point of view where a question that troubles the agent is unanswered with a commitment to a point of view that contains an answer to the question can, if the demands put on acceptable answers are well conceived, avoid the anxiety about subjectivity that led Dewey to think of inquiry as the transformation of indeterminate situations to determinate situations. Pathological cases of doubting and believing occur. These call for therapy rather than inquiry. Dewey and I agree on this point. I disagree, however, with Dewey's claim that it is the situation rather than the point of view that is transformed through inquiry.

According to the reform of Dewey's view of inquiry and the role of logic in it that I am proposing, the agent begins in a state of commitment (to full belief, probability judgment, value judgment, etc.). These commitments are changed or created by the actions of the agent. Such actions may be bodily or linguistic behaviors, fits of conviction, or the acquisition of dispositions to such things. The actions taken generate changes in commitments much as promises or contracts do. What the changes in commitment amount to depends on the agent's initial state of commitment and the context in which the agent acts. In this respect, the actions that change commitments do, indeed, resemble Deweyite transactions. In the case of full belief, the logic of full belief commits agent X to fully believe all the logical consequences of X's full beliefs, to conform to the dictates of positive and negative introspection and judge as seriously possible all and only those potential beliefs to whose negations the agent is not committed. The agent changes this doxastic commitment by engaging in linguistic behavior or in other forms of action that express a coming to full belief or coming to doubt. The dispositions and behaviors that fulfill these commitments are in general specifiable only in a very limited and partial manner and in a highly context-dependent manner. Although the agent who undertakes a commitment must perform some action, there is no specific type of action that is necessary to the undertaking.

If agent X is committed to fully believing that h but behaves in a manner that reveals anxiety and doubt as to whether h is true or false, X's performance fails to fulfill X's commitments. Such behavior could be pathological in the way Dewey describes. Pathological or not, X is in need of some form of therapy to bring X's behavior into better conformity with X's commitments. Similarly, if X fails to recognize the logical consequences of X's full beliefs, X stands in need of therapy, lessons in logic, or good computational or other prosthetic devices in order to improve X's performance.

I have proposed an alteration in Dewey's view of the "ultimate subject matter" of logic. Instead of considering transformations of *situations*, I suggest considering transformations of *commitments to points of view*. In doing so, I exploit an idea already to be found in Dewey—to wit, the idea that attitudes are commitments characterized by the principles of logic.

I think this modification of Dewey's vision improves the clarity of Dewey's account at least to the extent that it brings into focus some problems with his understanding of logic. It also avoids the mysteries of Dewey's naturalism at which I gestured before. And yet, it commits no hostages to the forms of supernaturalism for which Dewey quite rightly had little use.

NOTES

1. In his acute comment on my views concerning dispositions, J. Persson (2006) alleges that I overlook Elster's insistence that disposition predicates do not, in general, figure in covering laws. In my reply, I pointed out that in my account a disposition predicate is relative to a kind of trial S and outcome R. There can thus be a disposition to R on a trial of kind S and a disposition to fail to R on a trial of kind S*. I take this to be compatible with Elster's account of disposition predicates. What is incompatible with

Elster is my insistence that inquiry should endeavor to replace such disposition pairs with an account in some explanatorily adequate theory and Elster's refusal to do so.

2. I initially suggested that principles of rationality characterize a normative equilibrium and that the study of changes in states of probability judgment and states of full belief are a normative analogue of the study of comparative statics in thermodynamics or the theory of consumer demand (Levi 1970). Brian Ellis (1979, pp. 4–5) introduced the notion of a rational equilibrium that was to serve both as a physical and as a regulative ideal. In contrast to Ellis, I am skeptical of a useful comparative statical account understood as a kind of explanatory theory. For me, the equilibrium is normative. To emphasize this, I suggested thinking of such equilibria as analogues to states of health. I think of rational agents as being committed to being in such states of rational health.

REFERENCES AND FURTHER READING

Davidson, D. 1980. *Actions and Events*. Oxford: Oxford University Press.

Dewey, J. 1972. *John Dewey, The Early Works, 1882–1898*. Vol. 5, 1895–98, *Early Essays* (EW 5). Edited by Jo Ann Boydston. Carbondale: Southern Illinois University Press.

———. 1991. *John Dewey, The Later Works, 1925–53*. Vol. 12, 1938, *Logic: The Theory of Inquiry* (LW 12). Edited by Jo Ann Boydston. Carbondale: Southern Illinois University Press.

Ellis, B. 1979. *Rational Belief Systems*. Oxford: Blackwell.

Elster, J. 1983. *Explaining Technical Change*. Cambridge: Cambridge University Press.

———. 1989. *Nuts and Bolts for the Social Sciences*. Cambridge: Cambridge University Press.

———. 1999. *Alchemies of the Mind*. Cambridge: Cambridge University Press.

Frege, G. 1964. *The Basic Laws of Arithmetic*. Translated and edited by M. Furth. Berkeley: University of California Press.

———. 1979. *Posthumous Writings*. Translated by P. Long and R. White, and edited by H. Hermes, F. Kambartel, and F. Kaulbach. Chicago: University of Chicago Press.

Hinzen, W. 2006. "The Mind We Do Not Change." In *Knowledge and Inquiry*, edited by E. J. Olsson, chap. 17, with reply by I. Levi. Cambridge: Cambridge University Press.

Levi, I. 1967. *Gambling with Truth*. New York: Knopf. Reissued, Cambridge, MA: MIT Press, 1973.

———. 1970. "Probability and Evidence." In *Induction, Acceptance and Rational Belief*, edited by M. Swain, 134–56. Dordrecht: Reidel.

———. 1980a. *The Enterprise of Knowledge*. Cambridge, MA: MIT Press.

———. 1980b. "Induction as Self-Correcting according to Peirce." In *Science, Belief and Behaviour: Essays in Honour of R. B. Braithwaite*, edited by D. H. Mellor, 127–40. Cambridge: Cambridge University Press.

———. 1991. *The Fixation of Belief and Its Undoing*. Cambridge: Cambridge University Press.

———. 1997. *The Covenant of Reason*. Cambridge: Cambridge University Press.

———. 2003. "Dispositions and Conditionals." In *Real Metaphysics*, edited by H. Lillehammer and Rodriguez Pereyra. London: Routledge.

———. 2004a. "Beware of Syllogism: Statistical Reasoning and Conjecturing according to Peirce." In *The Cambridge Companion to Peirce*, edited by C. Misak, 257–86. Cambridge: Cambridge University Press.

———. 2004b. *Mild Contraction: Evaluating Loss of Information due to Loss of Belief*. Oxford: Oxford University Press.

Levi, I., and S. Morgenbesser. 1964. "Belief and Disposition." *American Philosophical Quarterly* 1: 221–32

Olsson, E. J., ed. 2006. *Knowledge and Inquiry*. Cambridge: Cambridge University Press.

Peirce, C. S. *Writings of Charles S. Peirce: 1872–1878*. Vol. 3 (WCP 3). Edited by C. J. W. Kloessel. Bloomington: Indiana University Press, 1986.

Persson, J. 2006. "Levi on the Reality of Dispositions," In *Knowledge and Inquiry*, edited by E. J. Olsson, chap. 20, with reply by I. Levi. Cambridge: Cambridge University Press.

8.

The Fecundity of Naturalism: Reflections on Dewey's Methodology

James Gouinlock

Dewey's naturalism is not defined by a single doctrine; there are several issues that comprise the meaning of his philosophy. An appreciation of this cluster of concerns will display the fecundity of this mode of thinking. In what follows immediately, much of the material will be familiar, perhaps, but I submit the review as a necessary prelude to exhibiting a method that is remarkably resistant to dogma and futility and is inherently productive. There are other dimensions of a naturalistic program of which Dewey is insufficiently cognizant. They offer still more vitality to naturalistic inquiry; so I will also attend to them. Finally, by way of illustration, I will review some of the recent prominent philosophies whose guiding method is precisely contrary to that of Dewey. I intend to suggest to you the unavoidable fatuity of these nonnaturalistic methods.

One learns from a deluge of his writings that the principal component of Dewey's methodology is to supplant any and all extant philosophic methods with those of science. The unwary reader is apt to miss the richness of this idea; so we must examine it. Dewey's most systematic treatment of method is in chapter 1 of *Experience and Nature,* in both the first and the revised editions. He makes a distinction between "gross" and "refined" experience, otherwise called "primary" and "secondary" experience, where gross (primary) experience denotes the state of experience one might have antecedent to any sort of analysis about matters immediately at hand. If and when such inquiry occurs, cognitive ideas are produced concerning the nature and behavior of selected features of the objects of primary experience. These ideas are refined experience; but their truth value cannot be determined without returning by way of prediction and observation to the materials of primary experience. This is elementary experimental method. A man gazes into the starry heavens with great wonder. He hasn't a clue what these beings are or what they do. This is his primary experience. He produces all manner of speculation to satisfy his wonder. This is his secondary experience. In the present instance, to be sure, his cognitive ideas are going to be false. What does he know—or care?—about scientific method?

When Dewey speaks of experience, he means the experience that we have independently of anyone's *theory* of the nature of experience. He means the real-life experience that we undergo day in and day out in common life: matters of work and play, love and hate, beauty and ugliness, aspiration and disappointment, striving and idling, and so on indefinitely. All human practice is a matter of experience, and the experience is often cumulative; so we speak of experienced physicians, mechanics, teachers, and so forth. Typically, all this is alternation or coincidence of "experience in gross" and reflection of some sort.

What has this to do with philosophy? Dewey urges that philosophical investigations begin and end in the same way as disciplined experiment: addressing problems that arise in the most salient phases of human experience and developing ideas that will clarify these self-same problems and discern instrumentalities that might yield resolution of them. Whether it be moral and political life, religion, the logic of inquiry, education, the arts, or the origin and nature of mind or language, the point of philosophy is to bring intelligibility and resource to the very problems that have given rise to stalemate and perplexity in the first place. Ultimately, the aim of such ventures is to provide clarity and power to the quest for human flourishing. These are "problems of men," with which philosophers might helpfully contend. They are not the problems of a hermetically sealed mode of philosophizing.

The philosophic standpoint for effective analysis is knowledge of experience and its status in nature, as we shall see. More often than not, however, philosophers impede such ventures, rather than advance them. The assumptions with which they begin their reflections are far removed from primary experience and serve to obscure it. Their underlying assumptions are theoretically derived, owing nothing to actual human travail; and they are never returned to gross experience for verification and utilization. In modern philosophy, for example, all philosophers supposed that experience is composed of inherently unrelated atoms of sensation. This view was mainly derived from the material atomism of Isaac Newton, not at all from primary experience, yet it became axiomatic and dogmatic.

It was united with an ancient presupposition, stemming from the Eleatics and Plato: to wit, the object of rational knowledge is the "really real" or "being in itself." True being is what is disclosed in this supposed rational knowledge, independent of experience. All that is not of rational knowledge is appearance, the merely subjective, the unreal, or the phenomenal; it is a distinct and lesser form of existence. Descartes axiomatically accepted this assumption. For him, the respective natures of matter and of mind are such objects of rational knowledge. Accordingly, mere objects of experience are wholly apart from them and cannot be predicated of them. Descartes is obliged to conclude that the material world is nothing but matter in motion, and mind is nothing but a thinking thing, the two sharing no properties with each other. With that, he is further compelled to say that nothing of sensory experience can be predicated of matter; that is, of nature.

Just the same, he can't very well deny that experience exists at all. He just encases all of that in subjective mind, from which it cannot escape. Hence the modern dualism of mind and body is born, and we may not attribute any of the traits of experience to a putative outside world. Indeed, in this thoroughgoing subjectivism, no individual has any consciousness of any other individual, however else it may seem to him. This of course is solipsism. Everyone (if anyone else exists) is in effect a perpetual somnambulist.

The idea of the atomistic nature of experience compounds the difficulties of Cartesianism. The atoms of sense must somehow be combined by some postulated subjective agency to produce a resemblance to the experience we actually have. As contrived in modern philosophy, to be sure, this a priori organization of atoms cannot consistently be said to be significant of anything but itself. Nature remains a conjecture beyond the dream of experience (to paraphrase Whitehead), but if there is anything out there at all, it is eternal and unchanging matter.

The incoherence and vanity of this modern philosophy! Apart from the tutelage of such philosophers, we witness orders in nature and discover her regularities. We do this not by an a priori grasp but by consulting that very experience which by philosophic definition cannot be indicative of nature. In addition, we witness nature not just in orderly patterns but convulsive and changing as well, producing disorder, novelty, and variation.[1] We witness the natural world running amok with qualitative change and displaying a staggering variety of powers, with which we must somehow contend. Natural processes have identifiable beginnings and endings. We might ally ourselves with them or be crushed by them. This organic convergence of natural forces determines the existence of ends and values in nature.

All this profusion is the scene of life and death, success and ruin, fulfillment and bitterness; but, according to the axioms of modern philosophy, things are not at all what they seem. Philosophers cleave to their initiating assumptions, let our real experience be what it may. Then they would impose their teachings on living beings. Is it any wonder that the literate public has little use for these oddly impertinent declarations? According to naturalists, on the other hand, there is always a presumption that things are what they are experienced to be; and this is the experience to which we naturalists attend. We are not speaking here of methodological niceties, per se. At issue is the basic subject matter of philosophy.

To show that the operative postulates of modern philosophy are without foundation is not to give an account of the ontological status of experience. That is a further inquiry. In Dewey's approach to this analysis, experience, replete with its powers and qualities, displays the potentialities of nature. They are real—just as we find them. These are potentialities that, to be sure, nature would not have if nature did not also have the potentiality to produce life—in particular, human life. The occurrence of qualities in nature is dependent upon a fairly definite sort of context, and when crucial factors are missing, qualities will not occur. Thus it is with all compound events: they are not eternal substances but the product of a confluence of processes. So far as Dewey is correct in such an analysis, he has indeed overturned the stubbornly enduring tradition of philosophy in Western thought.

If nature is the "buzzing, blooming confusion" (to adapt a phrase from William James), and not the sterile and lifeless thing stipulated by Descartes, then philosophy is challenged to formulate a conception of nature adequate to the reality. Hence, Dewey developed his naturalistic metaphysics. From the prolific, luxuriant, and variegated powers of nature he distinguished five generic traits: the stable, the precarious, qualities, ends, and histories. All of them were selected and elaborated in virtue of his concern with human fate and thriving. The nature and function of the events denoted by these terms, including their interrelations, are examined at length and in detail. The result is a remarkably coherent and organic vision of the nature of nature. This is nature as it defines the generic human condition.[2] Dewey called it naturalistic metaphysics. He might more suitably have named it a metaphysics of the human condition; but in any case it provides a vision of the ascertainable and salient traits of nature radically surpassing anything found in modern philosophy.

At this point it is evident that Dewey's concern with method is more than the desire simply for the experimentally responsible determination of truth—"warranted assertibility," in his gargantuan phrase. Important as that is, the identification of the resources of experience and nature that might remedy the practical and intellectual problems that prompt our various and urgent inquiries is of greater consequence. There might even be resources for massive fulfillments over a lifetime.

The greatest product of his philosophy, Dewey believed, would be the universalization of the use of rigorous intelligence in all of the affairs of common life. He typically used the idiom "social intelligence," stressing the intersubjective and collaborative phases of inquiry. Dewey was hopeful that all manner of formal and informal education would inculcate habits of experimental thought and practice in every learner. In his utopian enthusiasm, he declared that "incalculable" benefits in morals, politics, and all of daily life would follow from such learning; and he attempted much and taught much, as we know, in the reform of educational theory and practice.

Another good—one especially cherished by the philosophic mind—is the synoptic intelligibility that comes of a fully articulated naturalism, as in Dewey's naturalistic metaphysics. Dewey often complains of the cognitive dissonance created by philosophies. The typical student, including Dewey himself, finds it intolerable when philosophers instruct him that the world in which he suffers, loves, and strives has no resemblance to the way things "really" are. Of course, the prescriptions for conduct that issue from such philosophers are typically academic in the pejorative sense, and often harmful. The problem with modern philosophy is not just that it is false, and not alone that it is largely useless, but also that it makes a mockery of our experience. Dewey's naturalism comes to be defined, in part, by the demand that philosophy enlighten our life, rather than obscure it. As I will suggest later, philosophers have not mended their ways.

Dewey is by no means recommending that a philosopher should neglect the work of other philosophers. He learned much from his predecessors and colleagues, by way of both their successes and their failures. To pursue a truly instructive philosophy, in addition, one must have sufficient acquaintance with the relevant scientific knowledge of the subject matter; and—in most human matters—one must know a lot of history. Extensive worldly experience is a vital need, as well as the mother wit to use it.

I have been summarizing Dewey's accomplishment, focusing on his method; and certainly that has much to do with the fecundity of his thought. Setting aside his native brilliance, his insistence on starting with the traits, problems, and powers of real experience is indispensable to the fertility of his analyses; and so is his insistence on testing the adequacy of philosophic ideas by their relevance to lived experience. These methodological norms prove to be exceptionally fertile in light of the fact that philosophers—then and now—seem to be addicted to thinking in an experiential vacuum. Their primary subject matter is not experience but their personal predilections and the writings of current and like-minded philosophers.

The method of experience is not reserved to metaphysics alone. It can and should be used in virtually every field of philosophy. Dewey uses it as a matter of course in many of his specific treatises. Significantly, his most important work in ethics (*Ethics*, written with James H. Tufts) is subtitled *The Theory of the Moral Life*, suggesting that theorizing about ethics is derivative of analyses of moral experience in its vital social context. Dewey analyzes fundamental moral distinctions (such as rights, obligations, goods) for their functions, interconnections, and conflicts in coping with the typical needs and demands of the conduct of life. His great book in the philosophy of art, *Art as Experience*, displays exceptional insight into the phases and rhythms of experience in the revelations of the arts. His *Logic: The Theory of Inquiry* proceeds from the elementary tasks of problem solving in the context of lived experience, out of which emerge cognitive instruments. *The Quest for Certainty* displays familiarity with the procedures of working scientists, and *The Public and Its Problems* means to be predicated upon the actual dynamics of the public (more precisely, publics).

There are weaknesses in Dewey's discussions of method. A number of scholars have found that the distinction between gross and refined experience is unclear and perhaps at times unworkable. A "problematic gross experience" might be as broad as that of the nature and meaning of religion—a subject matter of many and varied dimensions and greatly extended geographically and historically. It would be peculiar, to say the least, to call this vast topic a matter of gross experience. But this is not a fatal reservation. Dewey's thought is always rooted in experience and always directed to experience, and religious beliefs and practices are a matter of the experience of a people in a given milieu. He could simply have retained his more accustomed distinction between the problematic situation and the consummation of inquiry. Occasionally he uses the expression "primary subject matter," and that might be the best choice of all. In any case, it would be essential to be clear that the primary subject matter is life experience—not theoretical postulates, nor a priori conclusions, nor professional journals. "The first and perhaps the greatest difference made in philosophy," he concludes, is "the difference made in what is selected as original material."[3]

There is a question to which I have already adverted, which Dewey recognizes from time to time but about which he says rather little. I am referring to the means of analyzing primary experience. This analysis is of first consequence, for it gives focus, direction, and meaning to subsequent investigation. What is actually problematic in a given situation, for example, might not be obvious. As a case in point, there is much talk that there is ruinous moral corruption in contemporary society, and many who hold this view say that the remedy for the problem lies in the recognition of moral absolutes. Such a claim is greeted with both passionate assent and contemptuous dismissal. "There are no moral absolutes," say the sophisticated, and some of them might even agree with the absolutist that without absolutes there is only relativism—everything is just a matter of opinion. The sophisticate, however, might welcome this conclusion, believing that it is liberating. In such a case, our man of the world will admonish us that there really is no problematic situation to begin with.

The controversy rages on. In explicitly philosophic circles, many will say that the ultimate solution to these vital disagreements lies in solving the is/ought problem, which, supposedly, brings an end to otherwise intractable disagreements.

Now, as a naturalist who has actually tried to address this sort of debate in its existential reality, I have asked, "What sort of problems in the primary subject matter actually underlie this passionate conflict?" There is not just one problem; there are many. The main one, I judge, is the universal need to maintain some kind of order in a society that will protect it from chaos, mayhem, and destruction. At best it will also provide for the pursuit of excellence and happiness. A morality of some description is a major component in satisfying these needs. We must have social stability—and vitality as well. To a naturalist, this urgent concern brings us to hold in abeyance the questions of moral absolutes, "is" and "ought," and the like. The question is more fundamental. The nature and conditions of a stable and even thriving moral order is a matter neither of armchair excogitation nor of religious faith. It is a multidimensional question of great scope and complexity; and it is notoriously difficult and controversial. It calls upon the examined results of many centuries of social experience and many formal inquiries, and it demands candor and sagacity of the philosopher. It is, for example, a question of historical knowledge, focusing on comparative analyses of distinctive moral orders—such as the implementation of differing systems of justice. We also must specify the forms of life activity denominated by moral terms, so that we might investigate the real and varying interrelations of these activities.[4] It is essential that we also undertake an honest inventory of our moral capacities and limitations, drawing from several fields of study, so that theory does not impose impossibilities or fail to demand appropriately high standards— hardly an untroubled investigation but the most important of all. All of these materials would be synthesized, more or less, to produce some guiding assumptions about the forms of moral conduct most suitable to whatever populations are in question.

The problematic situation gives the philosopher much to think about. What *are* the conditions of a vital and happy social order? In truth, we are trying to look candidly into the entire human condition. In humanistic reflection, the effective practice of naturalism requires that the philosopher be not simply a technician engaged in a craft. He must be a wise, informed, and perspicacious student of primary subject matter.

Aristotle, I would argue, is the best historic example of philosophy of this kind, but Dewey himself is of world-historical stature. There have been many others. As the case may be, one thinker botches the job while another does it well; but there is no univocal and unproblematic answer in any case. Moral practice will continue to display degrees of variation and conflict (and that, too, is a worthy subject of study for the moralist). Still, there is much very helpful knowledge to be attained. Even then, there will be many who will remain unconvinced and many others who will vehemently dissent. Such is the nature of things for a passionate, questioning, and disputatious race. Our naturalistic inquirer is not a philosopher-king. He becomes an *advocate* of a more or less well-defined position, and he might be an effective one. He formulates proposals for the norms of justice and right, let us say, and perhaps of duty and good and much else besides. He communicates his ideas to others and discusses them. Presumably, his moral ideas have some precedent in practice, and the precedents can be examined. He is able to suggest experiments in moral life, so that they may be evaluated. We may judge whether some semblance of an orderly, secure, vigorous, and happy social practice might result from such proposed arrangements. Any judgment must be provisional until it is well tested in practice. In any case no configuration of moral conduct will achieve universal concord and assent, but critical experience is ongoing.

My aim here is to offer some sense of what a naturalistic approach to the problem is. In a moment, I will contrast the approach of a naturalist with those who believe some single point, extracted from multifaceted, unruly, and often perplexing reality—or perhaps simply invented for the occasion—can be contrived to set our troubled minds at peace and agreement.

The point of such investigations is not to win a philosophic argument but to address the real root of matters, so far as possible, and engage the generic struggles and aspirations of humankind, rather than remain haughtily aloof from them. We might try our best, and we might pursue many lines of study, before we have anything helpful to say about consequent actions. The academic philosopher, on the other hand, will cavil: "Can you demonstrate that a harmonious and happy life is better than one that is solitary, poor, nasty, brutish, and short?" I would, in fact, have much to say in reply, but the short answer is this: "The fact of primary experience is that human beings much prefer the former to the latter."

Dewey, finally, *is* sometimes prone to assimilate method exclusively to the scientific variety, but that is an unwarranted reduction, and his own practice, in fact, repudiates it. Even granting that science requires a multitude of gifts—not least, a creative imagination—we should recognize that a philosopher requires multiple talents that cannot be reduced to those of a scientist. There are varieties of genius requisite to the analysis of various forms of experience, such as the aesthetic, moral, political, religious, or scientific; and some thinkers have the keenness for one or more of them but not for others. Whatever the subject matter, one requires at least a measure of catholicity in both learning and experience; and, as the instance demands, he must also exert such powers as sensitivity to actual human predicaments and must have a deep appreciation of human ideals and ideal achievements. The philosopher must have the intuitive powers to feel both the yearnings and joys of the heart and the core demands of human nature. He might have the wisdom to call upon the efficacies, delights, and vital teachings of aesthetic experience. As a sterling example, consider the analyses of religious life by Santayana in *Reason in Religion* and other writings. Santayana brings to the subject not just extraordinary learning but the intuitive imagination to see the underlying motives and values that drive a given religious belief or practice. If you are a Santayana, you are also astonishingly discerning in regard to the sources of the naturalistic ideals residing in supernatural religions.

With the exception of his trenchant observations of aesthetic experience and the conduct of inquiry, Dewey's analyses are, in my judgment, uneven and sometimes faulty. Even so, the merit of his philosophy of method is undiminished. If we think of philosophy as addressing real predicaments of humankind, in both their practical and intellectual phases, directly relevant to the perplexed and hungry heart—or even to the routinely concerned heart—then Dewey's naturalism has made the definitive, if not the final, statement. A point of objection that we might raise with regard to his legacy, all the same, is that it has failed to bring about much change in the practice of philosophy; but Dewey himself is not to be held at fault for this (except for the fact that he was not, on the whole, an effective writer). The determinants of philosophic trends are difficult to discern, but one of them has to be the bureaucratization of the profession and even the degradation of the entire university culture. Professional advancement and status are dependent upon the trendy and the prevailing ideologies. Perhaps, too, part of the problem is that there are intelligent human beings who just love to establish philosophic positions with little if any reference to the conditions on the ground, as we say. Sheer excogitation is so satisfying to the ego.

In my writings, especially my last two books, I have contended at some length that all of the academically prestigious books over the last several decades in ethics and political philosophy are founded on little more than thin air.[5] None of them actually looks to the conditions that define the moral life and moral struggle. The result is that no light is shed on the actual consternations, resistances, accommodations, and aspirations of mortal life, nor on the means by which moral uncertainty and conflict might be helpfully addressed. At the same time, we may be sure, any attempt to introduce the nostrums of such philosophies into a real population would be met with anything from derision to furious rejection. Curse of the ivory tower, indeed!

Consider a few examples of more or less recent vintage. G. E. Moore and the many who have followed him believe there are irreducible moral properties. For Moore, the irreducible property is *good*, which cannot be identified with any other property. Friendship is good, for example, just because it possesses this nonnatural property. It is not good because it is characterized by, say, the properties of common affinities, affection, admiration, sharing, and trust. Indeed, if good were predicated of friendship *because* it had these properties, then we would have to confess that it is *these* properties that determine the goodness at issue, and not good. If this cipher of a nonnatural property were the one and only determinant, then there would be no reason why it might not be predicated of undeserved suffering, for example, for there could be no rival determinant. Why should this alleged good be valuable and precious to us? Moore never gives so much as a clue. This is a theory that with but a single, isolated (and surely mythical) concept would settle all the puzzles of ethics—the rest of the world and our passions be damned.

An equally futile foray into moral philosophizing grew out of ordinary language philosophy. Perhaps R. M. Hare is most noteworthy here. He asserts that the justification for the universalization of prescriptions derives from our language. If one uses "ought" he commits himself to a perfectly impartial view. Ordinary English usage, Hare continues, requires this impartiality, but only in regard to preferences when they are prudent and weighted according to their intensity. How many native speakers knew that? Very few, if any, I am sure. (In fact, it tramples on moral experience.) In a more serious vein, why shouldn't we ask *why* this judgment is required by our language. How, if at all, did the mother tongue get this way? As the vernacular was evolving, Hare's arguments were not available to its users. One would suppose, actually, that the meanings of discourse evolved *in consequence* of moral experience. Linguistic usage is saturated with values, to be sure, but their mere existence, as such, is not a warrant to accept them. The Nazis developed many new terms and meanings and incorporated them in a dictionary. Would Germans therefore be obliged to accept them? Happily, newspeak is not the method of philosophical naturalism.

A different appropriation of language has been undertaken by Jürgen Habermas, who derives the complete panoply of radical socialist prescriptions from the fact that we are language users, no more and no less. This is a procedure that reduces the empirical evidence appropriate to controversy about socialism to the vanishing point. Those with reservations born of moral experience have no legitimacy in objecting, presumably.

Robert Nozick's *Anarchy, State, and Utopia* (1974) is another much-admired contribution to political philosophy, and he has had many academic imitators. Nozick himself (contrary to Habermas) deduces a form of libertarianism. He presupposes the validity of "absolute" rights and then asks what kind of state would develop if these rights were honored. "A theory of a state of nature that begins with fundamental general descriptions of morally permissible and impermissible actions . . . and goes on to describe how a state would arise from that state of nature will serve our explanatory purposes, *even if no actual state ever arose that way*" (p. 7). In other words, no historical experience and no assumptions about human nature need be introduced. Yet we might ask whether there is just this one veridical conception of the state of nature, or how one would have the wisdom to conceive it without consulting the subjects of inquiry embraced by the naturalist. We can ask why such a state of nature should be taken as conclusive for civilizations that do not resemble it. It is noteworthy that the postulates of Nozick's fellow philosophers bear little resemblance to his. "Postulates" tend to be ideological prejudices, as we also see in the case of Habermas. Is there to be no discipline that comes from our experience with reality itself?

Work in moral philosophy over the past several decades has been appallingly sterile, even though its practitioners have a very high opinion of their output. Numerous further examples could be adduced, but I confine myself to just one more, the celebrated Rawls.

I needn't make a detailed analysis.[6] I merely point out that Rawls's theory is extremely radical, denying left and right the moral values that have sustained our constitutional culture. (E.g., the recognition of merit and desert and the institution of freedom of contract.) The denial is made possible by the contrivance of what Rawls thinks of as an ideal moral being (the "free and equal rational being") who legislates for everyone else. Just one example from among the many available: this moral being legislates the so-called difference principle, which ordains that there shall be no material inequalities except insofar as a given inequality serves to improve the condition of the least advantaged. That is, no inequality of wealth is permitted except in the service of those who are worst off. In truth, this is a prescription for a stampede to join the class of the least advantaged, a collapse in productivity among those remaining, universal poverty, and intense class conflict. Rawls himself expects no such result, to be sure, but, just in case, he endows the state with a powerful ministry of education.

This is a prescription for tyranny and a triumph for the thought police, but Rawls has no such dread. You see, the free and equal rational being represents the "true" moral nature of us creatures of nature and history. The nature of the free and equal rational being is constant and is no creature of history. Beneath our diverse exteriors and ornery natures lies our true being; so, in effect, conformity to the principles of justice is just another version of the old idea of forcing people to be free.

When ideal beings legislate behind the veil of ignorance, they are always in unanimity, for in their ideality each is exactly like the others. None is conceived to have the self-knowledge of a contingent historical person, and none has any knowledge of history. They are said to know that the implementation of the theory of justice will be feasible for any and all denizens on the far side of the veil, where unanimity will ultimately come to prevail, just as it does on the legislative side.

The analysis of free and equal rational natures is asserted to be derived from "our" intuitions; and the philosophic project is to keep sorting out and adjusting our intuitions until they become wholly coherent with one another. This is not an experimental and worldly process of putting our intuitions in order, testing how they would accord with one another in practice. An intuition as such, Rawls believes, is an irreducible moral judgment. The lonely intuition per se must be given place and priority relative to other intuitions. Thought is disciplined by the demand for coherence of intuitions, not by experience in the unforgiving course of events. Indeed, once it is finally articulated, the theory of justice is complete and unchanging. (It wouldn't do to regard it as experimental, for then the theory could be distorted by the fallen creatures of common life.) Following the inaugural ball, there is no going back.

The definition of Rawls's free and equal rational being is not determined with the benefit of historical knowledge or with, say, the hypotheses of evolutionary psychology. It's all a matter of Rawls's intuitions. With these he sees fit to promulgate universal and absolute law. But, truth to tell, this ideal moral being is anything but ideal, and it is a fiction. It is likewise a fiction that this phantom represents the true nature of historical man. The theory is an artifice. It never engages lived experience and lived natures. Its primary subject matter is the effete intuitions of someone who never freed himself from the rarefied air of the academy.

My theme has been the fecundity of naturalism. It is fecund because it rejects any disjunction of theory and practice, whatever the practice—be it moral, religious, artistic, scientific, historical, social, cultural, or metaphysical. Accordingly, so long as there is novelty in the ongoing course of nature, there must be reflective and perhaps wide-ranging philosophic response. We must continue to reflect on the meaning of the sciences, as they progress; we must be prepared to understand unaccustomed or novel situations, unrealized or unexpected potentialities in the human estate, for good or ill, or new-found understandings of our past. Present conundrums might be due in large measure to inherited ideas; so we are called upon to reconsider the heritage, as Dewey did so masterfully. In all such cases there is need for creative, wise, and disciplined inquiry. The philosophy of the naturalist might be as fecund as nature's own fertility in producing demands on our moral and intellectual capacities. In addressing problems of human experience, the naturalist is fecund in bringing clarity and efficacy to human striving.

The reflections of the naturalist are disciplined not only by the selection of subject matter but also by experimental test. In general, the naturalistic mind is chastened by the hard lessons of experience; and its inquiry is successful when the ills and resources of a problematic situation are properly identified, potential remedies for them discerned, and the remedies tested as far as possible in practice. Would a given moral theory, for example, yield the results that it promises, or might it bring disappointment or even catastrophe? Does the love of absolutism in moral theory, for example, lead to tyrannies in practice? The answers to such questions can be elusive; so inquiry into the primary subject matter must be continued. Especially in humane interrogations (as Aristotle admonished), we must have the wisdom to determine the degree of precision and certainty the subject matter admits of.

There seems to be, however, an overwhelming tendency among philosophers to run after problems that owe their existence primarily to the tunnel vision of other philosophers, and the rupture of theory and experience goes unheeded. By a mere "trick of logic," in Dewey's phrase, they would conjure quick academic solutions for matters that demand the most penetrating and comprehensive investigations of nature. The restoration of pertinence, vigor, and wisdom to philosophy awaits a renaissance in our thinking on the nature of philosophy itself.

NOTES

1. This is not to say that the laws of nature are suspended. Earthquakes, tsunamis, volcanoes, and nuclear explosions, for example, depend upon specific conditions and are in principle predictable; but they create massive forms of destruction and disorder for the areas within which they occur.

2. See chap. 3 of James Gouinlock, *Eros and the Good* (Amherst, NY: Prometheus Books, 2004), for a fuller analysis of Dewey's naturalistic metaphysics. To be sure, Dewey's seminal naturalism in metaphysics leaves room for growth and improvement.

3. John Dewey, *Experience and Nature,* vol. 1 of *John Dewey, The Later Works, 1925–1953,* ed. Jo Ann Boydston (Carbondale: Southern Illinois University Press, 1981), p. 20.

4. Notice that I am recommending distinctive forms of *activity* as primary subject matter, not concepts or vernacular language. We would investigate, for example, the ways in which the *practice* of duties, conceived in a specified way, would impinge upon, say, the *exercise* of rights understood in a specified way.

5. See James Gouinlock, *Rediscovering the Moral Life* (Amherst, NY: Prometheus Books, 1993) and *Eros and the Good.*

6. I have done so elsewhere. See *Rediscovering the Moral Life,* pp. 247–68.

9.

Pragmatism and the Naturalization of Religion

John Peter Anton

I.

My chapter discusses the search for religious truth in the context of American pragmatism. It is well known that from its very start this philosophical movement expressed a strong interest in the conduct fostered by religious beliefs. The question of their truth was raised early by Charles Sanders Peirce and continued in the writings of William James, John Dewey, and their followers. Philosophical interest in the case of religion was changing direction away from theology to a scientific study of the claims and ways of this type of conduct, including its objectives and especially its challenge to the truths of science. The issue that led to the change from theology to religious conduct was the impasse regarding the justification of the conception of the nature of the divine in monotheistic religions. The main target was to understand what religious conduct is, how it is manifested, why it is formed, and what its consequences are. Other disciplines such as psychology, sociology, history, and anthropology in their own way tried to investigate the field of religious activity. Philosophy had held a special interest in this field ever since philosophy first became associated with whatever support it could render to religious dogma, but when the alliance was weakened it made a sustained effort to extricate itself from such services. In this chapter I will discuss only the case of philosophical inquiry as the American

155

pragmatists understood it in their effort to provide new answers to questions of the nature and usefulness of religious beliefs.

II.

I will begin with a brief account of two ways of viewing religion, as well as placing religion in conduct and as a source of values, (a) in nature and (b) in experience. I will call these two ways of treating religion "naturalizing the religious experience." I will essay to show how both ways support the denial of the supernatural in religious beliefs. The naturalizing of religion abounds in the polytheism of the ancient Greeks. In sharp contrast, monotheism, especially that of Christianity, creates a tension between the divine as transcendent and also as beings present in the natural world. I concentrate on the solution that certain American pragmatists worked out to remove the tension by arguing that one can preserve the substance of religious practice and also dismiss all claims to truth for the supernatural component of Christianity and religion in general.

Although the practice of Greek polytheism and the theories of American pragmatists both constitute cases of religious naturalism, they differ in method and in outlook. In fact, their respective approaches to religion have very little in common. What accounts for the difference in the naturalizing of religion is the relation between two different ways of relating to the divine. In the case of classical Greece, there is no deliberate process in practice or in theory to naturalize religion. Whatever came under the rubric of rites, ceremonies, worship, sacrifices, prayers, and invocations was already "natural." As religious activities, they were happening within nature as encountered or imagined. Another way of saying the same thing is that the gods, their existence, and their interaction with humans were taking place within the natural world. The most the Greeks did intellectually with their religion was to speculate about the divine, in order to determine what perfections the immortal nature contained that were worthy of respect and admiration, to be celebrated and worshipped as sources of protection. The Greeks understood their divinities as being indestructible and as eternal as the universe itself and more often than not with a human face. Whatever refinements the Greeks brought to their understanding of the divine, they did so through the exercise of their *logos*, an intellectual attainment they came to call *theologia*.

When a different religious wave came in from the East in the form of Christianity, it brought with it a totally different outlook and a doctrine at the center of which was the belief in the existence of a supernatural God as the absolute and omnipotent creator outside of the world, directing the world and controlling the fate of humanity. The transcendence of the divine marked a radical departure from the object of piety in classical Greece. The East, in other words, imported concepts, practices, and linguistic elements totally alien to what Greek religious practices, already naturalized, could absorb, let alone understand. Actually, Christianity did not denaturalize the religion of the Greeks; their polytheism simply rejected Christianity in principle as unacceptable in whole as well as in part. The religious conflict spread and ended in the obliteration of polytheism, the ruination of the ancient temples, the destruction of the idols, and the aggressive imposition of new symbols and liturgical language suitable to salvation.

The new religion that spread to the West introduced a totally different view of the divine, namely, a God beyond the created universe, even if eternal, in fact an omnipotent God who in his absolute benevolence had also made humanity forever in need of salvation. Once this religious outlook was granted official recognition in the fourth century CE, its entire system of conduct became the standard institution. The supernatural remained in command. With salvation occupying the highest place in the Christian hierarchy of values, the naturalization of religion was declared sinful and hence unthinkable. Regaining the natural world on its own terms, as science was to do eventually, was worse than heresy. It meant disturbing the unity and harmony of the universe as God had ordained it.

With the advent of the Renaissance, the conflict between science and religion became divisive and unbridgeable. The protestant movement shifted the order of priorities and authorities. It sought and demanded the search for the meaning and enjoyment of God within the experience of the worshipper rather than through the authority of the established ecclesiastical dogma. In the centuries that followed, the naturalizing of religion became a major philosophical issue. With the growth of the sciences and the emancipation of the arts, both heralding new freedoms, saving Christianity from the rigidities of outdated dogma took the form of a philosophical desideratum.

From Kant to Hegel, to mention only two important theoretical landmarks, the religious impasse received considerable attention but the final solution was yet to come. The literature that this complex movement generated on the controversy concerning the place of the divine in human affairs and the search for a solution is simply staggering, to say the least. The developments in epistemology, the new attempts at cosmology and metaphysics, along with the challenges of the new developments in biology, physics, and psychology, made the problem even more pressing and open to continuous debate. Still, the supernatural in religion continued to play a dominant role in social and cultural affairs during the last two centuries. Naturalizing religion, that is, bridging the gap between the supernatural and the worldly concerns of Christianity, continued to be a pressing concern. This was especially felt as a leading demand in the New World of America, the new land of freedom and blessed country under God, established as a place for religious freedom away from the oppression of the fatherland. Bringing the realm of God in line with the realm of Nature, especially in a land rescued from the heathen, became an intellectual and cultural imperative. The diverse idealisms and other doctrines of rationalism that were eventually imported from England and Europe failed to resolve the stubborn difficulty. Religious faith resisted being naturalized without its attendant supernaturalism without running the risk of falling victim to the demonic powers of atheism and paganism. Enter American pragmatism.

III.

Most of the modern thinkers, especially the Americans, when they reached an impasse forced on them by their epistemologies, felt compelled to justify religion, especially after they realized that they could not prove or disprove the existence of their God. Let us remember in contrast that the classical Greeks, given their tolerant polytheism, having neither an organized clergy nor a system of religious dogma, were neither irreligious nor lacking in piety. But once Christianity came to prevail in the Greco-Roman world, it made different demands on every aspect of religious conduct, including the role of *theologia*. The chief purpose of the new *theologia* was to justify, not provide, beliefs, and when centuries later it reached a dead end, the intellectual demands for justification took another route: assigning to *theologia* a place within a general theory of cognition. As a result, the language of metaphysics entered a new phase, changing its initial course from being an inquiry into the first principles of being to a search for the foundations of experience. Eventually, metaphysics moved inward and became the servant of epistemology.

Here is where we find the American pragmatists trying with bold strokes to correct the course of philosophy and reconstruct the meaning of experience. By so doing, they showed a limited respect for the Greeks, but when they encountered serious difficulties in their efforts to naturalize religion, they refused to go to with the classical model. In fact, their own cultural upbringing would not let them do so. They were caught in the snares of their own religious inheritance. By the end of the nineteenth century, the naturalizing of religion had become more than an intellectual problem; it had become part of the general demand to find a place for God in the new interpretations of experience.

Kant had cast a heavy shadow over the philosophical enterprise by turning transcendence into a transcendental realm of pure reason. After the reinterpretations of experience that followed in the footsteps of the three *Critiques*, the quest for knowledge opened a new road for the justification of what had become an imperative in the way of life of the West: how to save religion. The Americans tried repeatedly to solve the problem by borrowing from the modern idealisms and realisms, sprinkled as they were with all sorts of rationalistic elements and the new trends of voluntarism in particular that Schopenhauer, Nietzsche, and other romantic luminaries supplied. But more was needed, namely, a novel interpretation of experience and a new organization of the powers of the human psyche, a new psychology, so to speak.

IV.

The preliminary work was done by such pioneers as Charles Sanders Peirce and a handful of his contemporaries, including Chauncey Wright. But the protagonists turned out to be William James and John Dewey, who came up with two diverging justifications of religion. Both had become champions of naturalized religion by finding a justifiable place for it within the range of human experience. Each offered his own solution but the twain never actually agreed. Both were convinced that they had made a major discovery that allowed them to provide a special place for religion in human affairs. Both solutions turned out to be accommodations, not discoveries of foundations. The justification, however, followed with relative ease.

I would like to offer a brief explanation of how and why the two pragmatic justifications of religion were again put into the service of the traditional cause. The Western religious tradition, by appealing to the authority of the Bible, asserted its superiority over all other faiths. The pragmatists had no choice but to respond. We may go back to Charles Sanders Peirce to trace the beginning of the call. He established the view that the truth of ideas is a function of useful consequences. As a new approach to the meaning of truth, this position provided the religious beliefs with a defense of their usefulness. But usefulness is an open-ended term and subject to a multitude of meanings, often turning into a confusing and divisive program of action. In the case of the pragmatist's justification of religion, there operates in the background an optimistic article of good faith that ultimately religious perceptions, once clarified and morally sustained, converge into an ideal with its accompanying virtues of charity and humility. However, given the variety of Christian sects and practices, the ideal is rarely if ever attained. Furthermore, as a pursued ideal, it has to compete with the urgent demands of so many other forces of the soul, the appetites and desires, as Plato would say, or the constant tempting power of the original sin, as the biblical story would have it.

After identifying the flaws in the alternative justifications of religion, Peirce insisted that its proper sense can arise only from "the religious sensitivity" (*Collected Papers* 6, p. 433). When appreciated through what he called "musement," the "pure play and lively exercise of one's power," it can become religious meditation and "retain the perfect candor proper to Musement" (ibid., p. 458). In Peirce's evaluation of the idea of God's reality, he appealed to a rather peculiar use of pragmatism, one that made religion a *normal* and *instinctive* belief in God's reality: "Any normal man who considers the three Universes in the light of the hypothesis of God's Reality . . . will come to be stirred to the depths of his nature by the beauty of the idea and by its august practicality, even to the point of earnestly loving and adoring his strictly hypothetical God, and to that of desiring above all things to shape the whole conduct of his life and all the springs of action into conformity with that hypothesis" (ibid., p. 467).[1]

The "reality of God" has the makings of a liberated theology using a rational pragmatic mold to serve a synthetic vision of experience. Peirce's view of religion did little to prepare the grounds for Santayana's treatment of the same and less for James's own position. But it did help Dewey, who stayed closer to Peirce when he sought in his later years to identify religion as embedded in a mode or quality of experience. Religion was now made a normal and instinctive source of a special belief.

V.

James and Dewey also "invented" a religious quality in experience. Like Peirce, they appealed to a qualitative element to recognize religion as functioning in a special way in the human soul. It seemed so unproblematic to them to turn what had formerly been a dictum of dogma into a property of a power, be it initial as with James or final as with Dewey. Such a move would have shocked Aristotle, particularly if viewed from his theory of the soul in the *De Anima*. Because of this religious quality in experience, once they accepted it, the pragmatists could not go back to the Greeks for a more reasonable solution. Nor could they ignore the cultural imperative to justify the place of religion in human affairs, whether as salvation or as moral command. Both thinkers were in fact part of the American cultural outlook and its age-old indebtedness to the biblical commitment. So they forged a solution through their respective pragmatisms. One of their contemporaries, George Santayana, refused to go their way. If there was anyone who came close to the Greeks, it was Santayana, perhaps owing the favor to his Mediterranean origins. Anyway, he resisted the pragmatist way of naturalizing religion. James did not hesitate to charge Santayana with separating the realm of existence from the realm of value. Of course, Santayana did not accept the criticism.[2]

The pragmatic naturalizing of the divine was on its way. It did not take William James (1842–1910) long to see the new promise of pragmatism, except that its scope needed considerable widening. After writing his *Principles of Psychology* (1890) and bringing his findings into line with his lectures on *The Will to Believe* (1897), he concluded his approach to religion in his *The Varieties of Religious Experience* (1902). He had modified the Nietzschean "will to power" to support and justify religion as rooted in the will to believe. The "will" as a faculty had figured largely in Kant's ethical thought as well as in Schopenhauer's philosophy. By changing this will to power into the will to believe, James's position proved important to many Americans in providing an explanation of the psychological origins for the practice of religion, an institution so dear to them ever since the first colonists came to the new land.[3] For James, theology became secondary as he essayed to make the warfare between science and religion a side issue. He gave the seat of honor to the practice of religion. The pivotal point in his pragmatism was shifted from truth to meaning, from science to experience. With the tension between science and religion relaxed, the supernatural lost its forcefulness in opposition to science. Supernaturalism is "meaningful" though not true. By treating beliefs as hypotheses, James became convinced that he offered "a science of religion" in the place of a "philosophy of religion." Confident that his argument was correct, he also sought to strengthen his position by applying the evolutionary concept of the "survival of the fittest" to the religious beliefs that had become dominant in his time.

Switching from truth to meaning was a radical step in a direction different from the way Peirce understood it. In his 1897 *Will to Believe*, James offered a defense of the position of adopting beliefs as working hypotheses, even if their truth cannot be demonstrated.[4] It is sufficient to show that such a belief is useful and satisfactory. There is no reason why one cannot have religious beliefs as hypotheses so long as their consequences are satisfactory. After all, as hypotheses they can neither be proved nor be disproved. We accept them not for their logic but for their effectiveness. Later, in *The Varieties of Religious Experience,* James wrote: "The pivot round which the religious life . . . revolves, is the interest of the individual in his private personal destiny. Religion, in short, is a monumental chapter in the history of human egotism. . . . Science, on the other hand, has ended by utterly repudiating the personal point of view."[5]

It was in 1902 that James wrote his magnum opus on the psychology of religion, *The Varieties of Religious Experience*. In a letter he wrote to Miss Frances Morse, James told her: "The problem I have set myself is a hard one: *first*, to defend . . . 'experience' against 'philosophy' as being the backbone of the world's religious life . . . and *second*, to make the hearer or reader believe, what I myself invincibly do believe, that, although all the special manifestations of religion may have been absurd (I mean its creeds and theories), yet the life of it as a whole is mankind's most important function."[6] His plan was to give "a descriptive survey of man's religious propensities." And in *The Varieties of Religious Experience*, Lecture II, "Circumscription of the Topic," James wrote:

> Religion, whatever it is, is man's total reaction upon life. . . . Total reactions are different from casual reactions, and total attitudes are different from usual or professional attitudes. To get at them you must go behind the foreground of existence and reach down to that curious sense of the whole residual cosmos as an everlasting presence, intimate or alien, terrible or amusing, lovable or odious,

which in some degree every one possesses. This sense of the world's presence . . . is the completest of all our answers to the question, "What is the character of this universe in which we live?"[7]

The chief result of religious experience is the attainment of saintliness, the highest virtues of which are asceticism and charity. The purpose of the science of religion, James insists, is "to test saintliness by common sense, to use human standards to help us decide how far the religious life commends itself as an ideal kind of human activity." The verifying evidence, for James, is found in the surviving religions to which he refers: Buddhism, Islam, Judaism, and Christianity. They have met the "survival of the fittest" test. These religions are at least living as historical experiences that allow us "to test saintliness by common sense, to use human standards to help us decide how far the religious life commends itself as an ideal kind of human activity."[8]

James's argument, in which he appeals to a special sense of the "fittest," is but an extension of the meaning of this term from biological evolution to cultural and historical contexts. As such, the argument is specious. When it is coupled with his religious preferences and commitment, its claim to fit into a "science of religion" becomes void. It is quite a concession to dogma to convert a religious practice into a religious ideal, as James does with saintliness. To say the least, his proposal reads like a concession to irrationality, glossed over as the faculty of Will, no matter what he claims by appealing to intersubjectivity for its general presence. As such, it reads more like a rather adulterated psychological device with Kantian overtones.

In making a sharp pragmatic distinction between man as practical and man as theoretical, and in stressing the primacy of the practical, James was directly anti-Aristotelian. By so doing, and while realigning the practical with his own protestantism, James left out of his philosophy the entire classical tradition, just as he sought, again as an anti-Aristotelian, to minimize the role of the theoretical beliefs in the religious life. Again, by limiting his discussion to the surviving religions, Buddhism, Islam, Judaism, and Christianity, he had relegated Greek polytheism to the wastebasket of history.

VI.

There was still a slight chance of bringing back the Greek metaphysics of being to the effort to naturalize religion. James's own heritage proved an insurmountable obstacle. George Santayana (1863–1952), himself not a pragmatist, stated in his *Reason in Religion* (1905) that piety was "the most important moral lesson of religion" and "man's most reverent attachment to the sources of his being and the steadying of his life by that attachment" (p. 179). Still, religion with its illusions is much akin to the illusions of art, but while art is frank about its illusions, religion is not. While it serves a need, the worldview it indulges is bad geography. Christianity, Santayana noted, claims to have access to a supernatural world but it bears no close resemblance to the natural world. The result is that religion winds up espousing a sort of geography that promotes a set of misleading hypotheses for action while its expressions of aspiration are taken to be real causes of things on earth and in the sky. In general, traditional theologies, Santayana insisted, are simply untrue science and they rest on false descriptions of cosmic history. Taken as truth, religion is false, but taken as poetry it is compelling. The literal supernaturalism of religion is worthless, although its symbolic supernaturalism has a genuine value, but only if it gives expressive power to moral aims.

Despite its pretensions to ontology, Santayana taught, the justification of religion is moral. The moral values of religion are clothed in strong poetry. They persuade the faithful not through reason but by enchantment, not by argument but by a sense of deeper mystery. The moral lessons that religions have made their own essence turn out to be piety, spirituality, and charity. When piety is broadened and deepened, it may become piety to gods or humanity. There can be progress in religion, but it can be brought on by eliminating the magical and superstitious elements through an increasing knowledge of human nature and the universe. Yet, while carrying out this most difficult task, religion must still retain its persuasiveness for spirituality. It still must preserve the imaginative grasp of the human predicament in symbol and ritual. Reasonable religion preserves the basic religious attitudes and practices such as prayers, myths, piety, spirituality, and charity, but it does so in close cooperation with humanity's rational attainments in science, philosophy, and morality. If spirit is "aspiration become consciousness," then genuine religion leads to clarity, never to the emasculation of the mind in its love for all the excellence one can dream of. Clearly, Santayana was not antireligious but a serious critic of religious belief. In *Interpretations of Poetry and Religion*, he states: "The dignity of religion . . . like every moral ideal, lies precisely in its ideal adequacy, in its fit rendering of the meanings and values of life, in its anticipation of perfection. . . . Excellence of religion is due to an idealization of experience" (p. v).

Santayana had confidence in the attainment of a philosophical virtue, a piety that can come to have the universe for its object. It was a view that brought him close to a mixture of ancient and modern Stoicism. This was the closest he came to the religious naturalism of the Greeks. He stopped there and never entered the expanding mansions of pragmatism; he only flirted with some of its premises.

VII.

In 1908, Dewey published in the *Hibbert Journal* an article in which he spoke of the forms of religion in current times as suffering from falsehoods and pernicious supernaturalisms having serious moral implications that are in disagreement with the ways of democracy and science.[9] This caustic criticism of institutionalized religion continued throughout his career, and finally its various strands were brought together in 1934 when he published *A Common Faith*, a seminal work based on the Terry Lectures he gave at Yale University. The opening statement of the book provides a diagnosis of the malaise that has plagued religion for centuries:

> Never before in history has mankind been so much of two minds, so divided into two camps, as it is today. Religions have traditionally been allied with ideas of the supernatural, and often have been based upon explicit beliefs about it. Today there are many who hold

that nothing worthy of being called religious is possible apart from the supernatural. Those who hold this belief differ in many respects. . . . But they agree in one point: the necessity for a Supernatural Being and for an immortality that is beyond the power of nature. (p. 1)

What is stated as the object that preoccupies him is only the negative part of Dewey's approach to religion. His main objective, however, was the search for the point of origin of all religious conduct, to explain the how and why of "religion" versus "the religious," as the title of chapter 1, "Religion versus the Religious," states it. The result he expected to establish was that "for the first time, the religious aspect of experience will be free on its own accord" (p. 2). What appears on the surface of the pursuit to be revolutionary actually contains, as we shall see, a serious concession to a long historical practice in religious affairs.

At the heart of Dewey's approach is his view that the shared scientific experience, the expanded or to be expanded scientific cooperative association, is precisely what leads to a faith. It is religious, and more religious in character than any revelation or creed. There is more than a persistent effort to naturalize religion in Dewey's Terry Lectures; the rather surprising part is his determination to convert the term "religion" and give it a new linguistic turn by making "the religious" a quality in experience that can be shown to be the womb from which all such institutionalized practices and all historical dogmas issue forth into action. There is a daring but also a far-reaching claim in his premise, slippery and problematic, that has generated discussion. But aside from the difficulties of his position, it should be noted that Dewey was determined to bring the religious within the scope of his own theory of experience.

Since experience is one and continuous, there is no real difference in truths, given that truths are outcomes of intelligent inquiry. Yet, as we shall see, there is for Dewey a religious quality in all experience, something the defenders of supernaturalism fail to understand. It must be remembered that Dewey discussed religion in ways that excluded theology from those areas essential to the religious experience. More important than the exclusion of theology from the philosophical exploration of the religious quality in experience, as he calls it, is the further investigation of what Peirce and James had started in this field: identifying the origins of all religious conduct. *A Common Faith* is cast as such an inquiry and investigation into a vastly broad area at once social and cultural, the purpose of which was to ascertain the presence of "the religious" as an irreducible quality in all manifestations of human experience. Seen in another way, this work can be viewed as an attempt to reconfirm Dewey's radical reconstruction of pragmatism and as confirmation of a device that enables him to show how human experience can attain its final synthesis of whatever ideal values become available.

Given his theory of experience, Dewey had to pose the question on the nature of religious quality and the way to identify its features. His final answer came to this: "Any activity pursued in behalf of an ideal and against obstacles and in spite of threats of personal loss because of conviction of its general and enduring value is religious in quality" (p. 27). A few pages later, he informs the reader of how the element of faith occurs in connection with the religious quality in experience. "I should describe this faith as the unification of the self through allegiance to inclusive ideal ends, which imagination presents to us and to which the human will responds as worthy of controlling our desires and choices" (p. 33). The meaning of the act of unification allows Dewey to converge it with the idea of God: "It represents a unification of ideal values that is essentially imaginative in origin," referring to an earlier statement in which "god" is defined as "the unity of all ideal ends arousing us to desire and action (p. 14).

A difficulty arises as soon as the reader tries to envisage the criteria for a successful if not completed unification of one's ideal values, or, to put it differently, of one's discovery of God. The experimental notion of experience and the great variety of clusters of ideal values that enter such possible unifications should have alerted Dewey not only to the problematic character of his naturalization of religion but also to the implication of his conception of the divine as it leads to an open pluralism of the divine. Dewey's position opens the door to a novel form of polytheism, but one without grace or ritual. When naturalized in Dewey's way, God is restored not in nature but in human nature, limited and almost devoid of social significance. Defining the meaning of ideal values becomes as difficult as is the attainment of the Great Community Dewey had envisaged as the ideal end of the political pursuit.

It can be said that Dewey salvaged the institutions of religion by working with the traditions of monotheism and by extracting from them the constituents that could preserve what he acknowledged to be their valuable elements. Dewey responded in this regard to his own protestant tradition.[10] It seems that somehow Dewey never quite left the religious tradition of the West, although he essayed to liberate it from the impositions of theology and the burden of super-naturalism. Still he found a place for the concept of God in his broadened instrumentalism by endowing it with the role of the unifying principle of ideals in experience. Probably he did not quite understand that this principle had the marks of a proposal countering the Hellenic cultural ideal and the search for the unity of excellences as ideals. Plato's principle of the virtues, the ideal of justice, already included what the Christian religion recognized as one of them: piety. Santayana, as much as Dewey, recognized it as such but in its naturalized form. For Plato and the Greeks, however, excellence in religious conduct, piety, is but part of what is summoned to complete the unification of ideals, the *aretai,* as the perfections of the human character in *praxis*. For Dewey, the role of God emerging through the quality of experience may be the role of the supreme unifier, but not for the Greek philosophers. This is one lesson he could have drawn from Plato or Aristotle. His reservations about their philosophy, what he called their "spectator theory of knowledge," prevented him from seeing the merits of the classical way of naturalizing religion.

One can understand the intent of Dewey's recasting of the meanings of the terms *religion, faith,* and *piety* as transformations of their traditional usage. Actually, they turn out to be transpositions. All three terms were assigned new meanings in the context of the theory of experience as pragmatism understood it, but one wonders how discontinuous they were made by their strict assignment to serve in the pursuit of salvation. An obscure feature was left unattended, even after Dewey tried to free faith from its irrational performance so that it might stand for the persisting confidence in the imaginative perfections of intelligence. This confidence may be socially shared but not the idiosyncratic imaginative perfections that call for unification. Even in institutionalized religion, faith suffers from residual problems given the continuous rise of heresies as testimonials to the rational weaknesses in the structure of the dogma. Nevertheless, Dewey transposed the use of faith from the diverse religions to "the religious." Why this meaning of faith should have been chosen is more than a matter of linguistic action and anything but an accident. Rather, it is a deliberate move on Dewey's part to liberate a vital part in the scientific attitude, confidence in the procedures of scientific inquiry, from its irrational use when employed in defense of unquestioned attachment to a supernatural power. The misplaced use of faith in the practice of historical religions had a long history of uses and abuses, often supporting policies with catastrophic consequences as well as supporting innovations in the arts and the promotion of philanthropy. But the anomalous course of religious faith had to be changed. For Dewey, such a move called for the methodical transposition of the meanings of faith and God together with the naturalization of religion.

By following such a course, Dewey integrated his outlook on humanism by turning "the religious" into the foundation for a common faith, but a faith nevertheless. In a way, it may be seen as a way to state the modern deification of humanity when it acts at its best for the best.[11] As such, the course concerns the ideals as values. Dewey, in his reflections on ethics, had excluded anything that bordered on absolutes, transcendent or nonnatural. Ideals in the means-ends continuity were values perfected in imagination and reflectively invoked for their unification, thus providing the elements to be unified by "God" in the conduct of human beings. But we may still have to ask why it is necessary to refer to the integration of experience, clarified and consummated, as being in any sense "religious." One cannot help but wonder whether this was a concession to the long and powerful tradition in the West. Was intent dictated by the urgency of removing from the center of culture the effective and powerful role that institutionalized religion continued to play in the intellectual and political affairs of the Western world? Whatever the answer to this, another question looms large in the mind of the reader: is this where pragmatism ends, that is, in the task of elaborating and deepening what has hitherto been a misguided use of faith in the historical religions? Pragmatism as a way of naturalizing religion was meant to effect a transition from the ontic idealization of the divine to the principle of the unification of the ideal values in experience. The move was brought about through the search for the efficient cause. Peirce and Dewey located it as quality in experience; James found it in the will to believe.

Why did Dewey write his obscure and perplexing book on religion, so much unlike his usual way of philosophizing? Did he think it intellectually compelling to justify religion while freeing it from the elusive passion for the supernatural? He declared that he had established "for the first time the religious aspect of experience" so that it might develop freely "on its own accord." Dewey did not confine his efforts to the naturalizing of religion. He went as far as to assign it a purpose that neither science nor art, not even philosophy, can accomplish: a special consummation of experience. He actually restored religion to its traditional throne but without a de facto omnipotent God. But why did he decide to save religion as "the religious" from its old sins? Let us remember that Dewey had set limitations on the instrumental uses of reason, thus creating a problem for the epistemic range of experience. He used his own reasoning to question whether reason in its epistemic function can rise above its mediating role to serve as the unifier of all ideal values and thus perform the role of God. How strange this position turns out to be when trust in intelligence becomes confined to the performance of tasks limited to its own cognitive functions. How self-conscious and how non-Greek is Dewey's position. At the end of the day, philosophy lands in the realm of puzzling paradoxes. Reason is instrumental, but God alone can effect the unification of all ideal values. Presumably the set of values includes the ideal of reason, in which case for it to be ideal it must transcend its instrumental limits. God, once again, works mysteriously in experience by effecting the unification without the immediate and direct participation of reason. Once again, God works in mysterious ways.

VIII.

Before closing, I would like to risk a view on how to naturalize religion as experience without the traces of paradoxical surprises. I came to the conclusion that I had learned a lesson from Dewey's idealization of the divine. Since this concept belongs to "the religious," we may turn once again to the efficient rather than to the final cause, to speak with Aristotle. It may well be that religious sensibilities are traceable to imaginative responses to the multitude of needs human beings have from the moment of their birth. As sensibilities they affect ways of conduct that tend to use the power of reasoning, once it develops beyond its early feeble manifestations, by requiring it to support the imaginative symbolic objects that are needed for the justification of beliefs acquired through unresolved fears regarding present and future inexplicable events. The stronger the passions when facing threatening circumstances, the weaker the employment of reason. The same holds in the case of the blessings associated with utter gratification and unexpected rewards. The formation of habits of response to such conditions eventually consolidates its functioning in subsequent conduct. This is the material in experience that at some point will have to be brought to symbolic order in hope of delivering consolation, protection, gratitude, and perchance peace. Calling it salvation of one kind or another is but one type of response. Still, the beginnings of the materials for the formation of any religious outlook are inescapably human events, initially inexplicable, events that when left unexplained pass over into the realm of the mysterious. An understanding of this area of conduct, if that is what is needed in the case of religion, is better sought in a more complete inquiry into human nature and its total range of functions. Perhaps this was the investigative program that the second generation of pragmatists was expected to undertake. Whether they accepted the challenge and to what extent they succeeded is another story for another study.

NOTES

1. See, on this point, Willard Arnett's interpretation, in *Religion and Judgment* (New York: Appleton-Century-Crofts, 1966), p. 243.

2. As we see him doing in *Interpretations of Poetry and Religion* (New York: Charles Scribner's Sons, 1900).

3. As Hollinger has argued persuasively, the setting James assumed for his view on religion was to be the essence of the manifestations of religions in their variety, but he used Protestant examples extensively. See D. Hollinger, "Damned for God's Glory: William James and the Scientific Vindication of Protestant Culture," in *William James and a Science of Religions: Reexperiencing the Varieties of Religious Experience*, ed. Wayne Proudfoot (New York: Columbia University Press, 2004), pp. 9–30.

4. Hollinger, "Damned for Glory of God," pp. 1–2, has aptly raised the question of how the 1902 *Varieties* is related to the 1897 *Will to Believe*. Hollinger sees the link between the two works in James's "scientific vindication of Protestant Culture."

5. This quotation is taken from William James, *The Varieties of Religious Experience: A Study of Human Nature* (New York: Modern Library), p. 480. The Modern Library edition is a reprint of the 1902 edition.

6. Ralph Barton Perry, *The Thought and Character of William James*, vol. 2 (Boston: Little, Brown, 1936), pp. 326–27.

7. James, *The Varieties of Religious Experience*, Modern Library edition, p. 35. The subtitle was "A Study of Human Nature." Dewey expounded on the subtitle in his *Problems of Men* (New York: Philosophical Library, 1946), p. 392.

8. James, *The Varieties of Religious Experience* (Cambridge, MA: Harvard University Press, 1985), pp. 266, 277, 295, and 297, quoted by Hollinger. James's focus on surviving religions reflects his lack of interest in classical religious practices, mainly on account of their deficiency in saintliness. This is a weak point in James's general approach, namely, the preference for saintliness as the religious ideal. In the same way we can explain his lack of interest in classical philosophy. Neither in his *Principles of Psychology* nor in his later works does James show scholarly familiarity with the classical tradition.

9. "Religion in Our Schools," *Hibbert Journal*, July 1908, pp. 796–809; reprinted in John Dewey, *Characters and Events,* ed. Joseph Ratner (New York: Henry Holt, 1929), vol. 2, pp. 504–16.

10. See Ralph W. Sleeper, *The Necessity of Pragmatism: John Dewey's Conception of Philosophy* (New Haven, CT: Yale University Press, 1986), pp.

28–29 and 42–43, for Dewey's religious family background and the Christianity of his parents.

11. H. S. Thayer has given an interpretation of Dewey's conception of "religion" that is close to the one presented here. He writes as follows: "Inquiry is a sign and condition of human growth. It was not surprising that Dewey should find in inquiry the possibilities for a genuine religious outlook—one wanting only an imaginative projection of the essentially communal function of inquiry and its premium on socially shared experience. Nor was Dewey ineffective in giving expression to this intellectual deliverance; it was not a resuscitation of the eighteenth-century religion of Reason, but a reasonable faith. In serving intellectual and social-class differences in the dry husks of orthodoxy, inquiry, as thus interpreted by Dewey, is a radical agent of unification and social cohesion. In inquiry men achieve communion. . . . For Dewey, religion has its vital source and exercise in the shared experience of the community. Inquiry, since it is the compelling resource of human growth and renewal of values, is thus a fit object of religious reverence; just as its continuous workings are essential conditions of a human and liberal existence." H. S. Thayer, *Meaning and Action: A Critical History of Pragmatism* (Indianapolis: Bobbs-Merrill, 1968), p. 200.

REFERENCES

Arnett, Willard. 1966. *Religion and Judgment.* New York: Appleton-Century-Crofts.

Demand, Irwin, ed. 1953. *The Philosophy of Santayana.* New York: Scribner's Sons.

Dewey, John. 1908. "Religion in Our Schools," *Hibbert Journal,* July 1908, pp. 796–809. Reprinted in *Characters and Events,* edited by Joseph Ratner. New York: Henry Holt, 1929, vol. 2, pp. 504–16.

———. 1925. *Experience and Nature.* Chicago: Open Court. Rev. ed., New York: W. W. Norton, 1929.

———. 1934. *A Common Faith.* New Haven, CT: Yale University Press.

———. 1946. *Problems of Men.* New York: Philosophical Library.

Eldridge, Michael. 1998. *Transforming Experience: John Dewey's Cultural Instrumentalism.* Nashville, TN: Vanderbilt University Press.

Gouinlock, James. 1972. *John Dewey's Philosophy of Value.* New York: Humanities Press.

Hollinger, David. 2004. "Damned for God's Glory: William James and the

Scientific Vindication of Protestant Culture." In *William James and a Science of Religions: Reexperiencing the Varieties of Religious Experience,* edited by Wayne Proudfoot, 9–30. New York: Columbia University Press.

James, William. 1890. *The Principles of Psychology,* 2 vols. New York: Henry Holt.

_____. 1897. *The Will to Believe and Other Essays in Popular Philosophy.* New York: Longmans, Green.

_____. 1902. *The Varieties of Religious Experience: A Study of Human Nature.* New York: Longmans, Green.

_____. 1907. *Pragmatism: A New Name for Some Old Ways of Thinking.* New York: Longmans, Green.

_____. 1984. *The Essential Writings,* ed. Bruce Wilshire. New York: State University of New York Press.

_____. 1985. *The Varieties of Religious Experience: A Study of Human Nature.* Cambridge, MA: Harvard University Press.

Peirce, Charles Sanders. 1935. *Scientific Metaphysics.* Vol. 6 of *The Collected Papers of Charles Sanders Peirce,* edited by Charles Hartshorn and Paul Weiss. Cambridge, MA: Harvard University Press.

Perry, Ralph Barton. 1936. *The Thought and Character of William James.* Vol. 2. Boston: Little, Brown.

Proudfoot, Wayne, ed. 2004. *William James and a Science of Religions: Reexperiencing the Varieties of Religious Experiences.* New York: Columbia University Press.

Rockefeller, Steven C. 1991. *John Dewey: Religious Faith and Democratic Humanism.* New York: Columbia University Press.

Santayana, George. 1900. *Interpretations of Poetry and Religion.* New York: Charles Scribner's Sons.

_____. 1905. *Reason in Religion.* Vol. 3 of *The Life of Reason.* New York: Charles Scribner's Sons.

_____. 1946. *The Idea of Christ in the Gospels.* New York: Charles Scribner's Sons.

_____. 1950. "Ultimate Religion." In *Readings in Philosophy,* edited by John Herman Randall Jr., Justus Buchler, and Evelyn Shirk. New York: Barnes and Noble.

Sleeper, Ralph W. 1986. *The Necessity of Pragmatism: John Dewey's Conception of Philosophy.* New Haven, CT: Yale University Press.

Thayer, H. S. 1968. *Meaning and Action: A Critical History of Pragmatism.* Indianapolis: Bobbs-Merrill.

PART THREE:
NATURALISM APPLIED?

10.

Eupraxsophy and Naturalism

Paul Kurtz

I.

The conference for which this chapter was originally written was a historic occasion, for it was the first time that so many philosophical naturalists gathered to reflect on the future of naturalism. Naturalism has been an influential outlook in American philosophy in the twentieth and twenty-first centuries; though today there are powerful forces attempting to undermine it. In this chapter I wish to reflect on the impact of naturalism—past and present—on the broader culture and on the possible directions that might be taken in the future to clarify its meaning and extend its influence.

In one sense, naturalism is synonymous with modernism. Beginning with the Renaissance there was a new emphasis on humanistic values. The scientific revolution of the modern world and the quest for a method of inquiry by scientists and philosophers has had a profound impact on modern consciousness. Insofar as science uses objective standards for testing truth claims, it assumes at the very least *methodological naturalism*: that is, it abandons the quest for "occult" causes and seeks natural explanations of phenomena. Notwithstanding the enormous influence of science and technology on modern life, recalcitrant antinaturalistic and antihumanistic forces seek to counter naturalism. Witness the recrudescence of fundamentalist religions in the United States and worldwide, religions that question the very foundations of the scientific outlook, as in the defense of intelligent design by right-wing evangelicals against the theory of evolution. "It is only a *theory*," they insist; but when we ask, "Is the theory of gravity *only* a theory?" we receive no response.

No doubt it was the Enlightenment of the eighteenth century that was pivotal in the application of naturalism to sociocultural institutions. Especially noteworthy were the Industrial Revolution; the democratic revolutions in France and the United States; and the progressive ideals expressed by Condorcet and *les philosophes*, who declared that science, education, democracy, human rights, and the secularization of values would emancipate human beings from *les anciens régimes* and religious intolerance. Today, strident voices in opposition to the Enlightenment continue to bleat, among them the postmodernist disciples of Heidegger, who denigrate the role of science and technology and the optimistic agenda of liberation humanism. Some critics have proclaimed that we are already in a postsecular era and that naturalism is being supplanted by a new religiosity.[1] They point to the fact that a renascent Islam will in time outbreed secular cultures in Europe, that orthodox religions are recovering ground in eastern Europe and gaining converts in Asia and Africa, and that spirituality is capturing the younger generation.

I wish to focus in this chapter on the continuing relevance of naturalism to civilization and the need for a New Enlightenment appropriate to contemporary conditions. For one who has spent a lifetime *engagé* on the barricades, so to speak, defending naturalism, humanism, and secularism against their detractors, the question is not simply academic but has real practical consequences.

I have entitled my chapter "Eupraxsophy and Naturalism," for I wish to focus on the direct relevance of naturalism to social values and institutions. We can debate analytic issues—important as they are. But we should, I submit, also appraise the relevance of naturalism to individual persons, social institutions, and the planetary civilization that is emerging.

I wish to defend pragmatic naturalism: that is, I wish to focus on the wisdom of *practice*, not simply the practice of wisdom. In my view, *praxis* should have equal standing with *sophia*; often, those concerned primarily with *sophia* never get the opportunity to influence the course of affairs. I consider myself a pragmatic pragmatist in the tradition of Sidney Hook, who dealt directly with practical moral and social issues. I wish to *institutionalize* naturalism and transform it from abstract concepts to concrete applications. Indeed, I have at times said "Au revoir philosophia" and "Bonjour eupraxsophia."

I have coined the term *eupraxsophy* by combining the Greek roots *eu* (good), *praxis* (practice), and *sophia* (wisdom); this is not the love of wisdom, but the practice of wisdom. Eupraxsophy differs from antiseptically neutral philosophy in that it enters consciously and forthrightly into the marketplace of human affairs. By saying this, I do not mean that we should not develop the capacity for critical ethical judgment, but that we should go further and provide a coherent life stance based on the naturalistic outlook and we should endeavor to deal with concrete decisions encountered in daily life.

At this point I should express the premise of this endeavor: to create alternatives to religion, new programs and agendas to cultivate inquiry and human enrichment, focusing on the meaning of life and providing passional-rational guides, instead of the cathedrals, temples, and mosques that have dominated the cultural landscape for so long. These ancient parables need to be replaced by new institutions based upon naturalistic science and ethics.

Unfortunately, naturalism is often identified by friend and foe alike as antisupernaturalism, simply equivalent to atheism. Naturalists find insufficient evidence or reasons for a transcendental realm, and least of all for divinely inspired knowledge of God, by means of revelation or mysticism. Naturalism rejects command-morality, the implication that one can deduce from the Fatherhood of God the moral obligation of human beings.

Naturalism is skeptical of God language, finding it unintelligible. To say "God exists" is not comprehensible, because *exists* is not a predicate; we do not know in what sense God exists. I'm not talking about the imminent God of historical revelation, which claims that God manifests himself in human history. This form of theism is meaningful, though *false*, for there are clearly identifiable prophets, or, in the case of Jesus, a divine person. This is different from the transcendental God of the philosophers. The case against God is of

course familiar to naturalists: the burden of proof rests with the theists; and we find the deductive arguments either fallacious or incon-
clusive. This applies to the classical cosmological, ontological, and
teleological arguments, but it also applies to recent arguments such
as "intelligent design" and "fine tuning," neither of which accounts
for the widespread extinction of species or the deal-breaker problem
of evil.

I think it important that we apply the tools of methodological naturalism to examine the Hebrew Bible, the New Testament, the Koran,
and the Hadith. The range of phenomena examined is natural, or at
the very least *paranatural*; it is amenable to empirical research.
Carbon-14 has been employed to date the historical artifacts of
archeology, and the linguistic examination of ancient documents has
been applied with devastating results. Today the scientific investigation of miracles, stigmata, relics, and shrouds provides naturalistic
explanations. I agree with Daniel Dennett that we need to press into
service our knowledge of the brain and consciousness, biology, and
genetics; I would add that we should draw upon all the sciences,
including the social sciences, to provide naturalistic explanations for
the persistence of religious beliefs and practices.[2]

II.

The term *naturalism* has been used primarily as a weapon in the
battle against religion: the existence of God, the existence of a nonmaterial spiritual realm, or the postulation of separable souls that
survive death.

Much has been made lately of "the new atheism." There is intense
public interest in books by authors Richard Dawkins, Sam Harris,
Daniel Dennett, Christopher Hitchens, and Victor Stenger.[3] This "new
atheism" connotes only a *negative* definition of naturalism, in terms
of what it is *against*. I think that we should put our best foot forward
and start with the *positive* case for naturalism. We should begin not
with God, a myth to be debunked or refuted, left over from the pre-
scientific age, but with *nature itself*, directly experienced, and with

our efforts to explain *the primordial world of diversity and plenti-tude that we encounter in living and interacting*.

Supernaturalism at first represented the attempt by the primitive mind to account for the mysteries and tragedies of existence. God was postulated as a hidden cause of inexplicable events. The human response to them was to supplicate hidden deities by prayer and sac-rifice in the pious hope that God would rescue human beings from the world of sorrow and weltschmertz.

Supernaturalism dug such deep roots in human culture because it had been institutionalized; beliefs were ingrained by indoctrina-tion, enshrined by law, and made virtually compulsory. Heretics were exiled, excommunicated, or burned at the stake. Richard Dawkins and Daniel Dennett attribute the persistence of religious beliefs and practices to *memes*, patterns of culture conditioned and transmitted from generation to generation. The classical religions derived from the so-called Books of Abraham—Christianity, Islam, and Judaism—were enshrined before the emergence of modern sci-ence (as were the historic traditions of Hinduism, Confucianism, Buddhism, and other Asian religions).

These are the questions that we need to address: Can naturalism provide a genuine alternative to theism? Can it create new institu-tions to promote this alternative? This is already happening in the modern world with the development of secular economic, social, legal, and political institutions, the growth of democracy, the emer-gence of consumer cultures that enable ordinary people to enjoy the goods of this life, and the opportunities for education at all levels. But we need to further develop other aspects of the secular naturalistic outlook—particularly an appreciation for the role of science and the introduction of thoroughly humanistic ethical values.

III.

There are three key normative principles of naturalism that can pro-vide an effective alternative to religion.

The first is *methodological naturalism*, which recommends the use of scientific methods as broadly conceived as the most effective way of justifying beliefs, hypotheses, and theories. Hence, every effort is made to be impartial in evaluating, testing, and validating claims to knowledge. This entails theoretical and mathematical coherence, an appeal to evidence, and the use of experimental prediction. What are the grounds for accepting a claim to knowledge?— that it must be corroborated (or replicated) by competent inquirers in the field under study. It does not depend on subjective caprice or arbitrary authority. Unlike religious claims, scientific knowledge is open to revision in the light of new discoveries or theories. It is fallible, according to Peirce. Thus some skepticism is intrinsic to the very process of scientific inquiry.

Many naturalists take the natural sciences as the only area where reliable knowledge has been achieved; this presupposes that only natural entities or processes exist and/or are dependent on physical causal processes. Here the physicalist reductive model reigns supreme. My caveat is that the methods of justification should not be narrowly construed, for the strategies of investigation and confirmation may vary from field to field, depending on the context under inquiry. The natural sciences—physics, astronomy, chemistry, geology, and so forth—surely stand as an ideal model, using a physicalist framework. The biological sciences, however, introduce new concepts and theories not reducible entirely to their physical-chemical substrata. Similarly, the behavioral sciences of psychology and the social sciences, such as economics, political science, and sociology, introduce new constructs and theories, and their modes of confirmation may not be as precise as those in the natural sciences. I share the general hypothesis that all "mental" processes are dependent on physical processes and that knowledge of the underlying physical causes is a necessary condition for full understanding; but it may not be sufficient. At this stage of human knowledge, we cannot hope to understand how the economy functions by monitoring the micro-nerve patterns of billions of brains; rather, we need to correlate market forces with the rise or fall of interest rates or earnings, and supply-and-demand on the macro level. The need is similar for other fields of inquiry.

What is especially important is the practical need to educate students and the general public to think critically, and this is an extended sense of the application of scientific methods. In my view, scientific methods grow out of the practical ways in which people cope with the world and solve problems: as Dewey pointed out, it is continuous with common sense. Methodological naturalism in the final analysis is a prescriptive principle tested by its pragmatic consequences.

It is a normative recommendation based upon effective methods of inquiry; though the corroboration of claims to knowledge may vary from field to field. We should strive for physicalist explanations wherever we can, but these surely need to be supplemented by others at various levels of inquiry. I will illustrate the need for a plurality of strategies of research by reference to the projects pursued by researchers at the Center for Inquiry.

I am here referring to efforts we have expended in our three decades of investigating anomalous phenomena, paranormal claims, parapsychology, and cognate fields. Following in the tradition of philosophers such as William James, Henry Sidgwick, H. H. Price, C. D. Broad, and Curt Ducasse, and the Society for Psychical Research in England and Cambridge, Massachusetts, we have continued the scientific investigation of the evidence for ESP, telepathy, clairvoyance, precognition, and psychokinesis (PSI)—which, according to its proponents, such as J. B. Rhine, could not be explained by reference to natural scientific causes and may open us up to a realm of non-natural phenomena. To his credit, J. B. Rhine (whom I debated at the Smithsonian Institution three decades ago) wished to use the experimental methods of the psychological laboratory to test PSI. CSICOP (now CSI, the Committee for Skeptical Inquiry) has investigated anomalous phenomena in cooperation with (and criticism of) parapsychologists, and we've tested mediums and psychics, examined communication with the dead, ghostly apparitions, near-death experiences, and other alleged evidence for survival. We've gone even further and dealt with extraterrestrial visitations, the newest form of space-age religion that has become popular in the contemporary world. Although we've approached this area with an open mind, we are largely skeptical of the claims of paranormal investigators who are convinced that something strange is intruding in our universe. We have found a good deal of the data unreliable, based on anecdotal information and uncritical eyewitness accounts. Other difficulties that we uncovered were faulty protocols, experimental bias, the leakage of data to the experimenters, and errors in grading "hits."

The first question that we raised was whether such anomalous phenomena even exist. One cannot decide a priori that this phenomenon is impossible because it contradicts naturalism, as C. E. M. Hansel, the noted skeptical psychologist, assumed. He surmised that since it contradicted our understanding of the natural world, fraud was involved, which he attempted to uncover.[4] I dissented. We cannot prejudge. Thus I was interested in examining the empirical data. The first criterion that we used was a demand for reliable evidence, not merely hearsay testimony that cannot be substantiated by impartial investigators or replicated in the laboratory. Most often we did not find that the anomalous phenomenon existed. Insofar as people insisted that it did, we sought causal explanations to fit the alleged observed data. These turned out to be perfectly explicable in prosaic normal terms! I have spent more years of my life than I intended in examining the claims of mediums, faith healers, astrologers, palm readers, dowsers, and UFOlogists that strange phenomena were occurring. Those involved in our work were able to evaluate the claims by using powerful investigative techniques, not necessarily reducible to a physicalist model. We detected psychological and sociological processes of deception and self-deception. We could not find a physical mechanism for telepathy or clairvoyance; these were attributed to elusive "extrasensory" perceptions, so we drew upon *both* psychology and physics.

Another vital area where scientific methodology has been used with effectiveness is the examination of sacred religious texts—in opposition to the general view that science cannot deal with matters of faith or revelation. Historically, revealed theology was supposed to be accepted on the basis of faith.[5] We, however, examined the evidence for the virgin birth, exorcisms, and the Resurrection, all pivotal to Christianity, in the light of their historical or scientific credibility—was there an original body of reliable empirical evidence? I doubt it. The utter speciousness of the evidence for Revelation has by and large been ignored by philosophers, yet the contemporary reexamination of biblical claims demonstrates the factual inadequacy of the sources, and demonstrates that it involves "news from nowhere," transmitted by unreliable sources. None of the writers of the Gospels in the New Testament, for example, were eyewitnesses. Their accounts were based on hearsay, derived from a second- or thirdhand oral tradition, and hence are highly suspect. The criterion here is the need for corroboration of extraordinary claims of divine origin by impeccable eyewitness testimony, and/or the careful drawing upon circumstantial evidence that provides inductive evidence that is independently verifiable. The results of this painstaking research now over two centuries old have thrown doubt on the birth, ministry, and resurrection of Jesus, let alone his existence. None of the four Gospels—Matthew, Mark, Luke, John—were written by those who witnessed the miraculous events. They were most likely written by propagandists for a new faith; hence they are Gospels of fiction, not reliable historical accounts. Yet a powerful religion is based on these claims.

Similar considerations apply to the accounts of the life of Muhammad in the Koran and the stories of his life by his alleged companions, as related in the Hadith. Meticulous historical research demonstrates that there were many Korans, that we do not know whether the received doctrines about the life of Muhammad are accurate. Thus we are able to cast skeptical doubt on the traditional accounts of his divine calling. Similar considerations also apply to the Hebrew Bible. We at the Center for Inquiry have spent almost thirty years in this area of biblical and Koranic research. Such historical research is impartial; it is a form of *Wissenschaften*, though it does not strictly reduce to the natural sciences. Hence the need for various strategies of research to establish whether claims made are credible. We have again found that the psychology of deception is very important in reconstructing the readiness to believe.

I move on to a second form of naturalism, which I call *scientific* rather than philosophical naturalism. This form of naturalism entails another normative recommendation, the importance of describing and interpreting the body of scientific knowledge at any one time in history. This requires generalists who are skilled in uncovering overlapping interdisciplinary generalizations, common concepts and theories, and shared assumptions and presuppositions. I think that philosophers working closely with scientists are well qualified to participate in this important task. The eventual goal of scientific inquiry is to achieve, if possible, the "unity of the sciences"; that is, to develop comprehensive theories from which all subdisciplines can be deduced. This might entail, as Ernest Nagel said, "bridge hypotheses" between various disciplines. An ambitious goal, no doubt, and perhaps never achievable. We are well aware that philosophers today have some trepidation about spinning out metaphysical systems encompassing everything in the universe. The metaphysical conjectures of the past often turn out to be untested speculative ontologies, which are discarded as new discoveries are made or when radical paradigm shifts occur.

What should concern us is that today there is an abysmal lack of information among members of the general public and indeed among scientific specialists themselves about scientific discoveries. Botanists may not be familiar with what astronomers have discovered, mathematicians of what is going on in crystallography, neurologists of what is going on in economics or genetics. Indeed, it is especially unfortunate that our political and corporate leaders display abysmal ignorance about the basic sciences, and all too often they turn to religion, or literature, or the arts to develop an understanding of nature or human life. Scientific illiteracy is rampant. That is why we need to provide general outlines of our knowledge of the universe as far as we can. Most often it is scientists rather than philosophers—for example, Carl Sagan, Isaac Asimov, E. O. Wilson—who make contributions to the public understanding of science. E. O. Wilson, in *Consilience: The Unity of Knowledge*,[6] draws upon the nineteenth-century English philosopher of science, William Whewell, who recommends that we seek "consilience instead of coherence." This means a "jumping together of knowledge, by linking of facts and fact-based theory across disciplines to create common groundwork of explanation."

According to Whewell, consilience occurs "when an induction obtained from one class of facts coincides with an induction . . . from a different class."[7] All of this is an extrapolation; yet I submit that it is important to develop a kind of synoptic view of the universe at any one time in history. This is sometimes described as the quest for the "generic traits of nature" (to use the words of John Herman Randall

Jr.) or the "general categories" or "presuppositions of science." I prefer myself to label it as the quest for *empirical descriptive accounts* of what has been discovered across the sciences.

In this venture we draw from physics and chemistry first, in order to provide the bedrock of a wide range of systems. I quote from the famous physicist Richard Feynman in one of his famous lectures at Cal Tech. Feynman asked, "If, in some cataclysm, all of scientific knowledge were to be destroyed, and only one sentence passed on to the next generation of creatures, what statement would contain the most information in the fewest words?" His response to this was, "I believe it is the atomic hypothesis, or the atomic fact, or whatever you wish to call it, that all things are made of atoms. Little particles that move around in perpetual motion, attracting each other when a little distance apart but repelling upon being squeezed into one another."[8] Feynman is alleged to have said that if we take that one sentence and throw in imagination and thinking, we have the history of physics. In other words, physics uses reductionism, understanding complex things in terms of their constituent parts, and it has been extraordinarily successful in that inquiry. Physicalist explanations apply on the macro as well as the micro levels. Physicists and astronomers observe the behavior of large bodies in our solar system, calculating precisely the orbits of the planets around our sun. They have extrapolated this theory, using the principles of mechanics and gravitation, to other planetary systems. The question of scale is crucial, as we go from the micro to the macro level, yet the basic principles of physics still seem to apply, though they are adapted to very large physical systems, including galaxies.

The biological sciences depend upon physics and chemistry, but a high-level law, the Darwinian principle of natural selection, has been formulated to explain the evolution of species. Many think that physics and chemistry are the primary sources of the basic laws of nature; yet there are other fundamental regularities that have emerged in the life sciences—for example, the theory of evolution. Of course, micro-level explanations are relevant—such as the discovery of DNA and the genetic determinants of behavior. But there are principles that have emerged on the macro level that are not simply reducible to micro causality.

I have called the interaction of explanations *coduction*, where we draw upon many factors or causes to explain phenomena. The logic of coduction recognizes that to understand a living system we need to use *both* physics and chemistry, in which the atomic, molecular, and cellular functions of organisms are observed, but also on macro-like laws as in natural selection, where chance mutations, differential reproduction, and adaptation are essential in our understanding of biological systems. Both provide us with sets of explanation that are extremely useful. In some species we find that social behavior emerges—as in a beehive, an ant colony, or human society—and here other higher-level principles are relevant in explanations of behavior.

Does our understanding of human consciousness reduce experience entirely to the micro structures and functions of the brain, or do we not at the same time seek to understand intentional behavior, the role of cognition, and the psychology of motivation? Many find the concept of *emergence* relevant here, for there are systems in which new properties and qualia manifest themselves. Explanations drawn from sociology and the social sciences also help us to comprehend sociocultural institutions.

Many naturalists have assumed that hard determinism is the ultimate presupposition of all scientific inquiry. The classical thesis was that if you knew the exact state of the physical universe at any one moment, you could predict the future course of all events. This presupposes that all things in the universe are interconnected. This I submit is an oversimplification, which does not apply if we view the universe as an open, pluralistic scene in which order and disorder, contingency and regularity, determinism and indeterminism, chaos and stability, accidents and catastrophes are observed. I hope that I am not dealing in metaphorical language by saying that contingencies are real: I think that they reflect the evidential facts of nature. Are they contingent because we are ignorant of the causes, or does brute facticity include chance and indeterminacy? I submit that contingency is not only found in human affairs, where calamity and distress may suddenly engulf a tribe or nation-state, or in the struggle of competing species to adapt and survive or be vanquished by forces beyond their control—like the dinosaurs, the saber-toothed tigers, the mammoths, or the intricate, exquisite forms of life uncovered in the Burgess shale in Canada, which became extinct some 500 million years ago. Is contingency manifested in the crash of meteors, comets, and asteroids into our solar system, the birth and collapse of planets and stars, and the collision and explosion of galaxies in the universe at large, as viewed through telescopes, where we also observe a receding universe expanding at terrific speeds, black holes, and dark matter? The earlier conviction of scientists that nature was perfectly ordered in terms of deterministic laws hardly seems to accord with nature as we find it, in which the polarities of order and disorder seem manifest.

Scientific explanations are contrived by human beings in order to make sense of the world. The great ongoing adventure of scientific discoveries both advances our knowledge and introduces new puzzles, such as the discovery of over 250 planets outside of our solar system (in 2007) and the understanding that there most likely are billions and billions of planets and billions of galaxies, many of them involved in humongous collisions in outer space. So the notion of a fixed universe or the idea "that God would not roll dice in outer space" is perhaps a bias of the human mind, which demands order and perfection, whereas the evidence points to chance and contingency as facts of the universe at large.

In view of this, I wish to pose a series of questions for naturalists: Our age is the time when the human species confronts absolute death—not only death in terms of our own mortal existence as individuals but the likely death of our own species and solar system at some remote time in the future. Arthur Toynbee has graphically dramatized for us the rise and fall of past civilizations, with the clear implication that this likewise applies to our own. We have dethroned God and the planet Earth from the center of creation. The point is that science has shattered the anthropocentric religions of our forebears, but skepticism destroys any lingering conceit that our ideals will prevail throughout eternity. If God is dead because we killed him, so is the Human Prospect(s) in the long run bound to fail. In view of this, is the picture of reality presented by the sciences too bitter a pill to swallow, and will this lead to despair and hopelessness in the general public? This is the question that William L. Craig, the theistic theologian, hurled at me when I debated him recently.[9] He said that secular humanism led to nihilism. I denied that accusation.

What are the implications of methodological and scientific naturalism for life as lived? Both involve normative recommendations. The first requires a vigorous code of epistemological austerity, skeptical about speculative flights of faith and fancy. It wishes to extend the rigorous methods of corroboration to all claims to truth. This applies to secular ideals no less than to theistic; it admonishes us to be careful. We should not leap in with unfounded wishful thinking. Continuous peer review of ideals and values may kill off any humanistic agendas of liberation and undermine the audacity of hope.

The second form of naturalism presents us with a universe in which the God delusion is whacked to death (we cheer!) and religion is exposed as poison (hear! hear!), a universe that is without purpose, rhyme, or reason, indifferent to human ideals and values. It just *is*.

The response of secular humanists is that although nature has no intrinsic purpose or meaning, life presents us with opportunities (within limits) to create our own meanings, plans, and projects for ourselves and our fellow human beings. Countless generations have found life intrinsically worthwhile for its own sake; they have lived their lives full of satisfaction and happiness unmindful of the ultimate nature of an evolving biosphere, without any worry that humans do not have a privileged place in a vast mysterious universe of expanding galaxies, devoid of any illusions of immortality. The good life is achievable, we insist. But we are the only species apparently aware of its own death and the eventual degradation of our lovely habitat, the planet Earth. What is the meaning of life, we ask, as viewed from the galaxariums of the future?

This leads to the third form of naturalism, *ethical naturalism*, which focuses on human values. Naturalistic ethics came under heavy criticism in the early part of the twentieth century—from G. E. Moore onward. This criticism is now widely accepted. We cannot deduce what we *ought* to do from what *is* the case; we cannot derive our values from the facts. For example, if it is the case that the human male is prone to aggression in competition for females, it surely does not follow that it is morally permissible to act aggressively. If the universe has no special place for humans, how shall we assert our own significance? Human life is an audacious expression of how we choose to become what we want. What is the relevance of nature to our decisions?

May I present a *modified form of ethical naturalism* that survives the critique of naturalistic ethics: I submit simply that the facts of the case are relevant to our moral values and principles, and that we need to take them into account in decision making. We need to understand the limits and constraints, opportunities and openings, in the environments in which we live, the circumstances and facts within the contexts of choice. The consequences of our choices may persuade us to modify them, and the relevance of the means at our disposal help us to evaluate our ends. These considerations are value neutral; yet they are relevant to the things we hold dear, cherish, and esteem, a form of objective relativism. I have called this the *valuation base* and I submit that we can make reasonable value judgments in the light of it.[10] Hence, there is an intermediary relationship between values and facts, an *act-ductive*, if not deductive or inductive, relationship of facts and values to actions. Accordingly, naturalism has direct relevance to the decisions we make and the values we select.

Theists complain that a person cannot be good without God; that secular ethics is groundless, hence unreliable. I deny that. I maintain that both methodological and scientific naturalism have profound implications for a meaningful life. However, this depends on the flexible application of the naturalistic method and outlook to life. I submit that philosophy is a stepping-stone to normative morality, but it needs to be transformed directly into *eupraxsophy*. As I view it, eupraxsophers are skilled in the art of living and their recommendations have behavioral implications for the practical life.

Unfortunately, there has been considerable opposition to this agenda from philosophers and scientists. First, the lion's share of philosophical ethics—I call it formalistic or abstract ethics—has been focused on meta-ethics, in two senses: first the definition of normative terms and concepts, such as *good* or *bad*, *right* or *wrong*, *valuable* or *worthless*. There is a philosophical prejudice against redefining normative terms. This is a kind of definition-mongering, we are admonished. Why should I accept your definition? Is that not a form of *persuasive* definition, and is that not largely *subjective*? Philosophy, we are told, needs to be neutral and not engage in rhetorical definitional games. There is no rational ground for arbitrary fiat, they say. Second, there is another fallacious move, we are told, in proposing criteria, standards and norms, to be appealed to in order to justify valuational judgments. It is surely one thing to carefully analyze the logic of formulating practical judgments on the meta level, pointing out the pitfalls and/or advantages of one or more over others; it is another to seek to actually make judgments and recommend them to others as worthy. To do so, we are cautioned, is to descend into the battleground of moral disputes, to get entangled in the passionate, indeed often bloody, moral battles in the well-trafficked public square.

I concede that point, but I insist that it is important that we define our moral concepts, and also defend our moral principles and values in the process. In other words, naturalists need to advocate ethical positions in the *agora* of life as lived, and to *intellectually and passionately propose and defend them*.

Does this betray the philosophical position of neutrality and objectivity?—possibly; yet it is necessary to do so to satisfy the demand for meaning, the hunger for ideals, the quest for principles that deserve our devotion, the beloved causes that are worthy of our energy.

My response here is that "everyone is doing it, doing it, doing it—why not us?" If we do not defend the naturalistic outlook, try to apply it concretely, and seek to persuade others to accept it, then we have abandoned the melee and turmoil of controversy in order to seek refuge on higher ground—for fear of offending those in power who may disagree. The point is that the bishop and soldier, corporate president and senator, lawyer and rock star, teacher and nurse, worker and student *have* moral convictions upon which they act; so the *eupraxsopher*, if not the philosopher, needs to concentrate on real practical problems in an effort to help solve them; he or she will need to take moral and political positions; will speak out about abortion or same-sex marriage, war or peace, poverty or privilege, plutocracy or democracy, love or hate, joy or despair, the sense of the tragic or the promise of exuberance.

The reason why naturalistic philosophy has failed is that it has not ministered to the passionate needs of students, colleagues, co-workers, citizens in the communities in which we live, and to strangers in the broader community of humankind. We need, if I can borrow the metaphor, *eupraxsopher ministers of the soul, practitioners in the art and science and poetry of living*.

Ranged against naturalism, dealing in illusion and delusion, fantasy and nonsense are the priests and mullahs, rabbis and ministers, who seek to intrude, cajole, persuade, convert, and have no qualms about it. We also need to be forthright and bold about our deeply held convictions, which we need to vindicate.

The posture of the philosopher who is a professor in the university classroom is "Let's look at all sides of a question. We must never advocate, only analyze and explicate!"

That is why I have proposed *eupraxsophy* as a new branch of the applied sciences, which has broken off of the main trunk of philosophy to develop skilled expertise in the arena of valuation and action.

Bertrand Russell once said: "The good life is one that is inspired by love and guided by reason." To this I add that we need to be inspired by a *passionate commitment* to naturalistic humanism, as well as our devotion to reason.

NOTES

1. See Michael Novak's declaration. At a recent conference sponsored by *Telos* (June 22, 2007), he defended Roman Catholicism, and maintained that Jürgen Habermas has wavered on the secularist agenda in his dialogue with Pope Benedict. Many neoconservatives, especially Irving Kristol and his wife, Gertrude Himmelfarb, indict secular naturalism and believe that society needs religion to maintain the social order.

2. Daniel C. Dennett, *Breaking the Spell: Religion as Natural Phenomena* (New York: Penguin Books, 2007).

3. Richard Dawkins, *The God Delusion* (Boston: Houghton Mifflin, 2006); Sam Harris, *Letter to a Christian Nation* (New York: Knopf, 2006) and *The End of Faith* (New York: W. W. Norton, 2005); Dennett, *Breaking*

196 PART THREE: NATURALISM APPLIED?

the Spell; Christopher Hitchens, *God Is Not Great: How Religion Poisons Everything* (New York: Twelve Books, Hachette Book Group, 2007); Victor Stenger, *God: The Failed Hypothesis—How Science Shows That God Does Not Exist* (Amherst, NY: Prometheus Books, 2007).

    4. C. E. M. Hansel, *The Search for Psychic Power* (Amherst, NY: Prometheus Books, 1989).

    5. Richard G. Swinburne, the author of *Revelation* (Oxford: Clarendon Press, 1991) and *The Resurrection of God Incarnate* (Oxford: Clarendon Press, 2003), is a theist who accepts revelation on empirical grounds,

    6. Edward O. Wilson, *Consilience: The Unity of Knowledge* (New York: Alfred A. Knopf, 1998).

    7. William Whewell, *The Philosophy of the Inductive Science* (1840), quoted in Wilson, *Consilience: The Unity of Knowledge*, pp. 8–9.

    8. Quoted in Angier, *The Canon: A World Whirligig Tour of the Beautiful Basics of Science* (Boston: Houghton Mifflin, 2007), p. 87.

    9. See E. Garcia and R. King, eds., *God and Ethics* (Lanham, MD: Rowman and Littlefield, 2008).

    10. In the valuation base I have in my writings listed a whole number of normative principles, virtues, and values to which naturalistic humanists are committed: the common moral decencies (integrity, trustworthiness, benevolence, fairness); excellences (health, self-control, self-respect, high motivation, the capacity for love, caring for others, beloved causes, *joie de vivre*, achievement motivation, creativity, exuberance); altruism, impartial ethical rationality, human rights and responsibilities, the aphorisms of a good will, etc.

11.

Naturalizing Jurisprudence: Three Approaches

Brian Leiter

Gcerned with the nature of law and adjudication—has been
relatively unaffected by the naturalistic strains so evident, for
example, in the epistemology, philosophy of mind, and moral philosophy of the past forty years.[1] In this chapter, I want to sketch three
ways in which naturalism might affect jurisprudential inquiry.[2]

By naturalism here, I mean a *methodological* doctrine about how
we should approach philosophical inquiry. On this view, philosophy
proceeds (as the most familiar metaphor has it) "in tandem with the
sciences," that is, as the abstract and reflective branch of the empirical sciences as they limn the causal structure of the world. Such an
approach is agnostic about ontological questions: the sciences decide
those; and since, as Jerry Fodor has repeatedly emphasized, the
trend in the past fifty years has been toward the proliferation of the
special sciences, rather than toward a systematic reduction to a
basic science like physics, we should expect an acceptable naturalist
ontology to be comparably pluralistic—though, to be sure, we won't
find in it any moral facts or supernatural entities, since these play no
role in any scientific enterprise with the "predict and control" bona
fides of successful sciences.

There have, of course, been *substantive* naturalistic programs in
jurisprudence whose aim was to show that all the distinctive norma-

tive concepts of the law—"obligation," "right," "duty," and so on—can be explicated in terms that admit of empirical investigation and confirmation. The mid-twentieth-century movement known as Scandinavian Legal Realism (because of the nationalities of its proponents) is the primary example in the last hundred years, but one of H. L. A. Hart's decisive achievements was to demonstrate the failure of the Scandinavian program to account for the perspective of actors within a legal system—such a perspective, Hart argued plausibly, being essential to account for the social phenomenon of law.

From the standpoint of a methodological naturalism, there are three ways we might naturalize jurisprudential questions. Two of these pertain to questions about the nature of law, and one to the nature of adjudication, that is, the formal procedures by which courts and official bodies decide legal disputes. Like most branches of philosophy, philosophy of law has been concerned with the distinctive features of its subject matter: What demarcates legal norms from other kinds of norms, most notably moral ones? How do we distinguish human societies with law from those with other forms of normative regulation? And what kind of normative force is characteristic of legal rules? The most important work of twentieth-century jurisprudence was Hart's 1961 book, *The Concept of Law*,[3] which decisively displaced two influential alternative positions: on the one hand, Hans Kelsen's view that the nature of law was essentially tied to its use of sanctions, and that its normative force was only explicable by reference to a nonnatural transcendental fact, what Kelsen called the *Grundnorm*;[4] on the other hand, the Scandinavian program, mentioned already, which sought reductive definitions of all normative terms in law, that is, reducible to empirical predictions about official behavior. Hart's own philosophical outlook, as his student Joseph Raz has emphasized, was a naturalistic one.[5] Contra Kelsen, Hart thought one could explain legal systems and their apparent normative force in terms that were exclusively psychological and sociological—in terms of what legal officials actually do and their attitudes toward what they do—and thus without positing transcendental norms. He shared with the Scandinavians the naturalistic view that ours was a world without normative facts, but contra the Scandinavians, he did not think this required reductive definitions of all normative terms in law. The normative terms in law, Hart thought, can be understood noncognitively, and not simply as unsuccessfully referential terms. Talk of a "legal right" or "legal obligation" did not pick out properties in the world, but rather expressed the distinctive attitudes of actors within a legal system.[6]

In these respects, then, Hart's powerful articulation of a positivist theory of law—a theory according to which law depends on positive facts about official behavior—can be understood as itself informed by philosophical sympathies that are naturalistic in spirit.

Yet Hart's own method of inquiry is one that hardly looks to be naturalistically respectable. Influenced by the then-dominant "ordinary language" philosophy of J. L. Austin, Hart relied on appeals to intuitive claims about law manifest in ordinary language and in the understanding of, as he put it, a "modern municipal legal system" possessed by the ordinary man—or at least the "ordinary man" as conceived (perhaps correctly) by Oxford dons. Serious jurisprudence has, since then, been so spectacularly Oxford-centric that it would not be wrong to say that intuitions that ring true in the vicinity of Oxford's High Street have set the course of modern legal philosophy.

All of this calls to mind Robert Cummins's dismissive remarks about the "Twin Earth" industry in philosophy of mind, spawned by Hilary Putnam:

> It is a commonplace for researchers in the Theory of Content to proceed as if the relevant intuitions [about the Twin Earth cases] were undisputed. . . . The Putnamian take on these cases is widely enough shared to allow for a range of thriving intramural sports among believers. Those who do not share the intuitions are simply not invited to the games.[7]

Should legal philosophers be worried that the "intuitions" of those invited to the general jurisprudence "game" have been unrepresentative and thus unreliable? Perhaps they should. But before the question gets off the ground, a very different concern is likely to be raised: namely, what alternative could there possibly be to an appeal to intuitions about the extension of the concepts under investigation?

Quine famously suggests that naturalism is "the recognition that it is within science itself, and not in some prior philosophy, that reality is to be identified and described."[8] In that Quinean spirit, Cummins proposes:

> We can give up on intuitions about the nature of space and time and ask instead what sorts of beasts space and time must be if current physical theory is to be true and explanatory. We can give up on intuitions about our representational content and ask instead what [mental] representations must be if current cognitive theory is to be true and explanatory.[9]

That Quinean version of methodological naturalism about philosophical inquiry may work well where we have bona fide sciences—for example, space-time physics or cognitive neuroscience—to turn to for guidance. But how do we fare when we turn to social-scientific accounts of law?

Consider perhaps the leading predictive-explanatory theory of judicial decisions in the political science literature, Segal and Spaeth's "Attitudinal Model."[10] Developing ideas first broached by the American Legal Realists,[11] Segal and Spaeth argue that the best explanation for judicial decision making (more precisely, the making of decisions by the US Supreme Court) is to be found in the conjunction of the "the facts of the case" and "the ideological attitudes and values of the justices."[12] Segal and Spaeth identify the "ideological attitudes" of judges based on "the judgments in newspaper editorials that characterize nominees prior to confirmation as liberal or conservative" with respect to particular issues (for example, civil rights and liberties).[13] Looking at more than thirty years of search-and-seizure decisions—court decisions about the constitutionality of police practices involving arrests of criminal suspects and searches of their cars, homes, and property—Segal and Spaeth found that their Attitudinal Model correctly predicted 71 percent of the votes by justices: that is, the ideological attitudes of the judge toward the underlying factual situations (and their variations) explained the vote of the judge nearly three-quarters of the time.

Of course, to show that their explanation is the best one, Segal and Spaeth must compare the Attitudinal Model with some alternatives—most importantly, with what they call "the Legal Model" of decision.[14] According to the Legal Model, it is valid sources of law, in conjunction with valid interpretive methods applied to those sources, that determine outcomes (the valid sources and interpretive methods can be called "the class of legal reasons"). The difficulty is that the class of legal reasons is indeterminate: it justifies more than one outcome in appellate disputes. Thus, as Segal and Spaeth write:

> If various aspects of the legal model can support either side of any given dispute that comes before the Court, and the quality of these positions cannot be reliably and validly measured a priori, then the legal model hardly satisfies as an explanation of Supreme Court decisions. By being able to "explain" everything, in the end it explains nothing.[15]

In other words, one can generate no testable predictions from the Legal Model because the class of valid legal reasons justifies, and thus predicts, multiple outcomes.[16]

Following Cummins, a naturalized jurisprudence might ask what must law be if the current social-scientific theory of adjudication (namely, the Attitudinal Model) is to be true and explanatory? For the Attitudinal Model to be true and explanatory, there has to be, among other things, a clear demarcation between the ideological attitudes of judges (which are causally effective in determining the decisions) and the valid sources of law that are central to the Legal Model's competing explanation of judicial decision making. Thus, implicit in the Attitudinal Model is quite plainly a concept of law as exhausted by authoritative texts (precedents, statutes, constitutions), which are the raw material of the competing Legal Model, and which exclude the ideological attitudes central to the Attitudinal Model. The concept of law, in turn, that vindicates this assumption is none other than Raz's "hard positivist"[17] notion of a rule of recognition whose criteria of legality are exclusively ones of pedigree: a rule (or canon of interpretation) is part of the law by virtue of having a source in legislative enactments, prior court decisions, or constitutional provisions. That is the view of law required by the Legal Model, and it is the view of law required to vindicate the Attitudinal Model as providing the best explanation of judicial decision making. Raz's hard positivism, in short, captures what law must be if the Attitudinal Model is true and explanatory. To be sure, this defense of hard positivism is very different from Raz's own—to which I'll return below—but for the naturalist it suffices that the hard positivist concept of law figures in the best explanatory account of legal phenomena.

Yet it is one thing to turn to space-time physics, whose explanatory and predictive success is extraordinary, to understand the "essential" nature of space or time; it is quite another to think that the feeble social scientific models churned out by political scientists are cutting the social world at its causal joints. The Attitudinal Model, for example, looking only at a limited range of cases, and making some fairly crude assumptions about the competing Legal Model, is able to predict outcomes only 71 percent of the time. Predictive success of 50 percent would be achieved by the "flip the coin" model. A 71 percent success rate is, in short, not the stuff of which scientific credibility is made. Yes, the Attitudinal Model requires the truth of the positivist concept of law. Given the predictive feebleness of that model, this should hardly be comforting to the naturalist.

If naturalizing jurisprudential questions about the nature of law by appealing to pertinent sciences of law is not a viable option, that still leaves unanswered the worries about the robustness of the Oxford-centric intuitions that undergird the claims about the nature of law and authority that are central to Anglophone jurisprudence. There is, however, a second possible way in which jurisprudential questions about the nature of law might be naturalized, namely, by taking a page from the experimental philosophers. If "ordinary" intuitions are to be decisive in fixing the extensions of concepts, why not investigate, empirically, what those intuitions really are? Why not find out, to borrow Hart's phrase, what the "ordinary man" *really* thinks?

Consider the Razian argument for the hard positivist doctrine mentioned above, according to which all norms that are legally binding are so by virtue of their source or pedigree. Raz claims that it is part of the concept of law that all law necessarily claims authority, that is, it claims the right to tell its subjects what they must do. But in order even to claim authority, Raz argues, legal rules must be intelligible without recourse to the practical considerations on which they are based—they must, in Raz's terms, be "exclusionary" reasons for action that preclude consideration of the reasons on which they are based. According to Raz, this is because the concept of authority appropriate to law is the "service conception," according to which a claim to authority is justified insofar as it helps those subject to the authority to do what they really ought to do more successfully than they would without the mediation of the authoritative directives.[18] If law, as a purportedly authoritative directive, were not intelligible with recourse to the reasons on which it was based, then it could not perform any service for its subject.

But are authoritative directives *really* exclusionary reasons? This is, quite explicitly, an intuitive claim about the nature of authority. It has been contested by a number of legal philosophers, who think that *authoritative* reasons are simply *weighty,* rather than *exclusionary,* reasons, and so nothing significant follows about the nature of law, they claim, from the fact that all law claims authority. I confess my own intuitions line up with Raz's, but so what? Raz himself emphasizes that the concept "law" is one "used by people to understand themselves," adding that "it is a major task of legal theory to advance our understanding of society by helping us to understand how people understand themselves."[19] It is curious, indeed, then, that no one has made any effort to figure out what "people"—as distinct from the subset of them who work in the vicinity of High Street—actually understand by the concept. General jurisprudence awaits, and stands in need of, colonization by experimental philosophy.

But now let us put to one side questions about the nature of law and turn to adjudication. Within American law, the most influential academic movement of the twentieth century was American Legal Realism, to which I alluded earlier. The American Legal Realists— lawyers and legal scholars writing most actively in the 1920s and 1930s—urged that we look realistically at what courts are doing when they decide cases. If we do so, they argued, we will find that many of the legal doctrines and arguments that judges give in their opinions do little to explain the results they reach; the published opinions more often conceal, rather than illuminate, the actual grounds of decision making. In fact, the judges are responsive to the underlying factual scenarios—what the Realists call "situation-types"—and craft responses to those situations in light of nonlegal norms of fairness and economic efficiency. The "legal arguments" they then give are post hoc rationalizations for decisions based on other considerations.

The details of the Realist theory do not really matter for our purposes here; what is significant is how they conceived their theoretical task. The Legal Realists thought that the task of legal theory was to identify and describe—*not* justify—the patterns of court decisions; the social sciences—or at least social-scientific-type inquiries—were to be the tool for carrying out this nonnormative task. There is a sense, then, in which we may think of the jurisprudence of adjudication that the realists advocated as a *naturalized* jurisprudence on the model of something like Quine's naturalized epistemology. Just as a *naturalized* epistemology—in Quine's famous formulation—"simply falls into place as a chapter of psychology,"[20] as what Jaegwon Kim calls "a purely descriptive, causal-nomological science of human cognition,"[21] so too a naturalized jurisprudence for the realists is an essentially descriptive theory of the causal connections between underlying situation-types and actual judicial decisions. (Indeed, one Legal Realist, Underhill Moore, even anticipated the Quinean slogan: "This study lies within the province of jurisprudence. It also lies within the field of behavioristic psychology. It places the province within the field.")[22]

Notice, in particular, that Quine and the Realists can be seen as advocating naturalization for analogous reasons. On one familiar reading, Quine advocates naturalism as a response to the failure of the traditional foundationalist program in epistemology, from Descartes to Carnap. As Hilary Kornblith aptly puts it: "Once we see the sterility of the foundationalist program, we see that the only genuine questions there are to ask about the relation between theory and evidence and about the acquisition of belief are psychological questions."[23] That is, once we recognize our inability to tell a certain kind of *normative* story about the relation between evidence and theory—a story about which theories are *justified* on the basis of the evidence—Quine would have us give up the normative project: "Why not just see how [the] construction [of theories on the basis of evidence] really proceeds?"[24]

So, too, the Realists can be read as advocating an empirical theory of adjudication precisely because they think the traditional jurisprudential project of trying to show decisions to be *justified* on the basis of legal rules and reasons is a failure. For the Realists, legal reasoning is *indeterminate*: that is, the class of legitimate legal reasons that a court might appeal to in justifying a decision fails, in fact, to justify a *unique* outcome in many of the cases. If the law is determinate, then we would expect—except in cases of ineptitude or corruption—that legal rules and reasons would be reliable predictors of judicial outcomes. But the law in many cases is indeterminate, and thus in those cases there is no "foundational" story to be told about the particular decision of a court: legal reasons would justify just as well a contrary result. But if legal rules and reasons cannot *rationalize* the decisions, then they surely cannot *explain* them either: we must, accordingly, look to other factors to explain why a court actually decided as it did. Thus, the Realists in effect say: "Why not see how the construction of decisions really proceeds?" The Realists, then, call for an essentially *naturalized* and hence *descriptive* theory of adjudication, a theory of what it is that causes courts to decide as they do.

This way of naturalizing jurisprudence will no doubt call to mind the Attitudinal Model, discussed earlier, though the use to which the theory is being put is now different. Whereas earlier we considered the possibility that we might look to social-scientific theories of adjudication to figure out which concept of law renders those theories true and explanatory, the Legal Realist proposal under consideration is more modest: it suggests that rather than pretending that the law *justifies* one and only one decision in the kinds of legal disputes that attract the most attention (e.g., decisions of the US Supreme Court), we would be better served—as theorists and as lawyers—in constructing explanations that make sense of the empirical evidence, namely, the patterns of decisions by courts across differing situation-types. That research program is a thriving one in legal scholarship,[25] though largely disdained by legal philosophers. But it may constitute the most successful instance of one kind of "naturalized jurisprudence" that we presently have on offer.

NOTES

1. Why that should be so is an issue I will return to briefly at the end of this chapter.

2. This will in large part comprise a précis of my recent collection, *Naturalizing Jurisprudence: Essays on American Legal Realism and Naturalism in Legal Philosophy* (Oxford: Oxford University Press, 2007).

3. H. L. A. Hart, *The Concept of Law*, 2nd ed. (Oxford: Clarendon Press, 1994).

4. Hans Keslen, *Pure Theory of Law* (Berkeley: University of California Press, 1960).

5. Joseph Raz, "Two Views of the Nature of the Theory of Law: A Partial Comparison," *Legal Theory* 4 (1998): 249–82; see esp. 252–53.

6. For the most systematic development of this idea, see Kevin Toh, "Hart's Expressivism and His Benthamite Project," *Legal Theory* 11 (2005): 75–123.

7. Robert Cummins, "Reflections on Reflecting Equilibrium," in *Rethinking Intuition: The Psychology of Intuition and Its Role in Philosophical Inquiry*, ed. M. DePaul and W. Ramsey (Lanham, MD: Rowman & Littlefield, 1998), p. 116.

8. "Things and Their Place in Theories," in W. V. O. Quine, *Theories and Things* (Cambridge, MA: Harvard University Press, 1981), p. 21. Quine, unfortunately, never seems to have noticed that the psychological science of the 1930s—to which he was wedded—was subsequently discredited.

9. Cummins, "Reflections on Reflective Equilibrium," pp. 117–18.

10. Jeffrey Segal and Harold Spaeth, *The Supreme Court and the Attitudinal Model Revisited* (Cambridge: Cambridge University Press, 2002).

11. Ibid., pp. 87–89.

12. Ibid., p. 86.

13. Ibid., p. 321. As Segal and Spaeth remark: "Although this measure is less precise than past votes, it nonetheless avoids the circularity problem, is exogenous to the justices' behavior, and is reliable and replicable."

14. Ibid., pp. 48–85. Segal and Spaeth's treatment of the "Legal Model" is, in several respects, crude; I have cleaned it up considerably for the purpose of presenting it here.

15. Ibid., p. 86.

16. This is because prediction tracks justification in the legal model.

17. Joseph Raz, "Authority, Law and Morality," *Monist* 68 (1995): 295–324.

18. Ibid.

19. Ibid., pp. 321–22.

20. W. V. O. Quine, "Epistemology Naturalized," in *Ontological Relativity and Other Essays* (New York: Columbia University Press, 1969), p. 82.

21. Jaegwon Kim, "What Is 'Naturalized Epistemology'?" *Philosophical Perspectives* 2 (1988): 388.

22. Underhill Moore and Charles Callahan, "Law and Learning Theory: A Study in Legal Control," *Yale Law Journal* 53 (1943): 1.

23. "Introduction: What Is Naturalistic Epistemology," in *Naturalizing Epistemology*, 2nd ed., ed. H. Kornblith (Cambridge, MA: MIT Press, 1994), p. 4.

24. Quine, "Epistemology Naturalized," p. 75.

25. See, e.g., Thomas J. Miles and Cass R. Sunstein, "The New Legal Realism," *University of Chicago Law Review* 75 (2008): 831–51, for a useful overview of pertinent literature.

12.

How Knowers Emerge, and Why This Is Important to Future Work in Naturalized Epistemology

Lynn Hankinson Nelson and *Jack Nelson*

1. SOCIAL FACTORS IN THE CREATION OF "KNOWERS"

In 1987 Alvin Goldman argued that the work done by "social" in the phrase "social epistemology" is less than entirely clear. He noted that there is considerable disagreement even among those who are convinced there are social factors relevant to epistemology about what those social factors are (Goldman 1987).[1] Seven years later, the collection *Socializing Epistemology*, edited by Frederick Schmitt, revealed that the disagreements Goldman identified remained unresolved (Schmitt 1994).

It seems they still are. Our focus here is the role, the very important role, of one social factor in epistemology, namely, that the ability of humans to know requires extensive and successful interpersonal interactions in infancy and very early childhood. Naturalized epistemologists have drawn heavily on the findings of cognitive scientists, neuroscientists, and empirical psychologists concerning the capacities and workings of the mature human brain. This knowledge is, of course, important to epistemology. We are suggesting, based on the research that we summarize below, that naturalists now also need to pay careful attention to more recent findings indicating that innate structures and/or inherent capacities of the human brain are often a necessary *but not a sufficient* condition for the development of a mature human brain capable of knowing.

This relatively recent research (much of it done in the last decade) indicates that the capacities required for knowing (holding beliefs, having coherent experiences, and so forth) develop over time—however much the infant brain is "prepared" to learn at birth—and that the processes involved require substantive social interactions to be successful. This research is broad in its focus, studying the development of motor skills, perception, and other abilities. We pay specific attention to research in neuroscience and developmental psychology that explores the structures and mechanisms involved in first-language acquisition. First-language acquisition is a singularly important developmental achievement; one that both nativists and philosophical behaviorists—however much they disagree about how a child acquires language—recognize as necessary for conceptualization, belief formation, and the transmission and reception of information (see Pinker 1997, 1999; Quine 1960).

Why, it is sometimes asked, is research into early brain and language development relevant to naturalized epistemology? One of two views usually lies behind this question. The first is the view that the capacity for language acquisition in infants and young children is so extensive that only a "trigger" or "nudge" is needed to get the business of learning a language going, and consequently that the social aspect of language learning is minimal, and therefore of little interest to epistemology. We will argue below that this view of language acquisition conflicts with the findings of recent empirical research—alluded to above—which show that the social component of language learning is extensive and essential.

Alternatively, the relevance of early brain and language development to epistemology is sometimes challenged by those who think that the only appropriate epistemological questions concern how those who have already fully mastered a first language can be said to know. Those who hold this view seem to hold that epistemology need concern itself only with adults who are capable of knowing.

Of this second group we would ask the following questions: Why wouldn't those advocating a naturalized epistemology be interested in how language—so important for cognitive development and capacities—is actually learned, how the brain changes during the process, and in what way social interactions are crucial to these processes? How could any comprehensive theory of knowledge, let alone one based on the premise that it is important to take relevant scientific research into account, ignore the recent and dramatic findings in the neurosciences and related fields concerning brain development and social processes that help to explain how knowers come to be?

Finally, as we are among those interested in feminist and social epistemologies, we are concerned with a number of normative questions often not addressed in philosophical epistemology, naturalized or not, concerning the social factors that impede knowledge as well as those that contribute to it. On every level, from knowing in the sciences to knowing in the domain of so-called common sense, social epistemologists and feminist epistemologists (these are, of course, not mutually exclusive groups) have demonstrated that epistemic individualism is at least impoverished.

The research we discuss below supports this view by highlighting the necessary role of social interactions in the very beginning of an infant's development. As we will show, the actual story, so far as scientists now understand it, of infant and childhood development relevant to the emergence of competent language speakers, learners, and eventually knowers has significant normative implications for education policy and social policies more generally. It is just not the case, or even close to it, that because newborns come equipped with brains eminently ready to learn language, they will, by virtue of biology alone and in the absence of any specific brain disorder, seamlessly or automatically acquire language. There will be significant differences between infants provided with appropriate and extensive stimulation and those not so provided. Moreover, the significant social interactions required for first-language acquisition have already occurred by the time a child enters its first institutionalized learning situation, typically at five or six. By this age, the research we outline indicates, the die has largely been cast in the sense of necessary brain development and language skills, and only significant and informed interventions can mitigate to some extent the loss for children who have not enjoyed the requisite stimulation. We endorse the call by many neuroscientists and psychologists that the factors required for brain development and language skills, as revealed in this research, need to be "broadcast" to parents, educators, and policymakers (see, e.g., Kuhl 2007a). We see no conflict whatsoever in using what epistemologists learn from scientists to engage in socially responsible philosophy. Nor, of course, are we alone. At the 2008 meeting of the Pacific Division of the American Philosophical Association (APA), a mini-conference devoted to how to engage in socially responsible philosophy of science included many papers and sessions that were well attended. We suggest that exploring how to engage in socially responsible epistemology is an equally viable undertaking.

Our discussion is organized as follows. In section II, we engage in a preliminary discussion of developments in neuroscience that have led some in that field, as well as in developmental psychology, to describe the human brain as "a social brain," and we show how this notion is drawn upon by researchers studying how infants and young children come to acquire language. In section III, we turn to quite recent research in neuroscience that, making use of new technologies that allow for the identification of brain states and brain development in infants and young children, is changing minds in linguistics, psychology, neuroscience, and education theory about first-language acquisition. This research indicates that not only are specific, extensive, and successful interactions between infants and language-competent adults necessary for the acquisition of language, but also that to be successful such interactions must occur substantially earlier than previously assumed. For example, the ability of a seven-month-old infant to discern vowels in the language it regularly hears and no longer pay attention to the vowels of other languages to which it initially responded is highly predictive of a child's language abilities up to the age of three. These abilities are stronger and develop more rapidly in infants who have "specialized" their hearing to focus on what will be their native language than in infants who at seven months are still paying attention to the vowels and consonants of a host of languages. Infants in this second group have considerably less language ability at the age of three (Kuhl 2007a).

In section IV, we engage in a brief discussion of "a natural experiment" involving several generations of deaf children in Nicaragua who created a sophisticated sign language, Nicaraguan Sign Language, or NSL (or Idioma de Signos Nicaraguense, ISN), de novo. The emergence of NSL is often cited by nativists as evidence that the brain is so language ready that little more than a nudge will evoke a child's mastery of a language. However, a closer look at the timeline and the processes at work in the emergence of NSL reveals the necessary role of extended interpersonal experience and actually supports the claim that it is early and extensive exposure to language, along with whatever innate predisposition the brain comes with, that brings about the understanding of syntax and the acquisition of vocabulary that largely constitute the acquisition of language. Like the research outlined in section III, the Nicaraguan case indicates that language acquisition does not occur just because the human brain harbors innate capacities for language, such as the presence of "a language organ," as some suggest (e.g., Pinker 1999). First-language acquisition must occur *early*; it involves *stages and processes*, and social interactions are *necessary* for it to succeed. In section V, we briefly consider ways in which naturalized epistemologists can contribute to current efforts to institute the changes in educational and social policies that neuroscientists and developmental psychologists involved in research into first-language acquisition are calling for.

II. THE SOCIAL BRAIN

The expression "social brain" is often used to describe models of brain organization and function that emphasize the connections and networks that allow neurons and areas of the brain to "communicate." But the expression is used in a more specific way by researchers studying features of the brains of some species that cause or allow an organism's neuronal states to mimic those of another organism engaged in an activity. Key to this mimicking, many believe, are a special class of neurons, called "mirror neurons."

Some cautionary remarks are here in order concerning our use of research concerning mirror neurons. While a review of the relevant literature indicates that few neuroscientists or psychologists doubt the existence of mirror neurons, some are critical of what they regard as the "hype" surrounding their discovery and of what they view as inflated claims about the significance of these neurons and/or about the explanation of psychological capacities (e.g., empathy) in which they are invoked. As one such critic argues, the usefulness of the hypothesis that there are such neurons is often exaggerated by advocates and misunderstood or misused by those in other disciplines (Gopnik 2007). The only claim we make is that the research outlined in the next section into infant and early childhood language acquisition provides some support for the view, which is held by many of the scientists engaged in it, that mirror neurons do facilitate early childhood language acquisition. That said, it will also become clear that with or without such neurons, the claims we have made about first-language acquisition involving stages and processes that require substantial interpersonal interactions are supported by the research we later outline.

So, what are mirror neurons and what is the evidence for their existence?[2] The following account of the discovery of these neurons is not disputed. In 1991, a team of neuroscientists at the University of Parma, in Italy, were studying neuronal activity in areas of macaque monkeys' brains previously correlated with anticipating or engaging in movement. To track cell activity (neuron firings), researchers implanted electrodes in the areas of the brain they believed to be implicated in movement and connected the wires to a monitor that registered the firings of cells. They found, as their model predicted, that specific neurons in the identified areas fire just prior to a monkey's grasping or moving an object. But on one occasion they observed something their model did not predict.

A graduate student, the first to return from lunch, entered the lab in which a monkey was linked to the monitor recording neuron firings. The student was carrying an ice cream cone, and as he raised the cone to his lips, pings from the monitor indicated that neurons in the areas of the monkey's brain linked with movement were firing. This occurred even though the monkey had not moved; he had watched the student's movements. The lead researcher, Giacomo Rizzolatti, reports seeing something similar on an earlier occasion that involved a person eating peanuts in front of a macaque, but at the time he decided he couldn't have been right about what he thought he observed (Blakeslee 2006). But in subsequent experiments, the research group found that the same brain cells would fire whether a monkey brought a peanut to its mouth or observed a human or another monkey doing so. The researchers reported the same phenomenon when the activities involved cracking peanuts, peeling bananas, eating raisins, or manipulating a variety of objects.

After five years of additional research, the investigators published their findings and proposed that the brains of macaque monkeys have special kinds of neurons that fire either when a monkey carries out an action or when the monkey sees the specified action being carried out by another organism (Rizzolatti et al. 1996; cf. Rizzolatti and Craighero 2004). Since mirror neurons were first proposed, their existence and function have been supported by research devoted to a number of other species, including humans. The human brain, many neuroscientists propose, has more, smarter, and more plastic mirror neurons than other species now under study (species being studied include nonhuman primates, dolphins, and dogs). Some neuroscientists also point to evidence suggesting that, in the human brain, there are multiple mirror neuron *systems* that specialize not just in mimicking the actions of others but in understanding their intentions, the social meanings of their actions, and their emotions (Cochin et al. 1998; Oberman, Ineda, and Ramachandran 2007).[3] Mirror neurons, some neuroscientists believe, both reflect and contributed to the evolution of humans' sophisticated social abilities. Rizzolatti puts it this way:

> We [humans] are exquisitely social creatures. Our survival depends on understanding the actions, intentions, and emotions of others. Mirror neurons allow us to grasp the mind of others through direct stimulation, by feeling not by thinking. (quoted in Blakeslee 2006)

How, if at all, might mirror neurons or mirror neuron systems, together with other relevant factors, contribute to an explanation of first-language acquisition? Newborn infants do appear to have mirror neuron systems, though fewer such systems than do older children. Andrew Metlzoff at the University of Washington has published studies of the amazing ability of infants to mimic the facial expressions of adults, for example, to stick out their tongues when observing an adult sticking out his/her tongue at them (Metlzoff 1997). More to the point of the present discussion, some neuroscientists and psychologists propose that the acquisition of a first language depends in part on specific systems of mirror neurons present at birth. One such system, located in the front of the brain, contains overlapping circuitry for spoken language and sign language. In 1998, Rizzolatti and Michael Arbib of the University of Southern California proposed, based on their experiments, that the same brain machinery (machinery they take to include systems of mirror neurons) enables the complex hand gestures involved in signing as well as the complex tongue and lip movements involved in speaking (Rizzolatti and Arbib 1998). (Deaf infants engage in the equivalent of babbling common to hearing infants by gesturing with their hands.) The general hypothesis concerning the role of mirror neurons in childhood development is that these neurons enable infants and young children to internally simulate the actions of adults and imitate them, and that this capacity contributes to brain and behavioral development, including the developments associated with language acquisition. At the very least, *infants' interest in adults' actions and in imitating those actions is clearly involved in language acquisition*, as the discussion in the next section will show.

III. ACQUIRING A FIRST LANGUAGE

Until quite recently, investigations into how children learn language and, in so doing, start on the road to conceptualization and knowledge acquisition were limited to drawing inferences based on children's behavior coupled with one or another favored theory of mind.

Philosophical behaviorists, such as W. V. Quine, proposed a stimulus-response model of language acquisition, a process that takes the child beyond one-word sentences (such as "Red." and "Mama.") uttered, as Quine put it, "in appropriate presences, or as a means of inducing appropriate presences" (1960). Quine argued that it is the stimuli provided by interactions with language speakers that allows the child to move beyond one-word sentences, catch on to the recursive nature of language, and eventually produce original sentences.

In contrast, nativists such as linguist Noam Chomsky and evolutionary psychologist Steven Pinker maintain that children are born with an innate and highly structured capacity for language; for Pinker this innate structure is an adaptation, that is, the product of natural selection during the Pleistocene era and one "organ of computation" among many that together constitute the Stone Age (and current) human brain. In *How the Mind Works*, Pinker argues as follows:

> The mind is a system of organs of computation, designed by natural selection to solve the sorts of problems our ancestors faced in the foraging way of life, in particular, understanding and outmaneuvering objects, animals, plants, and other people. (Pinker 1997, p. 21; cf. Pinker 1999)

In describing the structural features of "the language organ," Pinker draws on linguistics to emphasize that information transmission in the human species requires the vocabulary and grammar and in particular the syntax that are the definitive features of language. And, in contrast with those who view language as just one among many capacities made possible by a form of "general intelligence," Pinker argues that the ability to catch on to these special features of language requires that there be parts of the brain that are dedicated to language acquisition and comprehension (Pinker 1999).

That the brain is, to some extent, specialized in the ways Pinker cites is supported by research in neuroscience that has long identified two areas of the brain as implicated in two tasks: the Broca area, which is implicated in the ability to produce language; and Wernicke's area, which is implicated in the ability to comprehend language. (Relatively recent brain imagery techniques can also pinpoint the growth of a neural loop, composed of a large number of nerve fibers, that develops between six and twelve months and connects the two areas [Kuhl 2007a].) Evidence for the role of these areas includes their activation when someone is speaking or listening, and the fact that damage to or lesions in one or both areas of the brain is strongly correlated with language disorders.

So the claim that specific areas of the brain are involved in language acquisition is supported by research in neuroscience. But questions remain. One is whether what we know about the brain's specialization constitutes prima facie evidence that language *is an adaptation*, and a *specialized* one. Noam Chomsky, who first proposed an innate language faculty to explain how quickly children catch on to the recursive structure of language, is among those who reject the view that language is an adaptation. Fortunately, whether any innate language faculty is or is not an adaptation is a question that can, for the purposes of this article, be safely left unanswered. A second question, and one we dare not ignore, is whether either the strong nativist or the strong behaviorist model of language acquisition is anything close to complete. In terms of the developing brain and first-language acquisition, there is substantial evidence that what actually occurs and is required is a robust interaction between a language-ready infant and competent language speakers. We would add, parenthetically, that we should not be surprised that an explanation of language acquisition and learning more generally involves complex interactions. The domains of the biological sciences are characterized by complex causal relations and interactions, including feedback loops and interactions among organisms and features of their environments.

Much of the research we summarize next is being done at the University of Washington's Institute of Learning and Brain Sciences. (Such research is also being undertaken in many other universities in the United States and abroad.) Researchers at the University of Washington, who come from several different sciences and specialties, are investigating the mechanisms and factors at work in the acquisition of a first language. At the institute (and at others like it), neuroscientists, biologists, and developmental psychologists have devised new methods and make use of new instruments to measure the brain activities and brain development of newborns and growing infants.

The infants involved in the research undertaken at the University of Washington institute are studied as newborns, again at 7 to 7½ months, then at 14, 18, 24, and 30 months. Patricia Kuhl, a neuroscientist who codirects the institute, reports that the findings of her group include the discovery that babies learn in ways we never imagined—and, in particular, that while some learning involves computation, there is often much more than computation at work and needed. We next summarize some significant findings that this research—at the University of Washington and elsewhere—has produced.

Initially, Kuhl and others have found, the brains of newborns are "equi-potential" in terms of the sounds of the world's 6,000 languages that they can hear, pay attention to, and will eventually be able to make. Together, the world's languages contain approximately 600 consonants and 200 vowels (Ladefoged 2001). Most recently, the initial equi-potential and subsequent specialization of an infant's brain have been studied using two methods: the infant's attention to sounds (behavior); and the infant's brain activity, measured by electroencephalograms (EEGs), which register neuronal firings, and, more recently, by MEG, or magneto encephalography, also known as magnetic source imaging (MSI). A very recent addition to the array of instruments used to study brain activity and development, MEG allows for far more precise pinpointing of brain states and brain activity than do EEGs and functional Magnetic Resonance Imaging (fMRI). MEG is also more appropriate for testing infants and young children than fMRIs (generally not recommended for children under five) because, with the exception of the language sounds it introduces to infants, it is relatively silent (Kuhl 2007a).

The experimental setup of the behavioral studies undertaken at the University of Washington institute is as follows. Infants are taught, typically over twenty sessions, to respond with a specific turn of the head when the sounds they are hearing (the sounds of individual vowels, for example) change; this training involves rewards for head turning when appropriate (e.g., the appearance of vivid puppets in the infant's field of vision).

Experiments involving behavior and brain imaging indicate that over a relatively short period of time, approximately 7½ months,

what was, in the newborn, an equi-potential brain becomes specialized in terms of its neural commitments. This commitment occurs as
the infant is immersed in a world where, typically, she hears one language. In terms of behavior, she no longer responds to sounds to
which she responded earlier (Kuhl 2007a; Kuhl 2007b). Relevant
experiments, many involving international teams of scientists and
making use of both behavior and brain activity, confirm this specialization. For example, a 7½-month infant raised in a Japanese-
speaking environment no longer, though she had earlier, responds
differently to "la" and "ra," although an infant at the same age raised
in an English-speaking environment retains the distinction. An
infant raised in a Japanese setting also responds—in terms of neuronal activity and behavior—to the five vowels Japanese contains,
but no longer to the multitude of vowels to which she initially, like
infants generally, did respond. An infant raised in an English-
speaking environment no longer responds, as she did initially, to distinctions in vowels that are part of Mandarin Chinese. And an infant
raised in an English-speaking environment maintains a distinction
between "pa" and "ba" that an infant of the same age raised in a
Spanish-speaking environment does not. The location of neuronal
firings (identified through the use of EEGs), and brain imagery (identified using MEG), indicates that a mapping of the infant brain takes
place over time and in response to auditory experiences—but not
any auditory experiences, as we shall later explain.

Linguist Judy Kegl, who is involved in research into sign language
acquisition and was one of the first linguists to study the emergence
of NSL in Nicaragua as it was occurring, summarizes the findings of
research into first-language acquisition in this way:

> Infants are born with "language-ready brains": a brain with an
> expectation of language and what language is like but requiring
> social input at specific stages for the neurological development that
> enables language. (Kegl 2002, p. 207)

That the "input" Kegl speaks of is interpersonal is supported experimentally. To Pinker's computational model, for example, we need to
add that although infants do engage in statistical thinking as they
listen to the sounds of language to determine which sounds to pay

attention to (i.e., sounds common to the language in which they are immersed), they apparently do not engage in such computations in the absence of face-to-face interactions with humans. Neither video recordings nor auditory recordings engage their attention or bring about the changes in their ability to respond to and discriminate among sounds as measured by behavioral experiments and brain imagery (Kuhl 2007a). Indeed, when six-month-old infants are tested using MEG, there is more brain activity related to discriminating sounds when an adult is simultaneously engaging the child with a variety of facial expressions and colorful toys (Kuhl 2007a).

Another experiment demonstrates the role of social interaction in language learning. As noted above, by the age of 7½ months, the sounds to which an infant's brain responds, and to which she responds behaviorally, have been "pruned down" to the vowels of the language to which she has been exposed (Kuhl 2007b). And as earlier noted, at this age, infants born into English-speaking environments show far less ability to recognize the different vowels of Mandarin than children surrounded by that language—though as we have seen, initially infants respond to all the vowels they hear. (Mandarin Chinese is quite different from English. It is a tonal language, in which it is the different pitch of a syllable that differentiates words.)

But experiments undertaken at the University of Washington institute indicate that if, between the ages of 8 and 10 months, these same infants (those raised in English-speaking environments) engage with speakers who, in the interactions, speak only Mandarin, they reacquire their previously "lost" ability to discriminate the vowels of Mandarin. The experiments introduce the infants to Mandarin speakers over twelve sessions, with each session involving four adults speaking only Mandarin and engaging the infants' attention by using play toys and books, exaggerating their vowels and consonants, and drawing the infants' attention to follow the adults' gaze to specific objects as words are spoken. After the sessions, the abilities of the infants to recognize, discriminate, and attend to sounds of Mandarin are indistinguishable from those of children of the same age raised in Taiwan. As one would expect, a control group meeting for the same amount of time with English speakers did not reacquire the ability to discriminate the vowels of Mandarin (Kuhl 2007a).

That human interaction, as both Kegl and Kuhl argue, is essential to language acquisition is supported by additional experiments, only some of which we can summarize here. In one such experiment, two adults stand or sit in front of an infant when an auditory recording of sentences from any language is playing. Only one of the adults moves his lips, and this is the only adult to which the infant will pay attention. Similarly, and as noted earlier, experiments show that infants do not respond, in terms of either neuronal activity or attention, to auditory recordings or to speakers on TV screens, even when the sounds are those of their "native" language. Kuhl and others attribute these differences to mirror neurons. Whether or not this is the correct explanation, it is clear that from infancy it is interaction with speaking persons that brings about the brain activity and development (however primed the newborn brain is) that ultimately result in language acquisition (e.g., Kuhl 2007a; Liu, Tsao, and Kuhl 2007). And, indeed, long before mirror neurons were discovered (or postulated), and long before the kinds of experiments currently under way were feasible, linguists and social psychologists offered compelling arguments for the claim that the acquisition of language requires extensive social interaction (e.g., Tomasello and Farrar 1986).

Kuhl's research group and others have undertaken voice analyses, involving pitch and physics, that compare "parent-ese" (or, as it is now called, "infant-directed speech," or I-D) with adult-directed speech, or A-D. The predominance of I-D in mothers and other adults when they interact with an infant is well documented. Voice analyses indicate that not only does I-D include more frequent changes in pitch than A-D, but vowel and consonant sounds are articulated for a much longer period of time, or are more stretched out, than in A-D. This extended time also allows caregivers to use their gaze, together with ostension, to draw an infant's attention to connections between sounds and objects. These factors, Kuhl and others hypothesize, serve to reinforce the sounds of what will be the infant's first language (Liu, Tsao, and Kuhl 2007).

There is additional evidence for the role of I-D in language acquisition. Second-language acquisition becomes increasingly difficult after the age of seven, declining precipitously with age, as the neuronal commitment that occurs early in life would predict. But using the findings concerning the role of I-D in promoting language acquisition in infants, researchers in Japan have experimented with using I-D rather than A-D to teach English to Japanese adults. While the adults do not respond to differences in pitch between I-D and A-D, they do apparently respond to the elongation of sounds and learn English more quickly (Kuhl 2007a).

Findings in the research we have summarized attest to the fact that the acquisition of a first language is a *developmental process that requires extensive interpersonal interaction*—however prepared the infant brain is to learn and embrace language. The most significant brain development occurs over a period of roughly three years and continues to the age of seven. This is also the case in terms of development in the two areas Pinker and others correctly cite as language centers: the Broca area and Wernicke's area. MEG tests indicate that there is neuronal activity in the Broca area in newborns, but apparently none in the Wernicke's area. With time and appropriate input, the Wernicke's area also displays neuronal activity, first at 6 months and even more so at 12 months, and between 6 and 12 months synchrony between the areas begins to occur and strengthen (Kuhl 2007a).

Finally, there are cases, including a relatively recent case, of infants and small children deprived of social interaction during the period critical to language acquisition, who, after being found, were never able to master more than a few vocabulary words or to grasp syntax. In the recent case, a child called "Genie" by the scientists who worked with her was raised in virtually complete isolation from other persons and language until she was discovered at age fourteen. Thus, her isolation extended beyond the critical period. For four years, a team of linguists and psychologists attempted to teach her language, but no amount of social interaction or language immersion was sufficient for her to acquire language; specifically, although "Genie" learned some vocabulary, she was never able to construct a syntactically correct sentence.[4] We can assume that, in many such cases, the relevant brain structures and capacities were present at birth, but the lack of appropriate and extensive social interaction, of the kinds outlined above, precluded the acquisition of language.[5]

In addition to the apparently crucial role of interpersonal interactions in enabling first-language acquisition, the research just summarized indicates that language acquisition proceeds *in stages* and *over time*. It is not solely the outcome of the infant's brain structures and capacities, and it is not immediate.

IV. "A NATURAL EXPERIMENT"

The apparent development de novo of a sign language by deaf Nicaraguan children has been cited by nativists and evolutionary psychologists as evidence of an innate "language organ" that needs little to "trigger" its development (see, e.g., Pinker 1997).

The generally accepted account of the development of NSL (Nicaraguan Sign Language) is as follows. After the Sandinista Revolution in the late 1970s, the Nicaraguan government embarked on an ambitious program to improve literacy. Included in the program were Nicaragua's numerous deaf children, who—because of cultural beliefs—had previously not been allowed to attend public schools (or were enrolled in schools for the "retarded"), not been allowed to socialize with other deaf children (or, for the most part, with hearing children, other than siblings), and not been allowed to marry. There were no schools for deaf children, no associations for the deaf, no social support systems for them or their families, and no sign languages.

Given these factors, and because most deaf children (99 percent) are born to hearing households, most deaf children in Nicaragua (as well as deaf adults) were what linguists term "language isolates": communication was limited to "home signs"—more accurately, gestures—typically idiosyncratic to particular families. The distinction between signs and gestures is important. Gestures are body signs, a form of nonverbal communication. In contrast, a sign includes syntax and a sign language includes syntactical rules and morphemes.

The first deaf children to attend schools for the deaf in Nicaragua were in their early to late teens. They showed a decided lack of interest in learning American Sign Language, or ASL, signers of which had been brought in to teach them sign language. They were far more interested in interacting with each other using the gestures ("home signs") they brought with them. As they worked to communicate, they increasingly used "pantomime-like" gestures, rather than the home signs with which they first arrived. Within several years (not immediately as some accounts would suggest), their vocabulary grew and their signs became less gestural and more fluid. Within a decade the first and second cohorts of children had developed a method of communicating distinct from ASL and unrelated to Spanish, the spoken language of the region. By the late 1980s, they had developed a sign language that included syntax as well as vocabulary—the first version of NSL (Kegl, Senghas, and Coppola 1999; Kegl 2002; Senghas 2005).

But it wasn't until the third and fourth cohorts, who entered the school in the 1990s at an average age of five to seven, that NSL developed to the point where it was as capable of communicating ideas and sentences as complex as those possible in ASL and spoken languages. For these younger children, who were being introduced to an *already existing* sign language and *during* the critical period for language acquisition, early communication was not difficult at all. Still within the critical window for mastering syntax, they began to impose stricter and more detailed rules on the language. The earlier cohorts, now adults, have not been able to master the syntax that the younger children imposed, and the older group's vocabulary is a good deal smaller than that of the younger group. Ann Senghas, a linguist who observed and studied the development of NSL, answers the question of "Why did NSL arise when it did?" in this way:

> More deaf people were socializing together than ever before. . . . They were meeting at a younger age. . . . Young deaf children had frequent contact with deaf adolescents for the first time. . . . Deaf people were staying in contact for a longer time, from childhood to adulthood. (Senghas n.d.; cf. Senghas 2005)

And, Senghas adds, "Nicaraguan Sign Language came from the same place that all languages came from—human minds, trying to connect with other human minds" (Senghas n.d.).

The nativist rightly claims that, in this case, there is support for an innate ability for, or predisposition to, language acquisition—a claim that interactionists such as we don't deny. And several aspects of this case strongly support a robust interactionist model, rather than a purely nativist model, of language acquisition. Whatever innate structures were in place, neither the older children of the first and second cohorts, nor the younger children of the third and fourth cohorts, acquired anything remotely resembling language *until* they were interacting with each other. Moreover, the lateness of the introduction of language to the older children explains why they have never caught up with the younger students in terms of the number of vocabulary words and syntactical rules acquired. And this is also (and sadly) true for deaf children born into hearing families in countries like the United States whose deafness is not immediately diagnosed and whose parents do not know a sign language. (Recall that 99 percent of deaf infants are born to hearing parents.) All too often, the delay and/or the lack of sign language on the part of these parents results in a child far less able to sign than are deaf children born to deaf and signing parents, or exposed early to others who are proficient in sign language. The link between gaze and ostension, noted above as facilitating hearing infants' acquisition of language, is seamless in the case of signing mothers, but labored and inconsistent in the case of hearing mothers, who are trying to simultaneously learn a language and teach it to their infant. Moreover, deaf mothers (and sign language–proficient adults generally) engage in I-D signing with infants, exaggerating through elongation the signs they present. As with language acquisition generally, studies show that if deaf children have not mastered a sign language by ten years of age, their skills will be very limited, as will be their sense of self and their ability to develop a theory of mind (see, e.g., Kegl 2002).

The general lesson is that both the early and the later versions of NSL, like language acquisition among speaking children and that among deaf children, did not emerge immediately. The emergence of NSL, like language acquisition generally, involved time and processes, including interventions on the part of adults who could hear and sign, and who introduced cartoons and other visual aids to encourage the children to use signs to tell the story they were watching or describe the pictures they were viewing.

V. IMPLICATIONS

We conclude with a brief discussion of what we take to be some epistemological and ethical implications of the research we have described. If, as we take this research to suggest, individualism in terms of language acquisition is untenable, that is, if language acquisition requires a robust social interactionism, then epistemologists who are naturalists should consider what implications this research carries for our efforts to understand knowing and knowers. We should as well consider the social/ethical implications of this research.

Some may want to insist on the inapplicability of the conceptual analyses characteristic of epistemology to social and ethical issues, relying perhaps on something like the traditional view that one cannot derive an "ought" from an "is." But this would be a very strange position, it seems to us, for a philosopher committed to naturalism to adopt. Any accounts of how children develop cognitively and acquire language skills, insofar as such accounts are based on empirical results and open to philosophical analyses of their implications, are obviously relevant to social and educational policies for they clearly suggest what will and will not help children to succeed in developing such skills.

Many neuroscientists and developmental psychologists view the research we have summarized as of fundamental importance to attempts to restructure social and educational policy. They have met with legislators and governors of their states, and spoken to parents' groups and educators to inform them of the practical implications of their research into language acquisition. (Indeed, Patricia Kuhl was one of several scientists asked to participate in a small conference devoted to childhood psychological development hosted by Bill and Hillary Clinton while Bill Clinton was president.)

Given all of this, why wouldn't a naturalist follow suit, having abandoned a priori reasoning in favor of empirical research results? Indeed, philosophical insights based in part on empirical research results are recognized as important in a number of areas—among them bioethics, cognitive science, and the philosophy of science—and frequently contribute to debates and analyses of issues in the relevant sciences and practices. Why shouldn't they also be advanced in those areas of childhood development crucial to the emergence of knowers?

Put another way, why shouldn't the future of naturalized epistemology include engagement with social and ethical issues to which our analyses of the implications of empirical studies are clearly relevant?

NOTES

1. Goldman's title referenced "social epistemics," rather than social epistemology, and this of course is significant, given that many self-described naturalists do not share Goldman's interest in retaining the traditional emphases on truth, justification, and related notions.

2. Indeed, the answers we provide here to these questions are highly truncated and general, as space limitations preclude discussion of the various kinds and locations of mirror neurons that neuroscientists identify. Those details are not important to the arguments we make here. But the articles we reference include substantial bibliographies that those interested can use to further explore the research.

3. The ability to gather evidence for human mirror neuron systems was considerably improved by the development of new technologies, including GED (which we discuss in the next section). fMRI's were not able to record more than activation in areas of the brain where it was thought such systems were. Cochin and colleagues 1998 are frequently cited as reporting on the breakthroughs and findings made possible by MEG.

4. There are several firsthand accounts of this case written by the scientists who were involved. Unfortunately, professional ambition seems to have played a role in the continuity of "Genie's" care, and the accounts often include finger pointing at others involved. See, e.g., Rymer 1994.

5. In the case of "Genie," it is unlikely that we will know, unless an autopsy reveals relevant details, whether she was cognitively challenged from birth (as her father believed; this led to his insisting on her isolation) or whether the extreme isolation she suffered until the age of fourteen was responsible for her inability to learn language. By the time she was fourteen, the kinds of test of brain activity and function available in the 1960s indicated spikes in the left hemisphere associated with mental impairment. But this does not, given today's knowledge of how the hemispheres develop, constitute evidence that the spikes were not the result of her extreme isolation.

REFERENCES

Blakeslee, S. 2006. "Cells That Read Minds." *New York Times*, January 10.

Cochin, S. C. Barthelemy, B. Lejeune, S. Roux, J. Martineau, et al. 1998. "Perception of Motion and qEEG Activity in Human Adults." *Electroencephalography and Clinical Neurophysicology* 107, no. 4: 287–95.

Goodman, A. 1987. "Foundations of Social Epistemics." *Synthese* 73: 109–44.

Gopnik, A. 2007. "Cells That Read Minds?" Special issue on Neuroscience and Neuroculture, *Slate*, April. http://www.slate.com/id/2165123.

Kegl, J. A. 2002. "Language Emergence in a Language-Ready Brain: Acquisition." In *Directions in Sign Language Acquisition*, edited by G. Morgan and B. Woll, 207–54. Amsterdam: John Benjamins.

Kegl, J., A. Senghas, and M. Coppola. 1999. "Creation through Contact: Sign Language Emergence and Sign Language Change in Nicaragua." In *Language Creation and Language Change: Creolization, Diachrony, and Development*, edited by M. DeGraff, 179–237. Cambridge, MA: MIT Press.

Kuhl, P. 2007a. "Early Learning, the Brain, and Society." The Provost's Distinguished Lecture, University of Washington.

———. 2007b. "Is Speech Learning 'Gated' by the Social Brian?" *Developmental Science* 10, no. 1: 110–20.

Ladefoged, P. 2001. *Vowels and Consonants: An Introduction to the Sounds of Language*. Oxford: Blackwell.

Liu, H., F. Tsao, and P. Kuhl. 2007. "Acoustic Analysis of Lexical Tone in Mandarin Infant-Directed Speech." *Developmental Psychology* 43, no. 4: 912–17.

Meltzoff, A. N. 1997. "Explaining Facial Imitation: A Theoretical Model." *Early Development and Parenting* 6: 179–92.

Oberman, L., J. A. Ineda, and V. S. Ramachandran. 2007. "The Human Mirror System: A Link between Action Observation and Social Skills." *Social Cognitive and Affective Neuroscience* 2, no. 1: 62–66.

Pinker, S. 1994. *The Language Instinct: How the Mind Creates Language*. New York: William Morrow.

———. 1997. *How the Mind Works*: New York: W.W. Norton.

———. 1999. *Words and Rules: The Ingredients of Language*. New York: HarperCollins.

Quine, W. V. 1960. *Word and Object*. Cambridge, MA: Harvard University Press.

Rizzolatti, G., and M. A. Arbib. 1998. "Language within Our Grasp." *Trends in Neuroscience* 21, no. 5: 188–94.

Rizzolatti, G., and L. Craighero. 2004. "The Mirror-Neuron System." *Annual Review of Neuroscience* 27: 169–92.

Rizzolatti G., L. Fadiga, V. Gallese, and L. Fogase. 1996. "Premotor Cortex and the Recognition of Motor Actions." *Cognitive Brain Research* 3: 131–41.

Rymer, R. 1994. *Genie: A Scientific Tragedy*. New York: HarperCollins.

Schmitt, F., ed. 1994. *Socializing Epistemology*. Lanham, MD: Rowman & Littlefield.

Senghas, A. n.d. "Where Did Nicaraguan Sign Language Come From?" http://www.columbia.edu/~as1038/L02-sign-langage.html.

———. 1995. "The Development of Nicaraguan Sign Language via the Language Acquisition Process." *Proceedings of the Boston University Conference on Language Development*, edited by D. MacLaughlin and S. McEwen. Boston: Cascadilla Press.

_____. 2005. "Language Emergence: Clues from a New Bedouin Sign Language." *Current Biology* 15: 12, 463–65.

Tomasello, M., and M. J. Farrar. 1986. "The Key Is Social Cognition." In *Language and Thought*, edited by D. Gentner and S. Kuczaj, 47–58. Cambridge, MA: MIT Press.

13.

Naturalism's Unfinished Project: Making Philosophy More Scientific

Randall Dipert

I. INTRODUCTION

It is not surprising that the scientifically informed progressives of the late nineteenth and early twentieth centuries surveyed human accomplishment over its history and across many domains—religion, the arts, history, literature—but saw in mathematics and the physical sciences the only places they thought had made genuine progress. With science progressing by fits and starts in ancient Greek society, and then rising and being more widely disseminated through printing in the late Renaissance and early modern era, it would have been hard for philosophically thoughtful people to look at most of human intellectual and cultural history and not to think of modern science and mathematics in a uniquely positive way. There exists in science and mathematics progress, pride, and genuine respect for competitors; and virtually no wars have been caused on their account. So many philosophers around the year 1900 who were knowledgeable about science saw almost at the same time that philosophy should do something more like *this*, to think like scientists do.

Naturalism, like pragmatism, is best described as a "big tent" movement, methodology, or clutch of metaphilosophical claims. Naturalism is a diffuse doctrine of such breadth and fuzziness as to be almost useless without a great deal of scrutiny. Nevertheless, naturalism in philosophy identifies something that broadly links together philosophers influenced by the methods and claims of the natural sciences. Its mainly American origins (at least under the label "naturalist") have merged in the mid-twentieth century with similar views concerning philosophy and science stemming from Mach and Helmholtz and then articulated by the Vienna and Berlin schools. In its originally American context especially, naturalism rejected supernatural explanations in natural evolution and cosmology.

Many authors separate the broad naturalist doctrine into at least two parts—ontological naturalism and methodological naturalism. Ontological naturalism makes a claim about the general metaphysical nature of reality and what science tells us about it. Roughly this has come to be articulated as the view that physical phenomena are causally closed: the causes of physical events are themselves all physical and the effects of physical events are likewise all physical. The former causal direction is more important, since all *explanations* of physical events are to be physical; one could apparently tolerate a physical world's influence on a nonphysical world. The second aspect of naturalism is typically called methodological naturalism, and it does not seek to import science-influenced metaphysics, but rather seeks to bring scientific methods to bear on philosophical problems. One way to do this is, for example, to use the conclusions or assumptions of the sciences in philosophy, but not to support ontological claims. I will have much more to say about methodological naturalism.

II. ONTOLOGICAL NATURALISM

First, some observations about ontological naturalism. In this view, the physical world is taken to constitute the whole of nature, and its structure—that which requires explanations—is exhausted by causal relationships. Curiously this view does not precisely rule out supernatural entities, for they could exist in their own, causally closed world. There could be a material world, a mind world, a world of gods, and a spirit world—or a Lewisian possible physical world—each causally isolated from the actual physical world but possibly not from each other. The modern interpretation of naturalism as causal closure thus does not precisely rule out what the antisupernaturalists intended to rule out, although it does block the causal influence of gods on the material world.

The recent interest in causal closure has centered not on perplexities of the interactions of the physical with gods, but on the interactions of the physical with minds, specifically on describing in naturalistic ways the exact connection between mental events and physical events.

But what exactly would be the epistemological status of this causal closure principle? Shouldn't we approach this principle with the "scientific spirit"—anticipating the methodological naturalism we will later discuss? Is the principle analytically true? Otherwise a priori? A posteriori and well justified by evidence?

The case for causal closure of physical phenomena, and thus the status of the principle, is, however, a disturbing one. One could say there is massive evidence for it—consisting of every physical event originally taken to have an occult cause but, after sometimes centuries of hard work, turning out to have a physical explanation. However, evidence is evidence, and it is then obvious that every as yet unexplained physical phenomenon should count *against* causal closure. This would include most of human psychology and certainly most social events: we do not even have remotely complete "local" laws of, say, the interaction of nations, or of a national economy. We certainly do not have any semblance of laws that connect these largely unexplained events to biological and historical facts, and these to chemical facts, and these to subatomic ones. One might suggest that we know enough to *surmise* that the relationship between international relations (or neurology) and biochemistry is like the relationship that once existed between chemistry and subatomic physics.

However, precisely that analogy, with chemistry and physics, is problematic. First, we do not have anything like general laws of the neurology of thought, or of international relations, that are like the extremely robust understanding of chemistry in about 1920. Second, and this is a bizarre story that is becoming better known, the story of the reduction of chemistry to physics is much more convoluted and strange than most would guess. In 1929, the British physicist Paul Dirac asserted that chemistry had actually been reduced to physics. Perhaps on closer questioning he would have said that the general ways in which chemical laws were related to physics were fully understood, and all that remained were the details.

The general theory of how chemicals combine is relatively well explained by valence and the organization of electron shells, and these and atomic weight and number were of course relatively well understood even in 1900. However, it turns out that most of the properties of medium-sized pieces of these pure elements or compounds, and how they are related to atomic and subatomic structure, were not understood at all. These are things like boiling and freezing points, heat of fusion, color, specific heat, ductility, electrical conductivity, and so on—almost everything we need to know in order to use these substances. A whole new field had to be developed, quantum chromodynamics, in order to calculate from diverse quantum and field effects what the ordinary physical properties of things were. It took some time after Dirac's statement until hydrogen, helium, and lithium were understood in this sense. An enormous amount of calculation is involved, solving hundreds of simultaneous equations using thousands of iterated operations. In the 1980s and 1990s, many more chemical properties of ordinary elements of medium atomic weight were "reduced" to their subatomic interactions, and since then the superficial physical properties of many simple compounds have been derived. The projections of quantum chromodynamics do accord with empirical results—but not yet for substances as complex as larger proteins. On the other hand, the physical characteristics of thousands of compounds were known empirically for hundreds of years, but an understanding in terms of the underlying physics of why, say, a compound is red or melts at 50°C has not been achieved until very recently or is still unachieved today. The difficulty has been twofold. First, the derivations were of astounding computational complexity. Second, the subbranch of particle physics itself, integrating quantum effects into the behavior of whole atomic systems, as opposed to quantum theories of the behavior of single photons or electrons, simply did not exist. And finally, in order to come out with results that matched those of an already perfectly mature empirical chemistry, many corrections had to be made to our precise understandings of the interactions of quantum and field effects.

Fine. This is a fascinating story, with the reduction of chemistry to physics more or less eventually triumphing in the way Dirac prematurely asserted. But my interest is this: what exactly was the epistemic status of "Chemistry reduces to physics" when Dirac said it in 1929 and during all the decades until a few years ago, with the maturing of quantum chromodynamics and vastly improved computational capacity? Essentially we couldn't during this period really explain some obvious observation like why chlorophyll is green. We are fortunate our students aren't more curious and demanding.

Dirac's assertion amounted, I think, at best to a hope or surmise. Or, more charitably, it was not a claim but a coach's motivational remark to his team that they will eventually win if they think they can. It cannot have been a reasonably justified scientific claim, and was some other sort of speech act.

Such claims as causal closure and determinism have, as nearly as I can determine, precisely and only the character of plausible motivational assertions for the home team of natural scientists. They are not empirically justified, they are not conceptually or intuitively true (in any worthwhile sense), and they are not necessary presuppositions of science. It is very important for the persistence of inquiry that one should always believe there is an explanation, ideally a physical one, for most or even all events. It may be noble and helpful to act in this way, but it doesn't make it true or even justified. I am not sure that we should even characterize our attitude to such propositions as properly belief: we do not, so to speak, act on them as a principle with a confidence that is exactly proportional to our justification; we act on them with vastly more confidence. And scientists do not really wonder if causal closure is true. I balk at calling such a principle a "belief": it is action-guiding enough for many pragmatists to accept it as a belief, but it does not prompt genuine inquiry and is not maintained to the degree to which it has evidence.

One of the few philosophers of science who has seen clearly that there is a theoretical problem with the exact status of such principles as causal closure and determinism was Charles S. Peirce. Ten years in advance of quantum theory, and for clear-thinking philosophical reasons rather than for reasons arising out of empirical or theoretical results, he rejected determinism. In some ways it is a natural outcome of his much earlier critique of Descartes' criteria of clear and distinct intuitions, and of his attack on the a priori method of fixing belief in his famous papers from the late 1870s. His immediate targets then were, of course, Kant's synthetic a priori truths of space and time and the principle of universal causation. We may indeed have strong intuitions that space is Euclidean and has three dimensions, but that is undoubtedly because that is all we need to get food and reproduce.[1]

Peirce's thoroughgoing methodological naturalism—before the term existed—is evident. A priori principles were the last bastions of the antiscientific rascals. A related theme was Peirce's fallibilism—but that is a subtle doctrine that we can't go into here. It was based on workaday laboratory methods rather than the "seminary" attitude he saw in people who endorse universal statements such as determinism or causal closure with weak evidence. In short, if you think a belief *in* causal closure is the essence of naturalism, get thee to a nunnery! On the other hand, most ghost stories have indeed turned out to be demonstrably false; I am not sure that amounts to a philosophical principle or a method.

There is much more that could be said about the issues connected with ontological naturalism. One task would be to deal with a whole raft of topics such as reduction, supervenience, emergentism, explanation, and so on. I think, however, that some preliminary spadework on simpler issues is necessary. Causal closure of the physical, after all, involves not *one* but *two* problematic notions—what a cause is and what counts as physical. I think it is wrongheaded to see scientific explanation as exclusively causal in any very simple sense. Does force cause acceleration, or does mass cause warping of spacetime, or does gravity cause the moon to stay in its orbit? The simultaneity of cause and effect seems to suggest not a classical notion of cause but a broader notion of functional dependence or grounding.

Likewise, if the *best explanation* of a repeated phenomena appears to be that the effect precedes the cause, then I would not rule this out a priori because of some bugaboo about backward causation. Causal relationships between events or event-types are one species of functional dependence in which time of occurrence occupies an argument position.

The problem of what precisely counts as physical is likewise not unproblematic. As Papaneu notes, action at a distance was once regarded as more aligned with theological than naturalistic explanations. In the late nineteenth century, the occurrences of magicians' tricks and of mental phenomena occurring independently of ordinary physical ones were taken seriously. Our mythology, religions, and literature require a fictional belief in minds without bodies and there does not seem to be any logical inconsistency in so supposing. Scientists like Leipzig astronomer J. K. F. Zöllner[2] and George Bruce Halsted proposed a fourth spatial dimension as a possible explanation—they argued that it was only a restriction to three-dimensional spatial conceptions of the physical that made mental phenomena appear nonphysical, whereas they were perfectly lawlike and causally integrated into a theory with four spatial dimensions. We laugh at them, but string theory proposes ten or more dimensions as an explanation of phenomena so that they can be better explained within a closed physical model. I myself think we'd do better to add dimensions to our explananda one at a time. Although various definitions of what is physical have been proposed, occurring or existing in space and time has a seemingly privileged place. I distinguish sharply the physical, which includes shadows, holes, surfaces, sounds, and many physical events and processes, from material entities. As we have just seen with the role of dimensionality in physical theory, adding dimensions can cover a lot of ill-understood territory without violating the spatiality of the closed "physical" world—but this is almost as suspicious as adding supernatural entities. At the same time I don't think naturalism, as the most scientifically motivated of ontologies, without regard to any empirical data, should assert that only laws with regard to three-dimensional space count as legitimate. The philosophers' simple criterion for physicality of "being in space and time" is not a simple matter: entities can have some but lack other spatial properties and the criterion's usefulness as an ontological criterion is extended into the realm of unfalsifiability when the notion of space is allowed to veer from classical physics with regard to dimensionality, locality and co-locality, topology, and discreteness.

III. METHODOLOGICAL NATURALISM

I would like to turn now to methodological naturalism, broadly described as the effort to import science into philosophy. This will also take us back to probe further underjustified intuitions. The importation of science into philosophy can occur in two ways: one is to require the theories of philosophy to accommodate mainly, or exclusively, scientific findings. The primary data of philosophy are simply to be the current data of the most successful scientific theories, preferably foundational ones. Such views are associated with Quine and also with more extreme views that are labeled scientistic. The second type of importation of science into methodological naturalism is the use of "something like" the scientific method in philosophy itself. On the face of it, this would seem very appealing. After all, scientific and mathematical investigations over thousands of years have produced a large body of widely agreed upon knowledge, if there is any knowledge. Philosophy, by contrast, has produced little or nothing that is widely agreed upon. (I believe there are conclusive results in philosophy concerning *flaws* with various theories, some sufficient conclusively to reject these theories altogether.)

I want to sketch two broad areas in which Anglo-American philosophy appears to have failed to be scientific. The first is a bit of a cheap shot and is what I would call a *collateral professional failure* to live up to naturalism. The second is by no means a cheap shot and is a more substantive and direct form of failure, or even a kind of false naturalism.

III. A. COLLATERAL FAILURE TO BE GOOD NATURALISTS

Most professional philosophers are primarily teachers. It is only through grossly inadequate or improper teaching that they can lose their jobs, and the nature of their largely implicit minimal contract with their institutions is to teach. But here is a striking contradiction: most naturalistic philosophers make no pretence of doing their teaching, this main activity of their professional activity, in a scientific way. This would presumably begin with the identification of some clear propositional- or skill-knowledge and then examine rationally, but especially empirically, what the best proven methods are for imparting this propositional- or skill-knowledge

For various reasons, the teaching of logic and critical thinking probably constitutes the area most amenable to these empirical methods, and thus constitutes the most conspicuous case of philosophers failing to be good naturalists. But is there something clearly identifiable as "thinking critically"? One indication that this is a real phenomenon or activity would be that we can measure it. But philosophers-as-educators are mainly of the "I know it when I see it" school and have scarcely ever wondered whether "critical thinking" is a coherent and real, measurable phenomenon in the world. Now let's assume it is (there is a Cornell Test of Critical Thinking, for example) and there is a great deal of evidence from the revised SAT, LSAT, and GRE that there are valid and stable factors strongly associated with analytical thinking. One would also think that, if philosophers were true to their claim to respect science, they would first attempt to identify and measure this skill (perhaps along multiple dimensions) and would then collect empirical evidence, or look for research on such evidence, on how best to impart this skill to students. In logic, or at least in the tasks of understanding notation and producing deductions, these are still more obviously measurable skills, and undoubtedly there are deductive theories and notations that are measurably more effectively taught by some methods. But except for isolated philosophers reading or writing for *Teaching Philosophy* and several individuals I know of through the Computers and Philosophy APA group, almost no one does this. Our textbooks or software do not advertise their approach in terms of anything like data supporting their effectiveness. We are clearly not being scientists here, despite naturalist philosophers' commitment to empirical investigation. Our teaching has more in common with praying: we pray or hope that there is something called critical thinking (and that it is generally intellectually desirable) and we pray especially that our teaching methods do indeed impart this skill. Many of us feel strongly about this. Actually there is a more precise analogy: it is more like traditional pottery making in the sense that we are practicing a trade and then using the methods that have been used on us, with minor changes.

Likewise, in our teaching and assessment practices we are often forced to use multiple choice and true/false tests. There are well-known, highly researched techniques for determining various respects in which such questions are good or bad from the resulting data. Social scientists—often the butt of many of our jokes—frequently use statistical analyses of testing very critically; to a lesser extent, natural scientists and mathematicians do too. Very few philosophers do: the data gathering is troublesome and the techniques of analysis are almost unknown to them. We continue to create miserable tests and judge students unfairly according to them. If only we would, as professionals, avail ourselves of a little empiricism and a little mathematics.

This critique of "collateral failure to be true to methodological naturalism" is flawed in minor ways. Machine-graded, in-class tests are now rare—although online tests would be even more amenable to statistical analyses. Also, such statistical methods are not worth the trouble if the number of students is relatively small. Furthermore, someone might protest that he is a thoroughgoing naturalist in his philosophical theorizing, but admittedly uses the scientific method rarely in everyday life; what I am demanding is more that philosophers be like educational engineers rather than scientists—applying the best available science to the design and use of artifacts. An automotive engineer who refused to apply his experience and theories in repairing his own car, and yet cared about the car's resulting state, would be a peculiarly flawed human being. My critique, if it is to stand, relies on what I would call a whole-person or life-integrated conception of what counts as being committed to naturalism. Others might argue that naturalist philosophers have a right to be unscientific in some areas of their lives. Cooking is enjoyed partly because it isn't chemistry. I do not find this view plausible here, for the simple reason that the quality of our teaching and tests has implications for others' skills and knowledge, which is in some clear sense our professional and civic responsibility.

III. B. SUBSTANTIAL FAILURES TO BE NATURALISTS

In this section I will primarily target the use of intuitions in ethics, but I will also make a few remarks about their use in ontology. As is well known, ethical theories are frequently supported, or undermined, by the use of supposedly clear and shared intuitions about test cases. These are lifeboat cases, trolley cases, and so on. The cases I am interested in are realistic like these, in a way that many thought experiments aren't. They are like the ordinary dilemmas we face, and it is even possible we will encounter situations relevantly like these; they are in nearby possible worlds where, if we have implicit rules or internal intuitive mechanisms, it is likely they arose to deal with cases like these. Likewise, scenarios to extract intuitions for military ethics are acceptable even if philosophers rarely carry their trusty M-4s. On the other hand, extracting intuitions about thought experiments like the Veil of Ignorance, about an experience machine, and perhaps about the evil demon and zombies, is more problematic. Whatever the intuiting faculties are here, they did not arise in order to deal with scenarios like these. In fact, it is hard to say how such faculties arose, what they are for, and how reliably they guide us to the truth. Ultimately, for a naturalist at least, a theory of the genesis of these intuitive mechanisms is extremely important. We, post-Darwin, cannot use moral sense theories. These latter situations are in remote, and in some cases, almost unimaginably distant possible worlds; we cannot meaningfully contemplate all the facts and physical laws that would have to be different for them to obtain.

It is relatively clear that in all of these cases, including the more realistic moral intuitions, these intuitions are used, science-like, as data points that support, confirm, or disconfirm a moral theory. Some authors are explicit about this use of an empirical, scientific method. A recent and positive development in contemporary philosophy, experimental philosophy, collects actual data about diverse people's intuitions, not just academic philosophers'; if we are using intuitions as data, it is surely more scientific to gather and analyze them in certain ways—honing the exact questions using statistical techniques and carefully collecting quantitatively significant data across cultures, languages, gender, and so on.[3]

A first objection to this supposedly scientific use of intuitions is that these are intuitions, and not physical facts of the normal sort, and that science uses public, observable, physical facts, not such mind-dependent data. (Of course psychology and sociology must use such reports, at least in part; but they are interested in the way people think and not something deeper or non-mind-dependent.) One reply of the naturalist-intuitionist is that sciences, even the physical sciences, use intuitions too. It is true that they often begin with the products of loose analogical mechanisms that resemble intuitions. Abduction is a mode of inference in which one attempts to come up with the most plausible hypotheses that would explain some given data. This is most readily seen in the diagnosis of a disease, especially in a case where the data are diverse, peculiar, and limited; and indeed many attribute intuitions or skills to good diagnosticians since they cannot articulate the exact rules that generate an explanatory diagnosis. However, the use of intuitions in the case of moral theorizing is quite different: in moral theory there is an attempt to use intuitions as data not in the abductive but in the deductive and inductive phases of inquiry, that is, as confirmation or disconfirmation of a theory itself. One of the difficulties in moral philosophy is that *apparently* we do not have access to anything like more reputable data that would aid a scientific investigation of moral principles.

The naturalist who scientifically gathers moral intuitions needs to push further into the natural world. How could these mechanisms of intuiting moral judgments have naturally arisen, and how are they ultimately related to what we are seeking—moral principles? There are essentially two ways in which I think these intuitions could have arisen, and neither is promising as a reliable source of real moral principles. The first is that they arose as a complex interaction among rules of thumb that we have extracted, or as a kind of Bayesian intelligence, from examples and instruction in our culture—encoded in slogans, folk tales, and literature. But then they represent at best a kind of cultural folk morality, perhaps memes selected over centuries and having a certain fitness for making societies work. They may even represent norms that have evolved and been selected as "equilibria" among competing interests that still allow the culture to survive and flourish. If collections of these intuitions are cross-cultural, they may either represent a central source from which all cultures derived them, or more likely, they represent the common rules of thumb that any human society must have in order to survive for a reasonably long time. The other, and probably less likely, source of the intuiting mechanism is in natural evolution of the brain itself—and Smith, Dawkins, and others argue that there is evidence of at least kin-specific innate altruistic inclinations. In the case of culture and its collective experience and collective moral wisdom, as well as in the case of evolved neurology, this does not get us very close to what we would recognize as real moral principles. First, the intuitions from cultures or physiology would at best be adept at helping us with scenarios that had often arisen in the past. Second, this implicit morality would have only reached points of relative equilibria of fitness in guiding the individual v. society dynamic: it would be as good as or better than competing cultures' implicit morality. Finally, the implicit morality of a culture would be guided exclusively by the goal of memotype or genotype survival. There is not much reason for thinking that such survival itself will embody large components of real moral principles. Imagine, for example, a highly successful but ruthless and restrictedly cruel culture. Note also that the cultural memes (or genes) are likely to encode either no advice or the wrong advice about how to treat individuals from other cultures—a conquistador ethic of eliminating threat and maximizing the spread of your culture. These cultural norms of behavior may have a certain fitness relative to those of their competing societies, but they do not *therefore* give us insight into true moral principles.

After a thorough naturalistic examination, I think the prospects are slim indeed for finding in moral intuitions anything like a faculty of sympathy. The faculty that generates moral intuitions is a dark cave out of which all manner of beasts fly and crawl.

Although I don't have time to examine them here, the prospects for ontological intuitions are also problematic. Consider a question I have recently pondered (and discussed with E. J. Lowe and in my metaphysics seminar): can there be physical events if there are no physical objects, or perhaps better: does the ontological level of events supervene, globally and even locally, on physical objects and their properties? For many this becomes something like the following: can you imagine events without objects, or events occurring and having properties independently of the properties that objects have? Here the intuiting faculty is one's "imagination." It is indeed hard to describe any such scenario, but this difficulty is itself suspicious because we customarily describe events by the objects they involve. It is extremely likely that all or most such intuitions arise from linguistic or cultural metaphysical folk wisdom and reflect a proto-ontology that was good enough for our predecessors' thought and communication most of the time. With an overly refined ontology, they would have been contemplating bare particulars instead of seeing that lurking tiger. Metaphysical intuition will have the accuracy to discern ontological truth that Peirce thought our spatial intuitions gave to Euclidean geometry—not much. In the case of experienced philosophers, it is also likely that their metaphysical "intuitions" derive from unforeseen implications, associations, and analogies with languages and cultures they have lived in, and theories and values they have already strongly endorsed—this, for example, is a major criticism of the egalitarianism that "emerges" from intuitions about what we would do in the Rawlsian Original Position.

Although I myself am not above using or at least rhetorically appealing to shared intuitions, I am, with Peirce, deeply suspicious of any such thing. We do not make ethics more scientific, or get closer to the truth, by empirically better surveying such intuitions, but not thinking about what the connection between intuitions and moral principles really could be.

And yet . . . I am still drawn to the effort to apply scientific and mathematical methods to the hardest philosophical problems in some way. How could it be done well? I have two examples that I think show some direction.

First, some notions of a summum bonum and what counts as an ideal human life are at the heart of a number of ethical theories: happiness, maximum sets of pleasures, contentment, eudaimonia, human flourishing, and so on. I believe there are important insights to be gained from philosophers' examination of what is now the extensive and high-quality literature in psychology on subjective well-being (SWB). By carefully examining this literature and its critics, I think we can begin to see much more clearly what such a summum bonum might consist in. The data help us to examine the components or dimensions of well-being, and the ordered importance of these components; and with a great deal of work, we can see from the correlates of reported happiness what the causes of happiness might be. There are many small problems with the exact nature of the data. Most notably this information is based upon reports of perceived happiness. As *reports*, such data have problems; and as *perceptions* of well-being, the problems with the data are compounded. However, many of these and other difficulties have been much reduced by careful and empirically guided crafting of questionnaires, and by statistical analysis that compensates for known errors of reporting and perception of mental states. What remains is something that remarkably concurs with hints in the philosophical literature about what an Aristotelian human flourishing or a Millian eudaimonia might look like. It is a pity that the way we treat ourselves, the way we treat others, our normative theories of both, and the social and economic policies we advocate aren't guided by something like a sophisticated and massively empirically supported theory of human well-being. This to me makes economic growth and even income equality look silly as overarching social goals.

The second example is also in moral philosophy and takes me back to my theme of the relative equilibria in societies that are provided by certain sets of memes or genes for moral inclinations and that might explain the phenomenon of moral intuition. In 2002, a National Security Strategy was announced at my former place of employment, West Point; it included a policy explicitly permitting preventive war. This was followed in 2003 by preparations and then the "preemptive" attack on and occupation of Iraq. The academic and especially the philosophical community roundly criticized the morality of any such preemptive or preventive war—but I thought in an extremely ill-considered and sloppy way. In addition to conducting a literature search, I set out to see whether preventive war could ever be a rational policy within game theory and in particular using variants of the iterated Prisoner's Dilemma. The usefulness of the iterated Prisoner's Dilemma as a simulation of international conflict was well known. Axelrod and Schelling had some time ago proven that the morally nasty-seeming strategy of tit for tat was fairly stable relative to other plausible strategies, and resulted in minimal long-term destruction to both the user and to the sum of all parties. I wondered if the even nastier-seeming preventive war strategy likewise, and *intuitively counter-morally*, constituted a relatively stable equilibrium when used by both parties. I wrote software that pitted various probabilistic preventive war strategies against parties with both that strategy and other variants of tit for tat. The results were rather surprising, namely, that even with the inclusion of such phenomena as accidental attack and incomplete or erroneous knowledge, there was indeed a relative equilibrium favoring a preventive war strategy when its use was wrong about an impending attack less than 10 percent of the time. My results are of curious but limited significance and have since been published.

I used, borrowing from Axelrod and Schelling and many others, various measures of conflict, errors in knowledge, and so on, that are based on increasingly detailed empirical results. This was the empirical part of my exercise. The rest of my exercise was a priori, although I cheated by using computer-assisted Monte Carlo methods rather than proving mathematical theorems about iterations of operations. What such results show about moral principles governing international relations is admittedly debatable. Such features as its being *rational* for the user of the strategy against others' likely real-world strategies and its reduction of total destruction if all parties employ it strongly suggest the possible moral permissibility of such strategies. Indeed, much nicer strategies result in far more total destruction if the other parties are minimally rational and sometimes exploit their advantages.

There are a few moral philosophers who understand and take advantage of such empirical-computational approaches, such as Phillip Pettit and my colleague Ken Shockley, but they are comparatively rare. I would argue that such methods at least struggle to be proper applications of scientific method in philosophy, and not merely scrupulously gathered but possibly irrelevant intuitions.

IV. CONCLUSIONS

My conclusions are these. First, the causal closure of physical phenomena and its cousin, determinism, are by no means justified beliefs; but they are very probably wise guiding principles. Second, the boundaries of what counts as physical are so nebulous as to be almost useless except against the most outrageous spiritualists. Third, many philosophers who would probably endorse the high road of science ignore this commitment in many of their teaching practices, an important part of their professional lives. Fourth, there are probably ways to "use" scientific and mathematical results in philosophy, but to employ scientific thinking directly in doing philosophy is difficult and liable to misuse. Finally, intuitions, except as first guesses, are very wicked things that often distract us from doing philosophy.

NOTES

1. We might guess that space deviates from this so rarely or to such small degrees that the evolutionarily efficient solution was to make it a strong inclination. The alternative would have been to have every baby crawling around and struggling to determine for itself the dimensionality and curvature of space. Observe that the unimaginability of an alternative may be an efficient solution, but that this has nothing to do with its necessity in any important philosophical sense—except perhaps for a strictly phenomenal space of humans with their present genetic makeup and cognitive inclinations.

2. J. K. F. Zöllner, *Transcendental Physics: An Account of Experimental Investigations. From the Scientific Treatistes of Johann Karl Friedrich Zöllner*, translated from the German, with a preface and appendices, by Charles Carlton Massey, 2nd ed. (London: W. H. Harrison, 1882).

3. A recent PhD dissertation at the University at Buffalo, under my direction, extensively explored these failed analogies: "Observation, Explanation, and Intuition: Two Arguments against Moral Realism," by Hitoshi Arima.

14.

Why Is There a Universe at All, Rather Than Just Nothing?

Adolf Grünbaum

In his 1697 article "On the Ultimate Origination of Things," Gottfried Wilhelm Leibniz posed a historic question: he demanded "a full reason why there should be any *world* rather than none" (1973a, p. 136). In a sequel in 1714, he famously asked more generally: "*Why is there something rather than nothing*?" [italics in original] (1973b, sec. 7, p. 199). And yet he spoke of the answer to this latter, more general question as providing a "sufficient reason" for "the existence of the *universe*," since the something that actually exists is indeed the universe in its most comprehensive sense [italics added] (1973b, sec. 8). Thus, presumably, Leibniz's two successive interrogative formulations can legitimately coalesce into my titular question: "Why is there a universe at *all*, rather than just nothing?"

In a 2004 article, I gave Leibniz's 1714 ontological query—"Why is there something rather than nothing?"—the title "Primordial Existential Question" (Grünbaum 2004, p. 563). I then employed the acronym PEQ to abbreviate the phrase "Primordial Existential Question." Thus, the locution PEQ denoted Leibniz's eighteenth-century question, "Why is there something rather than nothing?" Here, however, I shall employ the designation PEQ to refer alternatively to my more specific titular question, "Why is there a universe at all, rather than just nothing?" I trust that this alternative use in context will not incur the risk of confusion.

Within a Leibnizian framework, his 1714 version of PEQ must be refined to preclude its trivialization. As we know, Leibniz distinguished between a logically contingent entity, on the one hand, and a necessary being, on the other: a logically contingent object is one whose nonexistence is logically possible, and one that thus might well not exist. But, for Leibniz, a "necessary being" is one "bearing the reason of its existence within itself," a being whose nonexistence is thus logically impossible (Leibniz, 1973b, p. 199).

But if there is a necessary being, there can be no question for Leibniz as to why *it* exists, rather than not existing, because such a being could not possibly fail to exist. Therefore, it would clearly trivialize Leibniz's cardinal PEQ if the question were asked about a "something" that necessarily exists.

Thus, we can formulate Leibniz's nontrivial construal of PEQ as follows: "Why is there something contingent at all, rather than just nothing contingent?" And since Leibniz argued that God necessarily exists, he considered the being of God com-possible with (i.e., able to coexist with) a putative state in which absolutely nothing contingent exists.

Unlike Leibniz, the present-day philosopher Richard Swinburne claims that God exists only contingently. Hence, Swinburne believes that God is *also* absent from a world that is devoid of all contingent entities.

Like the philosopher Derek Parfit, I shall speak of the presumed logical possibility of there being nothing contingent as "The Null Possibility." And like him, I shall use the label "Null World" to refer to a logically possible world in which there is nothing contingent at all.

My major concern here will be, in due course, to provide a thorough critical scrutiny of Leibniz's time-honored PEQ, and then to develop the important ramifications of that critique. But to lay the groundwork for that, several preliminary admonitions are needed.

IS IT IMPERATIVE TO EXPLAIN WHY THE NULL POSSIBILITY IS *NOT* INSTANTIATED?

First, I need to comment on the gloss or twist that Parfit and Swinburne have given to Leibniz's PEQ. Almost a decade ago, Parfit wrote: "[W]hy is there a Universe at all? It might have been true that nothing [contingent] ever existed; no living beings, no stars, no atoms, not even space or time. *When we think about this ['Null'] possibility* [1998a, p. 420] . . . *it can seem astonishing that anything [contingent] exists*" [italics added] (1998b, p. 24). Thereupon, Parfit enthrones PEQ on a pedestal, saying: "No question is more sublime than why there is a Universe [i.e., some world or other]: why there is anything rather than nothing." Importantly, as I see it, Parfit's logical motivation for this cosmic version of PEQ derives largely from the insidious peremptory assumption that the actual existence of a contingent universe in lieu of the Null World is just not to be expected, and that the de facto existence of our world is therefore *inescapably amazing and perplexing*! A like attitude is expressed in a very recent Amazon.com review of the 2004 book by the Oxford philosopher Bede Rundle, which is titled *Why There Is Something Rather Than Nothing*. As the reviewer Erik J. Olsson of Lund University puts it: "The question 'Why is there something rather than nothing?' is a good candidate for being philosophy's most profound and disturbing question. Is it not a complete and utter mystery that there should be anything at all?" (Olsson 2004).

Swinburne shares Parfit's astonishment that anything at all exists, declaring in his 1991 book, *The Existence of God*: "It remains to me, as to so many who have thought about the matter, a source of *extreme puzzlement* that there should exist anything at all" (1991, p. 283). And, more recently, in his 1996 book, *Is There a God?* Swinburne opined: "It is extraordinary that there should exist anything at all. Surely *the most natural state of affairs* is simply nothing: no universe, no God, nothing" [italics added] (p. 48). Evidently, Swinburne's avowed "extreme puzzlement" (italics added) that anything contingent exists at all is driven by the same peremptory mind-set as Parfit's astonishment.

Turning to Parfit, I challenge his declared astonishment that anything contingent exists at all by asking him: Why should the *mere contemplation* of the Null Possibility reasonably make it "seem astonishing that anything exists?" I claim that it should not do so! Let me point out why indeed it should not.

If some of us were to consider the logical possibility that a person we see might conceivably metamorphose spontaneously into an elephant, for example, I doubt strongly that we would feel even the slightest temptation to ask why that mere logical possibility is not realized. I don't see anyone scratching his or her head about it. Why then, I ask Parfit, should anyone reasonably feel astonished at all that the Null Possibility, if genuine, has remained a mere logical possibility, and that something does exist instead? In short, why *should* there be just nothing, *merely* because it is *logically possible*? This mere logical possibility of the Null World, I claim, does not suffice to legitimate Parfit's demand for an explanation of why the Null World does *not* obtain, an explanation he seeks as a philosophical anodyne for his misguided astonishment that anything at all exists.

Let me tip my hand and tell you in advance that my very irreverent claim will be the complete deflation of PEQ.

CHRISTIAN DOCTRINE AS AN INSPIRATION OF PEQ

It now behooves me to explicate the implicit and explicit presuppositions of Leibniz's PEQ before challenging them in due course. This articulation is vital for a fundamental reason: if one or more of these presuppositions of PEQ is either ill founded or presumably false, then PEQ is aborted as a nonstarter, because it would be posing a nonissue (or a pseudoproblem). And, in that case, the very existence of something contingent, instead of nothing contingent, does not require explanation. For example, if Mr. X never committed a murder, it is ill conceived to ask him just when he did it, and it is fatuous to blame him for not answering this ill-conceived question.

In earlier writings (Grünbaum 1998, p. 16; 2000, pp. 5, 19) I have used the pejorative term *pseudoproblem* to reject "a question that rests on an ill-founded or demonstrably false presupposition" (2000, p. 19). But, since the German term for "pseudoproblem," *Scheinproblem*, was given currency by the Vienna Circle, I now reiterate my caveat that, in my own use of that label, "I definitely do *not* intend to harken back to early positivist indictments of 'meaninglessness'" (ibid.).

Yet the notion that a question is ill conceived because it rests on dubious presuppositions surely antedates the logical positivist disparagement of certain traditional philosophical problems as pseudo-questions. Thus, in medieval debates, some issues were dismissed as clearly unproblematic under the Latin rubric of *cadit quaestio*, meaning that the question falls by being undermined. Whatever this ancestry, the challenge from the Vienna Circle was timely, I believe, because sometimes a seemingly well-conceived question may not be warranted after all. Thus, a question may be misguided, because it is inappropriately generated by an assumption that was previously unrecognized as being very *misleading* indeed.

One of the main tasks that I have set for myself here is to show precisely how Leibniz's PEQ *is vitiated* by presupposing an altogether dubious corollary of an old Christian doctrine. Elsewhere (Grünbaum 2004, pp. 561, 571), I have formulated that unacceptable corollary as follows: spontaneously, the world *should* feature nothing contingent at all, and, indeed, there *would* be nothing contingent in the absence of an overriding external cause (or reason), because that null state of affairs is the "most natural" of all! For brevity, I say that this tribute to the Null World asserts "*the ontological spontaneity of nothingness*" (Grünbaum 2000, p. 5). And I have introduced the acronym "*SoN*" to designate the doctrine that avows this ontological spontaneity of the Null World. In this acronym, the *S* stands for *Spontaneity*, the *o* for *of*, and the *N* for the word *Nothingness*. And my reason for having articulated SoN is precisely that its claim will turn out to be a completely unwarranted presupposition of PEQ. Bear in mind that, in brief, SoN is the thesis that a null state of affairs is "the most natural" of all.

The traditional Christian doctrine that unilaterally entails SoN as a corollary axiomatically makes the following avowal: The very existence of any and every contingent entity, apart from God himself, is utterly dependent on God at any and all times. Clearly, this tenet of total ontological dependency has two immediate corollaries:

1. The first is SoN, which tells us that, in the absence of a supernatural external cause, the ontologically spontaneous, natural, or normal state of affairs is one in which nothing contingent exists at all.

2. The second corollary is that, without constant divine creative support—so-called perpetual creation—the world would instantly lapse into nothingness, as claimed historically by Aquinas, Descartes, and many others.

Thus, crucially, according to SoN, the actual existence of something contingent is a deviation from the supposedly spontaneous and natural state of nothingness. And, *qua* such deviation, contingently existing objects clearly require a creative external cause *ex nihilo*, a so-called *ratio essendi*, a reason for existing *at all*.

Furthermore, in accord with the traditional Christian commitment to SoN, creation *ex nihilo* is required anew at every instant at which the world exists, even if it has existed forever. Therefore, traditional Christian theism makes a major claim as follows: if any contingent entity exists, then its very existence in *some* form must have a creative cause *ex nihilo*, rather than being externally uncaused.

However, very importantly, as it stands, without its axiomatic theological underpinning, SoN can be strongly challenged by this counterquestion: "But why *should* there be nothing contingent, rather than something contingent?" And, indeed, why would there be just nothing contingent rather than something contingent? Moreover, why would there be nothing contingent in the absence of an overriding external cause? The Christian ontological axiom is question-begging.

Unfortunately, in the Christian culture of the Occident, both philosophers and ordinary people have imbibed SoN with their mother's milk. And it is deeply ingrained even in a good many of those who reject its received theological underpinning. But before Christianity molded the philosophical intuitions of our culture, neither Greek philosophy nor, notably, many other world cultures featured SoN (Eliade 1992). No wonder that Aristotle regarded the material universe as both uncreated and eternal.

In 1935, the French philosopher Henri Bergson aptly, though

incompletely, sketched SoN when he rightly deplored its beguiling role in the misguided posing of PEQ. As Bergson put it: "[P]art of metaphysics moves, consciously or not, around the question of knowing why anything exists, why matter, or spirit, or God, rather than nothing at all? But the question presupposes that reality fills a void, that underneath Being lies nothingness, that *de jure there should be nothing, that we must therefore explain why there is de facto something*" [my emphasis] (Bergson 1974, pp. 239–40).

Alas, Bergson's point that SoN vitiates PEQ was completely lost on Bede Rundle in his aforementioned 2004 book, *Why There Is Something Rather Than Nothing*. Thus, Rundle's rejection of PEQ, though correct as a conclusion, is left unjustified by him.

As shown by my articulation of SoN, Bergson's concise rendition of it needs to be amplified by the further claim that, in the absence of an overriding external cause or reason, the Null World would *spontaneously* prevail ontologically.

How then have the defenders of SoN tried to justify it in its own right, rather than just as a logically weaker corollary of the aforestated dubious Christian axiom of the world's total ontological dependence on the Deity?

A *PRIORI* JUSTIFICATIONS OF SoN BY LEIBNIZ, SWINBURNE, AND OTHERS

Some philosophers, notably Leibniz and Swinburne, have appealed to the presumed *a priori* simplicity of the Null World to argue that *de jure* there *should* be nothing contingent, so that the *de facto* existence of our world would provide an answer to the PEQ imperative. However, as I shall contend, the recourse to simplicity to defend SoN *a priori* is very unsuccessful, and, moreover, significantly, there is no empirical support for SoN either. Therefore, this twofold ill-foundedness of SoN will undermine PEQ precisely because PEQ presupposes SoN.

To mount an *a priori* defense of SoN, Leibniz and Swinburne maintained that the Null World is simpler, both ontologically and conceptually, than a world containing something contingent or other. This dual assertion of greater simplicity poses two immediate questions: (1) Is the Null World actually *a priori* simpler, and, indeed, is it the *simplest* world ontologically as well as conceptually? And (2), even assuming that the Null World *is* thus doubly simpler than a world containing something contingent, does its supposed maximum dual simplicity mandate ontologically that there *should* be just nothing *de jure*, and that, furthermore, there *would* be just nothing in the absence of an overriding cause (reason), as claimed by SoN?

In answer to the first of these two questions, let us assume for the sake of argument that Leibniz and Swinburne could warrant *a priori* the maximum conceptual and ontological simplicity of the Null World, as Leibniz avowed when he declared that "'nothingness' is simpler and easier than 'something'" (Leibniz 1973b, p. 199). Then my emphatically negative answer to the second of these questions is as follows: *even if the supposed maximum ontological simplicity of the Null World is warranted a priori, that presumed simplicity would not mandate the claim of SoN that de jure the thus simplest world must be spontaneously realized ontologically in the absence of an overriding cause.* After all, having the simplest ontological constitution does not itself make for the actualization or instantiation of the world featuring that constitution! Yet, to my knowledge, neither Leibniz nor Swinburne nor any other author has offered any cogent reason at all to posit such an ontological imperative (Grünbaum 2008).

ARE THE PHILOSOPHICAL FORTUNES OF OCCAM'S RAZOR HELPFUL?

Very interestingly, when Leibniz affirmed the ontological simplicity of the Null World, he made no mention at all of the early seventeenth-century enunciations of the injunction of simplicity that came to be known, by the mid-nineteenth century, as either "Occam's Razor" or "The Principle of Parsimony." Yet Leibniz may well have learned of the early seventeenth-century versions of

Occam's directive and may still have refrained from invoking them, perhaps because he did not think that they would strengthen his case.

Even more noteworthy is the fact that our contemporary Richard Swinburne, who was undoubtedly aware of modern appeals to Occam's Razor, completely passes over them in silence in two pertinent contexts: first, in his 1997 monograph, *Simplicity as Evidence of Truth,* and second, in his appeal to the supposed *maximum ontological simplicity* of the Deity as "an argument for God being the cause [*ex nihilo*] of the existence of the universe" in his 2004 book, *The Existence of God* (p. 138, n. 9)

Although neither Leibniz nor Swinburne mentioned Occam's injunction in their appeal to simplicity, the differing extant versions of the injunction may provide some perspective on their philosophical treatment of simplicity. Thus, let me comment on these versions of Occam's Razor.

William of Occam (1285–1349) worked during the first half of the fourteenth century. But, as reported by J. J. C. Smart, the formulation of Occam's Razor as "Do not multiply entities beyond necessity" was a seventeenth-century invention in its original Latin enunciation (Smart 1984, p. 118). However, the term *Occam's Razor* itself was first introduced in the mid-nineteenth century by William Hamilton, who also spoke of it as "The Principle of Parsimony."

Smart's 1984 gloss on Occam's original formulation is that it warns theoreticians "against an unnecessary luxuriance of [explanatory] principles or laws or statements of existence." As John Stuart Mill emphasized in this vein, the demand for parsimony is a rule of methodology mandating that we have evidence for our beliefs (ibid, p. 119). But this demand is emphatically not a viable thesis about the *simple* workings of nature, as Hamilton had erroneously claimed.

Smart declared somewhat soberingly, yet with quite insufficient caution: "I suspect that it is not possible fully to justify the idea that simple theories are objectively more likely to be true than are complex ones or even that they contain fewer arbitrary elements" (ibid.). However, he spoke very unguardedly and presumably enthymematically (leaving a crucial qualification unstated) when he referred *favorably* to "the idea that simple theories are objectively more likely to be true than are complex ones." As he stated it, this notion is surely *untenable* without *at least* an articulated proviso: after all, the ancient Greek Thales's monistic hydrochemistry of the chemical universality of water is staggeringly simpler than Mendeleyev's nineteenth-century polychemistry, but clearly the polychemistry is overwhelmingly more likely to be true.

THE FAILURE OF SWINBURNE'S SIMPLICITY RECIPE FOR VERISIMILITUDINOUS THEORIES

In *Simplicity as Evidence of Truth* (1997) and *Epistemic Justification* (2001, chaps. 3 and 4), Richard Swinburne argued strenuously that simplicity provides probabilistic evidence of truth by acting as a tiebreaker among conflicting theories as follows: greater simplicity is a criterion for "choosing among [competing] scientific theories of equal scope [or content] fitting equally well with background evidence and yielding the same data" (2001, p. 83). This choice of the simpler of two theories purportedly yields the theory that is more likely to be true precisely by *virtue of being simpler*.

However, in a lecture that I delivered in March 2006 at All Souls College in Oxford when Swinburne was in the audience, and also at the Royal Institute of Philosophy in London, I demonstrated at least two results that fundamentally subvert Swinburne's thesis, as he, in effect, conceded in the ensuing public discussion. To state my results, let me speak of a theory B that is more likely to be true than a theory A as "having greater verisimilitude" than A. Then two of my damaging contentions against Swinburne can be stated as follows:

1. His comparative simplicity ratings, which are to yield a verdict of greater verisimilitude, avowedly pertain to rival hypotheses of *equal content or scope*. Yet Swinburne, like Karl Popper before him, has left the implementation of this crucial content-parity requirement glaringly unfulfilled (Grünbaum 1976).

2. In *The Existence of God*, Swinburne wrote: "if there is to exist

something, it seems impossible to conceive of anything simpler (and therefore *a priori* more probable) than the existence of God" (2004, p. 366). Furthermore, he told us that "the [explanatory] choice is between the universe as [explanatory] stopping point [i.e., as existing *qua* brute fact] and God as [explanatory] stopping point [i.e., existing as a matter of brute fact]" (ibid., p. 147).

Thus, the God hypothesis is supposedly the conceptually and ontologically simpler option. And the avowed cardinal thesis of Swinburne's 2004 book, *The Existence of God*, is "an argument for God being the cause [*ex nihilo*] of the existence of the universe" (ibid., p. 138, n. 9).

Just for argument's sake, posit with Swinburne that in the class of all existential hypotheses, the theistic one is the simplest and therefore simpler than its atheistic competitor. It is then a patent corollary of the conclusion of the argument I presented in my 2008 paper titled "Is Simplicity Evidence of Truth?" that this supposed greater simplicity does *not* show theism to be inductively more likely to be true than atheism, absent some demonstration of the requisite content-equality of these two rival hypotheses.

Indeed, even if such content-equality were to be demonstrated, the supposed greater *a priori* simplicity of the God hypothesis would not confer any greater verisimilitude upon it: as I have argued elsewhere (2004, p. 573), *a priori* simplicity and *a priori* probability are not at all ontologically legislative, and thus Swinburne cannot milk any theological capital out of the purported *a priori* simplicity and *a priori* probability of the Deity, even if true! Yet his theism is explanatorily omnivorous, avowing very dubiously (Grünbaum 2004, sec. 2) that theism explains "*everything* we observe" (Swinburne 1996, p. 2).

Moreover, there are further difficulties: theory B might be simpler than theory A in one respect while being more complicated in another. But inter-theory comparisons of simplicity for assessing relative verisimilitude call for criteria of greater overall simplicity. Yet, elsewhere I have used a comparison of Einstein's general theory of relativity with Newton's theory of gravitation to impugn the feasibility of ratings of comparative *overall* simplicity for rival theories (Grünbaum 2008). However, differing verdicts from just such ratings are indispensable to both Swinburne's prescription for the greater verisimilitude of one of these theories and to philosopher J. J. C. Smart's aspiration to simplicity as an avenue to truth, an aspiration set forth above.

Indeed, if Einstein's theory of gravitation were held to be more complex overall than Newton's in virtue of the nonlinearity of its partial differential field equations, then its presumed greater verisimilitude is the death knell of both Swinburne's prescription and Smart's aspiration.

It has been said that scientists think they know when one theory is simpler than another overall as a matter of its greater beauty and elegance. But beauty is in the eye of the beholder, and, as Einstein aptly remarked, elegance had best be left to tailors.

THE DEMISE OF LEIBNIZ'S 1714 JUSTIFICATION FOR THE PRIMORDIAL EXISTENTIAL QUESTION (PEQ)

Now, let us come to grips with the specific 1714 context in which Leibniz formulated his PEQ and tried to justify it by relying carefully on both of the following two premises: (1) his well-known Principle of Sufficient Reason, for which I shall use the acronym PSR; and (2) his *a priori* argument from simplicity for the presupposition SoN, which is inherent in his PEQ, an argument I have articulated above.

Thus, Leibniz declared: "*the great principle* [of sufficient reason, PSR] . . . holds that *nothing takes place without sufficient reason*, that is . . . a reason sufficient to determine why it is thus and not otherwise. This principle having been laid down, the first question we are entitled to ask will be: *Why is there something rather than nothing?* For 'nothing' [i.e., the Null World] is simpler and easier than 'something.' Further supposing that things must exist, it must be possible to give a reason why they must exist just as they do and not otherwise" (italics in original) (Leibniz 1973b, sec. 7, p. 199).

These very ambitious avowals by Leibniz invite my clarifying comments:

1. Right after enunciating his PSR, Leibniz poses his PEQ "Why is there something rather than nothing?" as "the first question we are entitled to ask." However, immediately after raising that question, he relies on the supposed simplicity of the Null World to justify the presupposition SoN of PEQ, claiming, in effect, that the Null World would be spontaneously realized ontologically in the absence of an overriding external cause. As we recall, he puts it concisely: "For 'nothing' [i.e., the Null World] is simpler and easier than 'something.'" And, clearly, there is either something or nothing.

2. Evidently, Leibniz is not content to rely on his PSR alone to ask the truncated question "Why is there something contingent?" without the accompanying contrasting clause "rather than nothing." Instead, he uses SoN as presupposed in this contrasting clause to assert a dual thesis: (a) that the existence of something contingent *is not to be expected at all*; and (b) that its actual existence therefore cries out for explanation! As will be recalled, just this dual thesis was philosopher Derek Parfit's implicit rationale for embracing Leibniz's PEQ.

Thus, the soundness of Leibniz's justification of his PEQ evidently turns on the cogency of his PSR as well as of his *a priori* argument from simplicity for SoN. But we have already discounted his *a priori* argument for SoN above. Thus, we can now concentrate on appraising his PSR.

Consider the grounds in twentieth-century quantum theory for the demise within our universe of the universal causation familiar from Newton's physics as codified by Laplace's "determinism." This empirically well-founded quantum theory features *merely* probabilistic, rather than universal, causal laws governing such phenomena as the spontaneous radioactive disintegration of atomic nuclei, yielding emissions of alpha or beta particles and/or gamma rays.

In this domain of phenomena, there are physically possible particular events that *could* but *do not actually* occur at given times under specified initial conditions. Yet it is impermissibly legislative to insist, via Leibniz's PSR, that merely because these unrealized events are thus physically possible, there must be an explanation entailing their specific *non*occurrence and, similarly, a deductive explanation of probabilistically governed actually occurring events.

This admonition against PSR was not heeded by Swinburne, who avowed entitlement to *universal* explainability, declaring in *The Existence of God*: "We expect all things to have explanations" (Swinburne 1991, p. 287). In just this vein, we recall, Leibniz had demanded for every event an explanatory "reason [cause] sufficient to determine why it is thus and not otherwise." Hence, the history of modern quantum physics teaches that PSR, which Leibniz avowedly saw as metaphysical, cannot be warranted *a priori* and indeed is untenable on ultimately empirical grounds.

Thus, the discovery that the universe does not accommodate rigid prescriptions for deterministic explanatory understanding is not tantamount to scientific failure; instead, it is the discovery that positive reasons for identifying certain coveted explanations are phantoms.

As we saw, Leibniz had generated PEQ by conjoining his untenable PSR with SoN. Yet since his *a priori* defense of SoN via simplicity has also failed, it remains to inquire whether his avowed ontological spontaneity of the Null World might possibly be warranted empirically. My answer will be emphatically negative for the following reason: it turns out, as an induction from various episodes in the history of science, that SoN is altogether *ill founded empirically*, as we are about to see.

To examine the empirical status of SoN, it will be useful to reformulate it in Richard Swinburne's previously cited words: "Surely the most natural state of affairs is simply nothing: no universe, no God, nothing." But since our empirical evidence comes, of course, from our own universe (U), consider the corollary of SoN that pertains to U. This corollary asserts that it is natural or spontaneous for U not to exist rather than for U to exist. Contrary to any *a priori* dictum on the "natural" ontological behavior of U, the verdict on that behavior will now be seen to depend crucially on empirical evidence, and indeed to provide no support for SoN.

Two specific cosmological examples spell out this empirical moral, leaving aside some pertinent technicalities that I do not have space to develop here. Yet the point of my examples will be clear.

The first example is furnished by the *natural evolution* of one of the big bang models of the universe countenanced by general relativistic cosmology, the dust-filled, so-called Friedmann universe described by R. M. Wald. This universe has the following features relevant to my concerns (Wald 1984, pp. 100–101):

A. It is a spatially closed, three-dimensional spherical universe (a "3-sphere"), which expands from a punctal big bang to a maximum finite size and then contracts into a punctal crunch.

B. That universe exists altogether for only a finite span of time, such that no instants of time existed prior to its finite duration or will exist afterward.

C. As a matter of natural law, its total rest-mass is conserved for the entire time period of its existence. Thus, during that entire time, there is no need for a supernatural agency to generate that mass out of nothing and/or to prevent it from lapsing into nothingness, contrary to both SoN and to Thomas Aquinas and René Descartes.

Evidently, the "natural" dynamical evolution of the Friedmann big bang universe as a whole is specified by Einstein's empirically supported cosmology. Thus, the "natural" or spontaneous ontological behavior of big bang worlds is not vouchsafed *a priori*.

Second, the same epistemic moral concerning the empirical status of cosmological naturalness is spelled out by the illuminating case of Bondi and Gold's now largely defunct so-called steady-state cosmology of 1948 (Bondi 1960).

Assuming the mutual recession of the galaxies discovered by Hubble, the average density of matter ought to decrease with time. But in their 1948 theory, Bondi and Gold boldly postulated that, nevertheless, in a spatially and temporally infinite universe, as a matter of natural law there *is* large-scale, temporal constancy of the matter-density. Note that this conservation or constancy is not of matter but of the *density* of matter over time.

The conjunction of this constancy of the density with Hubble's mutual recession of the galaxies from one another then entails the following quite counterintuitive consequence: throughout space-time, and *without* any matter-generating agency, new matter (in the form of hydrogen) literally pops into existence, completely naturally, in violation of matter-energy conservation.

Hence, the Bondi and Gold world features the accretion or formation of *new* matter as its natural, normal, spontaneous behavior, yet terrestrially at a very slow rate. And although this accretive formation is indeed out of nothing, its complete spontaneity clearly precludes its being "created" by an external agency. Apparently, if the steady-state world were actual, it would discredit the doctrine of the medieval Latin epigram *Ex nihilo, nihil fit*, which means "From nothing, you cannot get anything," or more colloquially, "You cannot get blood out of a stone." But Bondi and Gold *could*.

The steady-state theory owes its demise to the failure of its predictions and retrodictions to pass observational muster in its competition with big bang cosmology. This episode again teaches us that empirically based scientific theories are our sole epistemic avenue to the "natural" behavior of the universe at large, though of course only fallibly so.

What then is the *empirical cosmological verdict* on the corollary of SoN that asserts that "it is natural for our universe *not* to exist, rather than to exist"? Apparently, there is no empirical evidence for this corollary from cosmology, let alone for SoN itself. Its proponents have not even tried to offer any such evidence for SoN, believing mistakenly, as we saw, that it can be vouchsafed *a priori* à la Leibniz.

PEQ AS A FAILED SPRINGBOARD FOR CREATIONIST THEISM: THE COLLAPSE OF LEIBNIZ'S AND SWINBURNE'S THEISTIC COSMOLOGICAL ARGUMENTS

Probably all of us who were reared in the Occident have wondered at some time: "Where did everything come from?" As we know, typically this question is not a demand for a statement of the earlier physical history of our existing universe. Instead, the question is driven by the largely unconscious assumption of SoN and is thus simply another version of Leibniz's PEQ. Yet as I have argued painstakingly, PEQ rests on the ill-founded premise SoN, as well as on Leibniz's very questionable PSR. Therefore, PEQ is an ill-conceived nonstarter that poses a pseudo-issue and does not warrant the quest for any sort of first cause as an answer!

But, as we know, both Leibniz and Swinburne raised PEQ as an imperative question, and thence they concluded misguidedly that the answer to it mandates divine creation. Indeed, in the May 26, 2007, issue of the German magazine *Der Spiegel*, journalist Alexander Smoltczyk tells us incoherently: "For most believers, God is neither a person nor a principle, nor yet an existing entity, but rather an answer to the question why there is something rather than nothing" [my English translation] (Smoltczyk 2007, p. 66). Thus, PEQ is invoked to generate incoherent theological capital in the culture at large: how, one needs to ask, can God not be an "existing entity" and yet be "an answer" to PEQ? Such is the desperation to give God a job to do.

However, PEQ evidently cannot serve as a viable springboard for creationist theism, because it is a pseudo-issue based on quicksand! By the same token, Leibniz's and Swinburne's cosmological arguments for divine creation are fundamentally unsuccessful.

Hence, I say to you: whatever philosophical problems you may have, it is my plea here that answering Leibniz's PEQ should *not* engage your curiosity, because his question is just a will-o'-the-wisp.

CODA ON RICHARD DAWKINS AND SAM HARRIS VIS-À-VIS PEQ

Despite all the telling arguments for atheism offered by both Richard Dawkins in *The God Delusion* and Sam Harris in *The End of Faith* and *Letter to a Christian Nation*, they both caved in altogether unwarrantedly by countenancing PEQ very misguidedly, as a searching question that rightly calls for an explanatory answer.

Thus Dawkins wrote: "Time and again, my theologian friends returned to the point that there had to be a reason why there is something rather than nothing. There must have been a first cause of everything, and we might as well give it the name God" (2006, p. 155).

Alas, entirely unaware that PEQ is an abortive nonstarter posing as a pseudo-issue, Dawkins replied unavailingly by actually allowing a "first cause, the great unknown which is responsible for something existing rather than nothing" (ibid.) but objecting most feebly that this notion of a first cause as "a being capable of designing the universe and of talking to a million people simultaneously, is a total abdication of the responsibility to find an explanation." However, this purported explanatory responsibility is a mere phantom, an ill-conceived contrivance of the ill-fated PEQ, as I showed in great detail in "The Poverty of Theistic Cosmology" (2004, sec. 1.9).

Relatedly, Sam Harris embraces PEQ to his detriment, declaring in *Letter to a Christian Nation* with misplaced intellectual humility: "Any intellectually honest person will admit that he *does not know* why the universe exists. Scientists, of course, readily admit their ignorance on this point" (italics in original) (2006, p. 74). But it is a direct corollary of my argument above that there is *no ignorance* at issue here of the kind that is in need of being admitted!

To boot, Harris writes: "The truth is that no one knows how or why the universe came into being. It is not clear that we can even speak coherently about the creation of the universe, given that such an event can be conceived only with reference to time, and here we are talking about the birth of space-time itself" (2006, pp. 73–74). At this point Harris offers a footnote pointing out that the physicist Stephen Hawking "pictures space-time as a four-dimensional, closed manifold without beginning or end." But, *in the very next sentence,*

Harris misguidedly capitulates to PEQ by making this previously cited ill-fated categorical declaration: "Any intellectually honest person will admit that he *does not know* why the universe exists" (p. 74).

Clearly, Harris applies this unqualified admission of ignorance to every instant at which the universe exists, *even if it has existed forever*. And evidently, he thinks that even Hawking's model of a universe whose time is unbounded though finite (like a circle) *cannot* purchase absolution from this challenge by PEQ, although that model undermines the particular question of how or why the universe came into being at a moment in the finite past. *A fortiori*, Harris again implicitly capitulates to PEQ in the case of other models of the universe, featuring other time-structures. Interested readers may consult my anticreationist account of the big bang universe in my essay "Theological Misinterpretations of Current Physical Cosmology" (1998).

ACKNOWLEDGMENTS

This essay is based on the presidential address I delivered in August 2007 at the thirteenth quadrennial International Congress of Logic, Methodology, and Philosophy of Science (DLMPS) of the International Union of History and Philosophy of Science (IUHPS), held at Tsinghua University in Beijing, China. It is dedicated to my late, beloved colleague Wesley C. Salmon. I extend my thanks to Thomas Cunningham and Balazs Gyenis for their helpful expository comments.

REFERENCES AND FURTHER READING

Bergson, Henri. 1974. *The Two Sources of Morality and Religion*. Translated with the assistance of W. C. R. A. Audra and C. Brereton. Westport, CT: Greenwood Press.

Bondi, Hermann. 1960. *Cosmology*. 2nd ed. Cambridge: Cambridge University Press.

Dawkins, Richard. 2006. *The God Delusion*. New York: Houghton Mifflin.

Eliade, Mircea. 1992. *Essential Sacred Writings from Around the World*. San Francisco: HarperCollins.

Grünbaum, Adolf. 1976. "Can a Theory Answer More Questions Than One of Its Rivals?" *British Journal for the Philosophy of Science* 27: 1–23.

———. 1998. "Theological Misinterpretations of Current Physical Cosmology." *Philo* 1: 15–34.

———. 2000. "A New Critique of Theological Interpretations of Physical Cosmology." *British Journal for the Philosophy of Science* 51: 1–43.

———. 2004. "The Poverty of Theistic Cosmology." *British Journal for the Philosophy of Science* 55: 561–614.

———. 2008. "Is Simplicity Evidence of Truth?" *American Philosophical Quarterly* 45: 179–90.

Harris, Sam. 2006. *Letter to a Christian Nation*. New York: Knopf.

Leibniz, G. W. 1973a. "On the Ultimate Origination of Things." Translated by G. H. R. Parkinson and M. Morris. In *Leibniz: Philosophical Writings*, edited by G. H. R. Parkinson. London: J. M. Dent & Sons.

———. 1973b. "Principles of Nature and of Grace Founded on Reason." Translated by G. H. R. Parkinson and M. Morris. In *Leibniz: Philosophical Writings*, edited by G. H. R. Parkinson. London: J. M. Dent & Sons.

Olsson, Erik J. 2004. Amazon.com editorial review of Bede Rundle's book, *Why There Is Something Rather Than Nothing*. http://www.amazon.com/gp/product/productdescription/B000QTD4GM/ref=dp_proddesc_0?ie=UTF8&n=283155&s=books.

Parfit, Derek. 1998a. "The Puzzle of Reality: Why Does the Universe Exist?" In *Metaphysics: The Big Questions*, edited by P. V. Inwagen and D. Zimmerman. Malden, MA: Blackwell.

———. 1998b. "Why Anything? Why This?" *London Review of Books*, January 22, 24–27.

Smart, J. J. C. 1984. "Ockham's Razor." In *Principles of Philosophical Reasoning*, edited by J. M. Fetzer. Totowa, NJ: Rowman & Allanheld.

Smoltczyk, Alexander. 2007. "Der Kreuzzug der Gottlosen" (The Crusade of the Godless). *Der Spiegel*, May 26, 56–69.

Swinburne, Richard. 1991. *The Existence of God*. Rev. ed. Oxford: Clarendon Press.

———. 1996. *Is There a God?* Oxford: Oxford University Press.

———. 1997. *Simplicity as Evidence of Truth*. Milwaukee, WI.: Marquette University Press.

———. 2001. *Epistemic Justification*. Oxford: Clarendon Press.

———. 2004. *The Existence of God*. 2nd ed. Oxford: Clarendon Press.

Wald, R. M. 1984. *General Relativity*. Chicago: University of Chicago Press.

About the Editors and Contributors

John Peter Anton is Distinguished Professor of Greek Philosophy and Culture at the University of South Florida. He has authored and edited over thirty books, including *Critical Humanism* (1981), *Categories and Experience* (1996), *Archetypal Principles and Hierarchies* (2000), and *American Naturalism and Greek Philosophy* (2005).

Mario Bunge is Frothingham Professor of Logic and Metaphysics at McGill University. He has published more than fifty books, including *Scientific Materialism* (1981), *Scientific Realism* (2001), *Emergence and Convergence* (2003), *Chasing Reality: Strife over Realism* (2006), and *Causality and Modern Science* (4th ed., 2008).

Randall Dipert is Charles S. Peirce Professor of Philosophy at SUNY Buffalo. He has published on the history and philosophy of logic, especially on Peirce and the development of pragmatism. In aesthetics, he has published articles on music theory, performance practice, and authenticity and is the author of *Artifacts, Art Works, and Agency* (1993).

James Gouinlock is Professor Emeritus of Philosophy at Emory University. A prominent scholar on John Dewey and pragmatic naturalism, he has authored *John Dewey's Philosophy of Value* (1972), *Rediscovering the Moral Life: Philosophy and Human Practice* (1993), and *Eros and the Good* (2004).

Adolf Grünbaum is Andrew Mellon Professor of Philosophy of Science and Co-Chairman of the Center for Philosophy of Science at the University of Pittsburgh. Among his books are *Philosophical Problems of Space and Time* (2nd ed., 1973) and *The Foundations of Psychoanalysis: A Philosophical Critique* (1984).

Paul Kurtz is Professor Emeritus of Philosophy at SUNY Buffalo and Chairman Emeritus of the Center for Inquiry in Amherst, New York. He has published forty-eight books, including *The Transcendental Temptation: A Critique of Religion and the Paranormal* (1986), *Philosophical Essays in Pragmatic Naturalism* (1991), *The New Skepticism* (1992), and *Skepticism and Humanism* (2001).

John Lachs is Centennial Professor of Philosophy at Vanderbilt University. A scholar of the history of American philosophy, he has authored *The Relevance of Philosophy for Life* (1995), coauthored (with Michael P. Hodges) *Thinking in the Ruins: Wittgenstein and Santayana on Contingency* (2000), and edited the *Encyclopedia of American Philosophy* (2008).

Brian Leiter is John P. Wilson Professor of Law and Director of the Center for Law, Philosophy, and Human Values at the University of Chicago. He is the author of *Nietzsche on Morality* (2002) and *Naturalizing Jurisprudence* (2007), and he has edited *Objectivity in Law and Morals* (2001) and *The Oxford Handbook of Continental Philosophy* (2007).

Isaac Levi is John Dewey Professor Emeritus at Columbia University. Among the more prominent of his many writings on epistemology and decision theory are *Decisions and Revisions: Philosophical Essays on Knowledge and Value* (1984), *The Fixation of Belief and Its Undoing* (1991), and *The Covenant of Reason: Rationality and the Commitments of Thought* (1997).

Joseph Margolis is Laura H. Carnell Professor of Philosophy at Temple University. He has published books in most areas of philosophy, defending pragmatic naturalism in such works as *Science without Unity: Reconciling the Natural and the Human Sciences* (1987), *Reinventing Pragmatism* (2002), and *Pragmatism without Foundations: Reconciling Realism and Relativism* (2nd ed., 2007).

Jack Nelson is Associate Dean for Student and Academic Programs in the College of Liberal Arts and Sciences and Professor of Philosophy at Arizona State University. He has published articles on personal identity, epistemology, and philosophy of science, and is coauthor with Lynn Hankinson Nelson of *On Quine* (2000).

Lynn Hankinson Nelson is Professor of Philosophy at the University of Washington. Working in feminist epistemology and philosophy of science, and philosophy of biology, she has published *Who Knows: From Quine to Feminist Empiricism* (1990) and is coauthor with Jack Nelson of *On Quine* (2000); she and Jack Nelson coedited *Feminism, Science, and the Philosophy of Science* (1996) and *Feminist Interpretations of W. V. Quine* (2003).

Nicholas Rescher is University Professor of Philosophy and Co-Chairman of the Center for Philosophy of Science at the University of Pittsburgh. He has published over one hundred books. These titles illustrate his work: *A System of Pragmatic Idealism* (3 vols., 1991–94), *Nature and Understanding: A Study of the Metaphysics of Science* (2000), and *Metaphysics: The Key Issues from a Realistic Perspective* (2005).

Sandra B. Rosenthal is Provost Eminent Professor of Philosophy at Loyola University, New Orleans. Her books include *Speculative Pragmatism* (1986), *Charles Peirce's Pragmatic Pluralism* (1994), and *Time, Continuity and Indeterminacy: A Pragmatic Engagement with Contemporary Perspectives* (2000).

John Ryder was Professor of Philosophy at SUNY Cortland, and presently serves as Director of International Programs at the State University of New York. He has authored *Interpreting America: Russian and Soviet Studies in the History of American Thought* (1999), edited *American Philosophic Naturalism in the Twentieth Century* (1994), and coedited *The Blackwell Guide to American Philosophy* (2004).

John R. Shook is Vice President of Education and Research and Senior Research Fellow at the Center for Inquiry, and Research Associate in Philosophy at SUNY Buffalo. Among his books are *Dewey's Empirical Theory of Knowledge and Reality* (2000), *Pragmatic Naturalism and Realism* (2003), *A Companion to Pragmatism* (2005), and *Dictionary of Modern American Philosophers* (2005).